Anticipating a Nuclear Iran

Anticipating a Nuclear Iran
CHALLENGES FOR U.S. SECURITY

Jacquelyn K. Davis and Robert L. Pfaltzgraff Jr.

Columbia University Press   New York

Columbia University Press
Publishers Since 1893
New York   Chichester, West Sussex
cup.columbia.edu
Copyright © 2013 Columbia University Press
All rights reserved

Library of Congress Cataloging-in-Publication Data
Davis, Jacquelyn K.
      Anticipating a nuclear Iran: challenges for U.S. security / Jacquelyn K. Davis
and Robert L. Pfaltzgraff Jr.
        pages cm
      Includes bibliographical references and index.
      ISBN 978-0-231-16622-5 (cloth : alk. paper) —ISBN 978-0-231-53594-6 (e-book)
   1. Nuclear weapons—Iran. 2. Iran—Military policy. 3. Iran—Politics and government—1997– 4. Iran—Foreign relations—1997– 5. United States—Relations—Iran.
6. United States—Military policy. 7. Deterrence (Strategy) 8. Security, International.
I. Pfaltzgraff, Robert L. II. Title.

UA853.17D38   2013
355.02'170955—dc23   2013016815

Jacket design by Noah Arlow

References to websites (URLs) were accurate at the time of writing. Neither the
author nor Columbia University Press is responsible for URLs that may have expired
or changed since the manuscript was prepared.

Two things, I confess, have staggered me, after long Parliamentary experience, in these debates. The first has been the dangers that have so swiftly come upon us in a few years, and have been transforming our position and the whole outlook of the world. Secondly, I have been staggered by the failure of the House of Commons to react effectively against those dangers. That, I am bound to say, I never expected. I never would have believed that we would have been allowed to go on getting into this plight, month by month and year by year, and that even the Government's own confessions of error would have produced no concentration of Parliamentary opinion and force capable of lifting our efforts to the level of emergency.

—Sir Winston Churchill, November 1936, Remarks in the House of Commons

CONTENTS

TABLES AND BOXES

PREFACE

This book is the product of several years of research and analysis, based on primary and secondary sources, interviews, focused workshops, and seminars. We benefited from the insights and ideas of many people, including members of the Institute for Foreign Policy Analysis's international board of research consultants and discussions with key leaders in the United States and allied/partner national security community. We wish to thank them all.

The idea for this book grew out of a project that was funded by the Smith Richardson Foundation. We owe a debt of gratitude to the foundation for supporting the initial work, without which this book would not have been possible. In particular, we wish to thank Dr. Marin Strmecki and Dr. Nadia Schadlow for their sustained encouragement and support, together with the Board of the Smith Richardson Foundation for having granted us the opportunity to explore the implications of a nuclear Iran for U.S. security planning.

We also wish to acknowledge our colleague, Dr. Charles Perry, at the Institute for Foreign Policy Analysis (IFPA) for his comments and ideas as we worked through subsequent drafts of this manuscript, as well as Professor Richard Shultz at the Fletcher School, Tufts University. We also want to thank and recognize Ilan Berman, Professor Paul Bracken, Michael Eisenstadt, Ambassador Robert Joseph, and Dr. Keith Payne for their insightful comments and suggestions on various drafts of this manuscript.

Last but not least, we owe thanks to Polly Parke for administrative support that was indispensable to this project and book, as well as to Jack Kelly and Ricky Trotman for their help in tracking down sources and to Christian Hoffman for graphics and layout.

Anticipating a Nuclear Iran

1
Introduction: Setting the Scene for Iran's Emergence as a Nuclear Power

Despite continuing international efforts to constrain or halt Iran's programs, there is growing evidence that Iran is determined to become a nuclear weapons state. If this cannot be prevented, or if it can be only postponed, the United States and other nations will face the need to coexist with a nuclear-armed Iran and to contemplate the consequences of this situation for U.S. and allied/partner defense and deterrence planning. It is widely assumed that an Iran with nuclear weapons would threaten stability in the politically fragile and potentially explosive Middle East. It would also challenge the legitimacy of the international nonproliferation order established in the second half of the twentieth century and codified by the Nuclear Non-Proliferation Treaty.[1] If we cannot dissuade Iran from becoming a nuclear weapons state, can we live with it? If so, how? Would a nuclear Iran be "deterrable," and are its leaders "rational actors" when it comes to calculations pertaining to crisis management and escalation control? Would the possession of nuclear weapons embolden Iran's foreign policy decisions, or would it serve as a defensive shield to protect Iran's vital interests? Answers to such questions may possibly be found in the way in which Iran goes about its nuclear development as well as speculation about alternative Iranian nuclear futures.

There are essentially three paths that Iran could follow to achieve nuclear weapons status. First, Iran could actually deploy nuclear weapons with credible evidence that it had done so. This approach would rely on Iran's fielding of specific systems—nuclear warheads and delivery vehicles—for all to see. Iran could, for example, adopt the "North Korean model," in which it chooses to demonstrate publicly its capability to deploy nuclear weapons by one or more tests, as Pyongyang has done. The publicity that Iran has given to its missile tests and nuclear reactor development is consistent with this idea. By adopting the North Korean nuclear model, Iran's leadership may believe that it might have a better chance of ensuring regime survival and hence avoiding the fate that befell the Qaddafi regime in Libya.[2] Just as important, however, might be an Iranian assumption that Iran would benefit politically from the overt deployment of nuclear weapons capability, particularly as it relates to regional political dynamics and its self-proclaimed leadership role on the international stage. In this respect, nuclear weapons quite possibly could embolden Iran's leadership in its conduct of foreign policy, providing a basis for taking risks that the country's leaders might otherwise not elect to assume. At the same time, Iran's possession of nuclear weapons might also ameliorate domestic opposition to the regime. Diverting public attention from difficult domestic challenges at a time when the regime faces increased criticism at home would create an opportunity to channel public discontent and anger away from domestic problems, allowing Iran's leaders to highlight Tehran's new international status.

Alternatively, Iran could adopt a stance of nuclear ambiguity, neither affirming nor denying a nuclear weapons capability based on a highly secret program that moved Tehran steadily toward the nuclear weaponization threshold.[3] In this sense, Iran could adopt the "Israeli model," in which nuclear weapons would be developed clandestinely and deployed in secret locations, away from Western observation. Iran could choose to refrain from showcasing its nuclear capability, much as Israel has tried to do for so long, and plausibly deny that it had developed a nuclear deterrent capability as a means of hedging its bets with the international community. This approach would be consistent with Iran's penchant for secrecy. It would also support a regime decision to protect itself against the inevitability of further Western (and UN-mandated) counter-measures that would likely be attendant upon adoption of the North Korean model. It would also provide Iran with a "defensive deterrent" or retaliatory capability should Iran ever be threatened with aggressive nuclear or conventional military action.

Finally, Iran could progress systematically toward nuclear weapons status while continuing to assert that its nuclear programs are intended only for peaceful purposes and entirely compatible with its membership in the Non-Proliferation Treaty regime. In this way Iran could remain officially a nonnuclear signatory to the NPT while moving toward but not actually deploying nuclear weapons. With this model, which has been embraced by Japan, Iran could develop a latent nuclear weapons capability without an actual deployed nuclear weapons force.[4] This appears to be the current Iranian approach. It is consistent with Iranian efforts to develop a sophisticated nuclear-technology base, which could be used to provide the basis for a nuclear "breakout" capability if and when a strategic decision to cross the nuclear threshold is taken. In the case of Japan, because that country is widely assumed to have the ability to produce and deploy nuclear weapons relatively quickly, it is said to possess so high a level of nuclear latency as to make it a virtual nuclear state. With its ongoing uranium-enrichment programs, a wide-ranging, indigenous missile-development effort, and an ambitious space-technology program, Iran may indeed be pursuing nuclear latency as the means to achieve its political and strategic objectives without breeching its NPT obligations. In the final analysis, the decision about whether to cross the nuclear threshold becomes a question of policy choice rather than technological capability. The necessary infrastructure and expertise are in place, ready to be activated when the political leadership decides to do so.

Whatever path the Iranian regime may be pursuing, it is important to realize that in Iran there is a broad domestic constituency in support of the development of nuclear technologies based on Iran's desire for international recognition as an important regional and global actor. There is a resurgence of Persian nationalism, which is fueling domestic support for Iran's mastering of nuclear technologies. To the extent that nuclear weapons have conferred a special status on nations that possess them, this line of thinking is driving some Iranians to support the nation's development of nuclear weapons technologies as well. In fact, as pointed out by Farideh Farhi,[5] some of the most significant decisions taken in Iran to advance the country's nuclear weapons–relevant programs came during the presidency of Mohammad Khatami, who is widely regarded in Western analytical circles as a "reformer," given the emphasis during his tenure on a "Dialogue of Civilizations" and his later position as cofounder of the Green Movement,[6] which emerged during the 2009 election campaign. Subsequently, during the tenure of Mahmoud Ahmadinejad,

Iran's nuclear development programs have advanced even further, with the support of Iran's Supreme Leader, Grand Ayatollah Sayyed Ali Hosseini Khamenei. All decision making about national security issues lies in the Ayatollah's hands, despite the highly fractured and personalized nature of Iran's political structures. Notwithstanding the 2013 election of Hassan Rouhani as president, Iran's conservatives are in charge, and, in any case, there is a national consensus supporting Iran's development of a nuclear technology base. In this, Iran's conservatives have been empowered by the military, which has emerged as a powerful element in Iranian society. It asserts great control over the levers of government and Iran's commercial enterprises, with Iran's Revolutionary Guards Corps (IRGC) dominating many of the country's nuclear programs, including those perceived as contributing to Iran's nuclear weapons effort. Moreover, the IRGC's Qods Force element has tightened control over weapons transfers to allies, including the embattled regime of Bashar al-Assad in Syria, and has assumed responsibility for the training of surrogates, notably Hezbollah in Lebanon and Hamas, and for providing them with weapons.[7]

Since the disputed election of 2009, the regime has remained firmly in control, although increasingly because of the tightening of the sanctions against Iran and the brutal suppression of the leadership of the Green Movement, it faces formidable political and economic problems.[8] Iran's dependence on imports of refined petroleum products makes it susceptible to the global energy market, and from this perspective the sanctions have been hurting everyday life. A great economic divide exists between the country's poor and uneducated population and those who are educated and comparatively wealthy. When the price of oil was high, Iran's structural economic problems could be hidden, but when depressed oil prices became a reality in 2008, Iran's reckless fiscal and monetary policies could no longer be concealed. Projected spending plans were roundly criticized, and the fund for the country's strategic oil reserve fell from around $200 billion to less than $7 billion. Making matters worse, Iran's rate of inflation exceeded 30 percent, and its jobless population reached almost 3 million, of whom 2.4 million were young people.[9] Indeed, some 70 percent of Iranians are under the age of thirty, and that "youth bulge" is creating additional pressures on Iran's economy and Iranian society and politics, contributing to an official youth unemployment rate of about 28.6 percent, although many economists believe that the percentages of inflation and youth unemployment may be even higher.

Empowered by the military, the Iranian regime has sought to use the nuclear issue to improve its domestic position and to direct public anger against the outside world, arguing that the imperialist powers are attempting to deprive Iran of the "dignity" and "respect" that it deserves. Both are emotionally laden terms for Iranians because they are associated with Iran's sovereignty, territorial integrity, and freedom of development.[10] In framing their arguments in these terms, regime leaders have been increasingly assertive in promoting Iran's interests and in their efforts to rectify widely perceived historic injustices inflicted on Iran by the more powerful "imperial" nations, including tsarist Russia, the Soviet Union, Great Britain, and, of course, the United States.[11] Allegations that "powerful nations" are keeping Iran from advancing technologically resonate deeply. Speaking before the United Nations General Assembly, President Ahmadinejad used the term "nuclear apartheid" to describe this phenomenon. Nuclear technologies are seen as a key imperative in Tehran for mitigating the country's formidable economic problems, i.e., the use of nuclear power for domestic energy needs and the export of Iran's oil and gas resources for revenues. Access to nuclear technologies is also considered to be a right conferred on Iran by articles 3 and 4 of the Non-Proliferation Treaty.[12] While the NPT does allow access by nonnuclear signatories to civilian nuclear-power-generation technologies, it also makes clear that such access is conditioned on the promise not to exploit these technologies for military purposes.[13] Iran, like North Korea before its withdrawal from the NPT, had been a member in "good standing," until its eight-year war with Iraq apparently helped convince its revolutionary leadership to reconsider the value of nuclear weapons to support and uphold the country's independence and to deter attacks. While publicly stating its intention to pursue nuclear technologies for peaceful purposes, behind this façade there is mounting evidence that Iran is developing nuclear weapons.

For many Iranians who lived through the Iran-Iraq war of the 1980s, there is another convincing rationale for Iran's pursuit of a nuclear weapons capability—although many who support this line of thinking argue that Iran should not breech the "nuclear threshold" by developing an actual weapons capability. Rather, like Japan, Iran should harvest all the technologies necessary to produce nuclear weapons but refrain from deploying them. Having such a virtual capability in hand would, it is argued, contribute to Iran's international prestige and provide the basis for a "break-out" capability were Iran threatened, as it was during the war with Iraq, during which time the international community lined up in support of Iraq against Iran. In Tehran's view, Iran was isolated and left to fend for itself during the war with Iraq. This legacy helps shape contemporary Iranian perspectives and may even lend support for the notion of an independent Iranian nuclear capability. According to this line of reasoning, nuclear technologies can contribute to a more independent Iran in possession of a strengthened scientific infrastructure. As part of this science base, an Iranian nuclear program is fully consistent with Iran's quest for independence and greater international stature and influence. As suggested by Farideh Farhi, "Framing the Iranian program in terms of the country's scientific and technological progress made it much more difficult to challenge domestically."[14] According to another Iranian scholar, Bahman Baktiari, "Iranians view science and technology as important components of a country's international status and prestige."[15] This suggests that any Western attempts to constrain Iran's development of nuclear technologies can be and have been portrayed as efforts to constrain or otherwise deter Iran's emergence as a first-world power.

While tapping into Iranian perceptions of the country's inevitable emergence as an important world power, Iran's pursuit of nuclear technologies may also be consistent with the country's identified foreign policy and national security goals. Not only would an advanced nuclear-power capability provide the means to achieve energy security, but it also might offer Iran a credible option to develop the means to offset Israel's nuclear weapons and protect the country from other potential nuclear or conventional adversaries. A nuclear Iran would be less likely to be invaded by the United States, a lesson also derived from North Korea's possession of nuclear weapons and the Qaddafi regime's decision to surrender its nuclear potential for Western trade and the lifting of sanctions against Libya. Having in hand a capability to deter enemy attacks and to ensure regime survival, therefore, appear to converge as powerful motivations for development of an independent deterrent capability. Even for Iranians opposed to the current regime, Iran's position as a Shia outsider in a predominantly Sunni Muslim world might provide a persuasive rationale for supporting a nuclear program and perhaps even nuclear weapons. In other words, national pride that cuts across broad segments of the population accounts for much of the domestic support for Iran's nuclear activities. However, to the extent that Iranians care about how Iran is viewed by the outside world, international legitimacy matters as well. This factor may in fact encourage the adoption of a more nuanced position on whether the regime should abrogate the NPT by overtly deploying a nuclear weapons capability or stop short of crossing the nuclear threshold and remain formally in compliance with the treaty. Arguably, an Iran that had not actually taken the final step toward nuclear weaponization but had the means to do so could have the best of both worlds, that is, continued NPT membership and the ability to deploy nuclear weapons quickly once the political decision to do so was taken.

Any Iranian decision to cross the nuclear threshold would be dependent on the state of Iran's nuclear programs and their likelihood of achieving the objective of development and deployment of a credible nuclear weapons capability within a specific timeframe. There have been numerous estimates and reports about Iran's nuclear programs. In 2007, the United States produced a controversial National Intelligence Estimate (NIE),[16] which concluded that Iran had terminated work on a nuclear warhead design program in 2003, supposedly as a consequence of the American military intervention in Iraq.[17] In 2010, however, that assessment was modified when a new NIE was delayed as a result of the emergence of new, ambiguous evidence about an Iranian nuclear weapons program. Since 2007, and indeed against mounting evidence to the contrary, including the revelation in 2009 of a secret nuclear site located near Qom (generally known as the Fordow facility), new information concerning Iran's enhancement of capabilities for uranium enrichment, and speculation about the testing of high explosives at the Parchin military complex—a development fueled by a November 2011 report of the International Atomic Energy Agency (IAEA), the group tasked with enforcement of the NPT's safeguards agreements—U.S. analysts have contended that Iran either never stopped its nuclear work or resumed it shortly after the fall of Saddam Hussein.[18] In either case, since 2007, Iran has continued its production of low-enriched uranium (LEU) at Natanz while installing new centrifuges to enrich uranium to even higher levels (of HEU) that would provide the basis for the production of weapons-grade fissile material. According to a February 2013 IAEA report, Iran had by that time produced 7,451 kilograms of low-enriched uranium at Natanz.[19] If further enriched, this quantity could produce enough highly enriched uranium for six or seven nuclear weapons. The question then becomes one of timing. How long after it makes a strategic decision to produce nuclear weapons would Iran be able to produce a bomb and weaponize it?

To date, there is no consensus on this issue, but the evidence strongly suggests that Iran is moving ahead with military programs designed to support a weapons decision. Since the publication of the controversial U.S. NIE in 2007, Iran has more than doubled its stock of 5 percent enriched uranium, while starting to enrich small quantities of uranium up to 20 percent, installing new centrifuges at Natanz and Fordow presumably for that purpose. At the same time, with the activation of the Arak heavy-water production facility, Iran appears to have opened up a second path (i.e., plutonium) for warhead development, leading to new concerns in the international community about an Iranian "breakout" capability sooner rather than later. In a January 2012 televised interview, Secretary of Defense Leon Panetta stated that the consensus on Iran is that "if they decided to do it, it would probably take them about a year to be able to produce a bomb and then possibly another one to two years in order to put it on a deliverable vehicle of some sort in order to deliver that weapon."[20] Israeli estimates point to a possibly even shorter time frame based on their calculation of the time needed to amass enough enriched uranium at the Natanz and Fordow sites. During his address before the 2012 United Nations General Assembly, Prime Minister Benjamin Netanyahu stated that Iran was six months away from amassing the necessary quantities of enriched uranium to produce a bomb and argued that Iran was putting itself in a position "to make a short, perhaps undetectable, sprint to manufacture its first nuclear weapon."[21]

U.S. and Israeli assessments of Iran's potential for a nuclear "breakout" are remarkably similar, even if press reports highlight differences over their "red lines," or the point at which even more substantive action must be undertaken to achieve their shared objective of denying Iran any nuclear weapons capability. U.S. and Israeli differences over the seriousness of Iran's possession of the technologies and materials to give it a nuclear weapons capability have created tensions between the two countries and are fueling debate among policy makers about Iran's real intentions. Is Iran seeking to become a nuclear power, or does it just want to give the impression that it is so technologically advanced that if it decides to become a nuclear power it can do so in a matter of months? By adopting this approach, the regime in Iran may hope to shape its engagement with the West without actually having to jettison a future option to cross the nuclear threshold. However, as the August 2012 IAEA report suggests, the circumstantial evidence is mounting that Iran hopes to have in hand a "breakout" capability sooner rather than later. By all accounts, and this includes its continued efforts to stockpile and enrich uranium, open a plutonium processing front at Arak, continue to resist efforts to inspect suspect sites, and work to design, develop, and produce nuclear triggers and warheads (for missile delivery), Iran will have enough fissile material to support production of six or seven nuclear bombs. When this happens, according to Israeli assessments, Iran will have become a virtual nuclear power, and the West will have lost any capacity to stop a nuclear breakout. In fact, with many of Iran's nuclear activities hidden from view in underground facilities, we may never know, except in a crisis, the extent to which Iran's nuclear program has advanced. So, from this perspective, the time to do something about this is before Iran's enrichment activities produce enough weapons-grade material to yield a real and not a virtual capability.

The question of timing relating to an Iranian breakout capability remains a contentious issue of debate among Iran scholars. Nevertheless, as the August 2012 IAEA report makes clear, Iran has increased its production of enriched uranium and has installed new generation centrifuges at Fordow and Natanz, beyond the requirements for medical research, the ground on which the regime has maintained the requirement for these programs. As Iran seems determined to sustain its nuclear programs without transparency, relying on underground facilities for its more modern production efforts, Western nations have variously tried to stop Iran's nuclear programs through a combination of measures, including negotiations, sanctions, and even the implementation of active measures designed to slow down or halt Iran's nuclear programs. Even as Iran's own indigenous nuclear-technology base has advanced, it has also suffered setbacks, including from internal problems with the functioning of older centrifuges and as a result of hostile actions to introduce a malware virus into Iran's centrifuges. Designated the Stuxnet virus, this malware appears to have been part of a calculated cyberwarfare attack on Iran's nuclear development.[22] Together with other measures, including the imposition of ever tighter and targeted sanctions against key individuals and industries as well as the assassination of key scientists in Iran's nuclear programs, cyberattacks against Iran's centrifuges have undermined Iran's nuclear efforts. Nevertheless, the programs remain intact and appear to moving toward the objective of providing the regime with a capability on which to base a weaponization decision. This reality has engendered protracted debate between those who believe that Iran can still be influenced to halt its nuclear program and those who contend that weaponization is not only inevitable but also a key element of the regime's military modernization and its aspirations for great power status in the Middle East and on the broader international stage.

To those who believe that Iran still can be dissuaded from going nuclear, continued efforts to engage the regime remain the key. Epitomized by Turkey and Brazil's attempt to reach an agreement over the reprocessing of Iranian fissile material outside Iran, as had been proposed earlier by the IAEA,[23] proponents of this "engagement school" argue that a "grand bargain" can still be struck with Iran based on a mix of incentives (i.e., "carrots") and inducements (i.e., "sticks") to convince the regime in Tehran that the West means business. Proponents of this approach argue that while it is important to keep credible military options (for preventive action) on the table, a more compelling negotiating strategy that answers Iran's legitimate energy concerns has a better chance of achieving the desired objective of stopping Iran's nuclear programs.[24] However, Iran's leadership has tried to shape the engagement process and use it to get around Western-imposed sanctions to maintain Iran's technology programs, and hence to keep in hand a credible option for weaponization if that strategic decision is made.

Above all else, Iran has been adamant that further engagement with the West is dependent on "confidence-building measures," which, as seen from Tehran, must include the removal of all sanctions. In table 1.1 we summarize the four rounds of sanctions against Iran that have been approved by the United Nations Security Council in an attempt to curtail its nuclear weapons development. As a result of the various sanctions, Iran's oil exports and trade have been reduced while its access to global financial markets has been curtailed, with transactions between Iranian banks and the outside world increasingly restricted. Undoubtedly, sanctions have slowed Iran's nuclear program; they have made it more difficult or impossible to import nuclear-related technologies. Nevertheless, sanctions have not halted Iran's indigenous efforts to develop nuclear technologies and to enrich and reprocess uranium or pursue the plutonium path. In addition to using illicit trafficking networks to gain access to restrictive materials, technologies, and know-how, Iran has benefited from differences among Western nations and at the United Nations over specific sanctions regimes and the extent to which sanctions should be employed as a tool to coerce Iran into negotiations on its nuclear programs. In this respect, China has continued to engage with Iran, probably because it needs access to Iranian energy exports to fuel its growing economy, and has been problematic when it comes to implementing and enforcing UN sanctions on Iran.[25] With their growing economic ties with Iran, Turkey and South Africa have made it more difficult to constrain Tehran's nuclear activities.

Moreover, in June 2008, there were reports suggesting that digitized blueprints for nuclear weapon designs might have been transferred illegally to Iran (among other countries) by members of the Tinner family of Switzerland working as part of the A. Q. Khan network.[26] Subsequently, an Iranian-based nuclear black-market ring was uncovered, using French and Chinese companies as cutouts to smuggle dual-use and sanctioned military items into Iran. In a report about the blueprints' discovery, Dr. David Albright, a former UN weapons inspector, observed that the blueprints are "troubling" because the designs they contain are "ideal" for Iran (and North Korea), both of which have faced "struggles in building a nuclear warhead small enough to fit atop their ballistic missiles, and these designs were for a warhead that would fit."[27] In May 2012, the Mujahedin-e Khalq (MeK), an Iranian opposition group, released a report citing Iran's work in the area of nuclear weapons design and testing.[28] According to published reports, some sixty individuals and eleven institutions are identified as having a role in Iran's nuclear weapons

Table 1.1 United Nations Security Council Sanctions Against Iran

RESOLUTION 1737 (DEC. 23, 2006)	RESOLUTION 1747 (MARCH 26, 2007)	RESOLUTION 1803 (MARCH 3, 2008)	RESOLUTION 1929 (JUNE 9, 2010)
Imposes travel and financial restrictions on twenty-two Iranian individuals and entities linked to the nuclear program	Bans all Iranian arms exports and expands UNSC 1737 to include twenty-five more individuals and entities linked to Iran's nuclear and military agencies	Imposes a travel ban on five individuals involved in Iran's most sensitive nuclear efforts and travel and financial restrictions on twenty-four others	Expands the arms embargo on Iran
Requires states to prevent the export of sensitive nuclear-related equipment and expertise to Iran	Targets specific individuals and entities linked to Iran's Revolutionary Guard Corps and Qods Force	Bans trade of critical nuclear-related materials and calls on states to monitor and report on Iranian banks suspected of facilitating Iran's nuclear activities	Tightens restrictions on financial and shipping enterprises related to "proliferation-sensitive" activities
Bars training of Iranian nationals abroad that could be applied to the nuclear program	Threatens additional penalties against Iran if it fails to suspend its nuclear program within sixty days	Authorizes voluntary inspections of cargo to and from Iran if there are "reasonable grounds" to suspect the transit of prohibited materials	Specific sanctions against forty-one individuals and entities, including one scientist (Javad Rahigi, head of the Isfahan Technology Center), IRGC members, defense-industry banks, and the national shipping line

programs, which has its headquarters in Mojdeh, near Tehran. The report also singled out another facility in Tehran's Pars neighborhood, which it said is responsible for building nuclear detonators to be tested at the Parchin site. Identified as the Center for Explosives, Blast Research, and Technologies, or METFAZ by its Persian acronym, this site is said to comprise divisions focused on uranium enrichment, warhead design and development, the production of materials for warhead development, nuclear-detonation technologies and materials, electronic calculations

RESOLUTION 1737 (DEC. 23, 2006)	RESOLUTION 1747 (MARCH 26, 2007)	RESOLUTION 1803 (MARCH 3, 2008)	RESOLUTION 1929 (JUNE 9, 2010)
Requires Iran to broaden cooperation with International Atomic Energy Agency inspectors and demands that it halt banned nuclear activities within sixty days	Vote: 15–0	Threatens to impose "further measures" against Iran if it fails to halt sensitive activities within ninety days	Includes creation of panel of experts to monitor implementation
Vote: 15–0		Vote: 14–0 (Indonesia abstained)	Addresses Iran's illicit trade and weapons smuggling
			Sanctions against Moshen Fakhrizadeh-Mahabadi, head of Iran's nuclear weapons program and the SPND facility in Mojdeh; Azim Aghajeni, Qods Force member; and Ali Akbor Tabatabali, IRGC/Qods Force leader, among others
			Vote: 12–2 (Brazil and Turkey), 1 abstention (Lebanon)

for warhead designs, and laser activities. If verified, the existence of this facility contradicts Iranian claims that it does not have a nuclear weapons program and indeed places into doubt recent efforts to engage Iran in negotiations to halt its weapons-related activities.[29]

While sanctions do appear to be having a deleterious effect on the Iranian economy, particularly its access to global financial networks, they apparently have not done enough damage to change regime behavior with respect to nuclear programs. They have, however, forced the regime to reengage with the West. Even major European countries and the European Union, whose dependence on Iranian energy imports is far greater than that of the United States, are stepping up to impose sanctions on Iran's banks and industries involved in regime activities. European insurance companies, for example, increasingly are denying insurance to port operators dealing with Iran, with the result that fewer shipping companies are willing to carry Iranian oil. As a result, by April 2012, Iran had entered into another round of negotiations (this time in Istanbul with the P-5 + 1, the five permanent members of the United Nations Security Council plus Germany) designed, from the Western perspective, to constrain Iran's nuclear programs and influence the regime to not cross the nuclear weapons threshold. From an Iranian perspective, Iran's leaders may have hoped to use these negotiations to buy time for its nuclear programs and to shape favorably their domestic debate over the sanctions issue. By all accounts, the Western powers stepped back from their previous insistence that Iran refrain from any and all (uranium) enrichment activity and, instead, adopted the position that Iran would be permitted to enrich uranium up to 5 percent—the upper end of the range for most civilian uses—with a new emphasis on getting agreement to constrain Iran's enrichment activities at the higher levels needed to produce weapons-grade uranium. This engagement strategy was built from a failed Turkish and Brazilian initiative[30] and included new ideas put forth by the Russians, who had previously offered a "step-by-step" plan for IAEA-supervised reprocessing of Iran's low-enriched uranium outside Iran.[31] The hope was that Iran could be persuaded to step back from the nuclear brink while saving face with the preservation of its civilian nuclear programs and its indigenous nuclear-technology base.

Since the Istanbul meeting with the P-5 +1 in April 2012, however, the Iranian government has shown little inclination to accept these terms. Despite its agreement to participate in subsequent rounds of talks in Baghdad, Moscow, and Almaty, Kazakhstan, official spokesmen for the Iranian government still insist that before any serious negotiation on Iran's nuclear programs can take place, the West must lift its sanctions and "normalize" Iran's nuclear file in the IAEA and at the United Nations. Indeed, this is the basis on which new talks were proposed, beginning after the 2012 U.S. presidential election and engaging only the United States and Iran on a bilateral basis, as has been suggested by Hossein

Mousavian, Iran's former nuclear negotiator and an ally of former Iranian president Ali Akbar Hashemi Rafsanjani, whose daughter was recently placed under arrest by the Ahmadinejad government.[32] Proponents of engagement argue that the Iranians are just posturing and are looking for "reciprocity" and a "face-saving" formula to cut a deal. After all, they argue, the Supreme Leader, Ayatollah Ali Khamenei issued a fatwa, or religious edict, against building nuclear weapons, and the West would be well served by engaging in a broader discussion of confidence-building measures, which could include issues such as defeating the Taliban, enhancing coordination in countering drug trafficking, and recognizing Iran's right to develop nuclear technologies for peaceful purposes.[33]

Thus far, proponents of engagement have little to show for their efforts, and even if the Iranians do continue to negotiate, the lack of transparency inherent in their society and government allows Iran to continue with its nuclear programs without limitation. Critics of this approach, including the prime minister of Israel, argue that without transparency and reciprocity, Iran is free to play a duplicitous game. In this context, and to checkmate Iran's nuclear efforts, another school of thought has emerged, and this one is based on the notion that "deterrence and containment" are the only plausible options for dealing with an Iranian nuclear weapon capability because engagement has yielded little or nothing and has probably actually advanced Iran's nuclear programs. This approach keeps the military option on the table, but it also emphasizes other proactive measures, including the tightening of sanctions against Iran, the use of cyberwarfare, and the creation of an elaborate system of alliances designed to minimize the political fallout from Iran's eventual emergence as a nuclear weapons state.

Opinion is divided, however, on whether containment and deterrence can work against a regime determined to achieve nuclear weapons status. It is more united in its support for such an approach after Iran attains nuclear status, although, as we hope to demonstrate later in this book, a nuclear Iran may in fact reject Western notions of deterrence and build its nuclear capability within a context that defies rational thought (at least from our Western cultural perspective). At the very least, proponents of a deterrence and containment strategy argue that U.S. (and Western) deterrence theory must be updated and its implementation reassessed in the face of new challenges. New ideas for allied/partner reassurance will be necessary, as will innovative approaches to dealing with emerging proliferation threats, including the extension of an Iranian nuclear umbrella over Hezbollah, a nonstate armed group and Iranian ally. It will also be necessary to consider new ways to degrade the regime's confidence in its own deterrent posture and to inject nontraditional elements into U.S. deterrence thinking, such as the use of cyberwarfare, missile defenses, and space as new aspects of U.S. deterrence planning.

Deterring and containing a nuclear Iran or an Iran on the nuclear threshold may even require the implementation of a preventive strike against Iran's nuclear complex. However, this is fraught with dangers and might only set back Iran's nuclear programs for an unspecified but limited period. For many in the United States who have grown weary of America's decade-long war in Afghanistan, the results of such action may not be worth the costs, unless such action was guaranteed to obliterate completely Iran's nuclear program. However, some in Israel may be prepared to accept even results that buy a short amount of time, based on the existential threat that a nuclear Iran would pose to Israel and the contention that even limited success would buy precious time by setting back the Iranian nuclear program perhaps by several years.[34] Barring a successful engagement strategy or an effective strike against Iran's nuclear infrastructure, deterrence and containment seemingly emerge as the best of the bad options for dealing with a nuclear Iran. The question then becomes one of how to deter and contain a regime leadership in possession of nuclear weapons.

A nuclear Iran might be emboldened to be more aggressive in a crisis, either by threatening to use nuclear weapons first or by extending a security umbrella over proxy forces such as Hezbollah, the armed organization created by Iran's Revolutionary Guards in 1982. It might also choose to provide an extended deterrence guarantee over Syria, with whom Iran maintains a mutual defense pact, in an effort to deter an attack or intervention against the embattled Assad regime. A nuclear Iran could empower Syria in Lebanon, or it could decide to augment Hezbollah's position in Lebanon at a time when Israel is under challenge on all fronts by the uncertain results of the Arab Spring.[35] Hezbollah might be prepared to engage more actively in irregular warfare under the protection of Iranian nuclear capabilities.[36] Whether Hezbollah, Hamas, or Syria, for that matter, could actually depend on a nuclear Iran for protection to deter Israeli retaliation is not clear, although such uncertainty could provide the basis for miscalculation as these actors contemplate their options in a setting in which Iran has nuclear weapons.

An Iran with nuclear weapons would also be of concern because of the possible transfer of weapons, fissile material, or scientific know-how to other states such as Syria or Venezuela or to Hezbollah or Hamas. Iran's apparent sanctioning (through payments to Syria) of Syria's transfer of Scud ballistic missiles to Hezbollah seems to indicate that Iran is prepared to proliferate weapons technologies. Would a nuclear Iran be less willing to proliferate nuclear technologies to nonnuclear entities? This might even include al-Qaeda, elements of which are fighting in Syria and have used Iranian territory to move money and operatives to South Asia.[37] Al-Qaeda still operates with a fatwa justifying the use of weapons of mass destruction as a means of striking infidels and generating mass casualties, and, notwithstanding the death of its leader, Osama bin Laden, it still seeks to acquire or produce such weapons. Despite Sunni-Shia tensions resulting in part from al-Qaeda's miscalculations in Iraq, together with Iran's growing influence there, this contingency remains plausible, as Tehran's current support for the Taliban, who practice a form of Islam closer to the Sunni tradition of Wahhabism combined with tribal practices, makes clear.[38] With the United States having completed its military withdrawal from Iraq and a similar drawdown proceeding in Afghanistan, Iran is stepping up its efforts to broaden its reach and presence in and beyond the region. Iran transferred weapons to its militia allies in Iraq and Afghanistan not only in anticipation of the American troop withdrawal but also to accelerate the exit of U.S. forces. Indeed, there is mounting evidence that Iran, either officially or via elements of the IRGC and Qods Force, has facilitated the training of the Taliban inside Iran, where recruits have been taught how to ambush NATO's International Security Assistance Forces (ISAF) in Afghanistan, to enhance the destructive potential of improvised explosive devices, and to evade capture and improve their attack techniques. In Afghanistan, Iran has provided the Taliban with weapons and training while, reportedly, allowing the group to open an office in eastern Iran, from which location it is also mounting operations inside Afghanistan.[39] In Iraq, Shia extremists are operating with Qods Force support both to influence Iraqi politics and to open an arms-supply bridge through Iraq to Syria. These and other Iranian initiatives fit into a pattern that suggests that Tehran is moving both to exploit opportunities presented by the withdrawal of U.S. power from Iraq and Afghanistan and to fill political vacuums created by uprisings across the Middle East. Iran supports such uprisings where they weaken U.S. influence and opposes them, as in Syria, where they would diminish Iran's position.

A nuclear-armed Iran would be cause for concern for other reasons as well. For one, it might accelerate regional and global proliferation, as Saudi Arabia, Turkey, and Egypt rethink their security strategies. It could also open the door to nuclear proliferation in Asia if nations there concluded that the credibility of American deterrence guarantees had eroded and that nuclear weapons possession offered the best means of ensuring their security. A nuclear-armed Iran would also have the potential to threaten the United States directly, either after having developed a long-range intercontinental ballistic missile (ICBM) capability or using air-burst weapons on shorter-range launchers to launch an electromagnetic pulse (EMP) attack from a missile over or near U.S. shores.[40] Tehran is reported to have conducted the kind of missile tests that would be needed for an EMP attack. Such an attack would have devastating consequences from which the United States might recover only with great difficulty.

In order to understand more precisely just how a nuclear Iran might act, we have developed three heuristic models: (1) a Defensive Iran, (2) an Aggressive Iran, and (3) an Unstable Iran. In assessing expected characteristics of Iranian behavior in each of these models, we have identified four issue areas: (1) the type of nuclear capability that Iran would likely field; (2) the conditions under which Iran might resort to threatened or actual nuclear weapons use; (3) the extent to which Iran's military strategy and declaratory policy relating to nuclear weapons possession might embolden Iran or its proxies to pursue more aggressive policies in the region and vis-à-vis the United States; and (4) Iran's potential to transfer nuclear materials to others in and outside the region and the implications of an Iranian weapon for a nuclear cascade, in which other states would acquire their own nuclear capability in response to Iran's crossing the nuclear threshold. These models are described more fully in table 1.2.

Table 1.2 A Snapshot View of the Three Models

MODEL I: DEFENSIVE DETERRENT	MODEL II: AN AGGRESSIVE IRAN	MODEL III: AN UNSTABLE IRAN
Key Attributes	Key Attributes	Key Attributes
Regime survival	Political tool	Technology transfer to states or armed groups is a concern
Territorial protection	Offensive first use	"Loose nukes" a possibility
Minimum deterrence posture	Extended deterrence	Factional control over nuclear weapons in or outside Iran
Defensive launch under attack	Assured-destruction posture	
	Robust and survivable forces	

It is conceivable that each model could describe an Iran whose approach to nuclear weapons changes over time, depending on the type of regime in power and the evolution of its defensive or expansionist objectives. For example, Iran might initially deploy a nuclear force configured out of necessity both doctrinally and operationally for inherently defensive purposes (Model I). As time passes, Iran's motivations for a nuclear weapons capability might evolve toward a more aggressive stance (Model II). Such motivations might be based either on specific goals that the regime sets for itself or on the opportunity afforded by a more advanced and powerful nuclear force. An Iran with nuclear weapons behaving in accordance with the characteristics of either Model I or Model II might eventually be subject to disintegrative forces, thus leading to the characteristics of Model III. Therefore, in assessing the implications of a nuclear Iran it may be useful to think about dynamic models that are subject to modification, either as the regime adapts to new circumstances or as the nuclear technologies available to Iran evolve. Model III could replace either of the other two models unless, of course, a regime in possession of nuclear weapons is successful in overcoming challenges to its ability to quell domestic unrest.

Our Model I may describe an Iran that has acquired nuclear weapons but has undergone regime change that at least moves Iran toward greater democratization. In this sense Iran would have shed revolutionary aspirations to become instead a democracy as envisaged, for example, by its Green Movement. Such a transformation is probably not likely before Iran achieves nuclear weapons status. Indeed, the nuclear clock in Iran is advancing at a much faster rate than the democracy clock in the aftermath of the June 2009 presidential election and protest movement, which was crushed by the current regime. This is a regime that is committed to Iran's technological advance and to a Persian nationalism that views the country through the prism of Iran's greatness. With that in mind, a nuclear Iran under the control of its present leadership would be even more difficult to challenge than an Iran without nuclear weapons or an Iran that has embraced secular, democratic governance. However, the assumption here is that Iran, even in Model I, remains a clerical state and seeks nuclear weapons to ensure regime stability. Conceivably, our Model I could also describe a country that has embraced limited government based on representative institutions with civilian control of the military and transparency with regard to military expenditures and defense strategy and policy, but that is unlikely to be the case unless and until opposition forces within the country unite to create a new form of governance or overthrow the regime. Under present circumstances it is far more likely that under Model I: A Defensive Iran, any decision to cross the nuclear threshold would be taken to underwrite a security policy far more modest in scope than would be the case in either of our other two models.

Our Model I also accommodates the idea put forward by the international relations theorist Kenneth N. Waltz that nuclear weapons instill greater caution rather than emboldening their possessors to take aggressive action. Waltz bases his hypothesis on the idea that nuclear weapons states are unlikely to go to war against other nuclear states because the stakes are so great. Nuclear states, in his view, become even more cautious in their dealings with other nuclear states, and this includes dealings with nonnuclear states that are clearly aligned with a recognized nuclear power. Contrary to the conventional wisdom set forth by opponents of nuclear proliferation, Waltz's theory asserts a stabilizing effect of nuclear proliferation.[41] If this logic holds, the emergence of a nuclear

Iran, followed by a nuclear cascade in other states in or around the Middle East, may result in a more stable regional balance of power or, at the very least, it would induce greater caution in decision making about foreign policy and security matters. Nuclear states fearing the possibility of annihilation are unlikely to attack other nuclear states. From this perspective, a world with many nuclear-armed states is likely to be more stable than a world without nuclear weapons. In the absence of nuclear weapons, the nuclear standoff that existed during the Cold War between the United States and the Soviet Union would probably have escalated to actual armed confrontation between massed conventional armies, or so this theory would suggest. Such strategic logic is entirely compatible with our Defensive Iran model, in which nuclear weapons protect only the most vital national interest, state or regime survival.

In contrast, in Model II: An Aggressive Iran, we introduce the assumption that the threat of mutual nuclear annihilation as the basis for caution is replaced, for example, by the apocalyptic idea of sacrifice on behalf of an afterlife. The threat of annihilation becomes an invitation to action rather than a basis for mutual deterrence. In this sense, the survival motivation that is central to Model I gives way to a fundamentally different assumption: namely, that in place of the core national interest of survival there is an ideological/religious belief that a beckoning redemptive future lies beyond present existence. In Model I, Iran is a normal nation-state in possession of nuclear weapons. In Model II, Iran is a messianic revolutionary state whose approach to nuclear weapons and their possible use on behalf of posited goals encompasses self- and group sacrifices—the mentality of a suicide bomber extended to a larger group, the nation, or at least to portions of such a nation. It is more likely that an Aggressive Iran with nuclear weapons would embark on a foreign policy designed to expand Tehran's influence within and beyond the Middle East. Nuclear weapons would be seen as giving Iran greater options to act below the nuclear threshold, confident that its enemies would be cautious in responding out of fear of escalation to the nuclear level. Such a calculus carries with it the risk of miscalculation and therefore heightened crisis instability, although from an Iranian perspective it can hardly be considered to be irrational or implausible.

In Model III, we have elements of unpredictability and instability based in this case on the assumption of chaos and ungovernability within a nuclear-armed Iran. Such capabilities could fall into the hands of nonstate armed groups with widely divergent and differing interests, values, and goals. Some might be imbued with the jihadist religious/ ideological fervor leading to possible nuclear use against nonbelievers and other perceived enemies. Some might be prepared to make such weapons available to other terrorist groups who would have little hesitation to use them against the United States and its allies. Within this model there is great potential for the realization of the so-called loose nukes phenomenon, as well as for an "insider threat" that could lead to a nuclear detonation inside or outside Iran, based on the emergence of competing factions for government control or the transfer of nuclear weapons or component technologies to proxy agents. In subsequent chapters these models are explored in greater detail, but here it is useful to sketch out, in an introductory fashion, the major characteristics of the models in relation to their preferred deterrence concepts and force posture considerations.

Model I: A Defensive Iran assumes a commitment to a minimum nuclear-deterrence posture. If we must contemplate a nuclear Iran, this would obviously be the best case from the U.S. perspective. Iran would deploy a nuclear force that is small and whose principal objective would be to deter an attack on Iran or its regime. Quite likely in this circumstance, the Iranian leadership would issue a declaratory policy that specified the conditions under which Iran would use or threaten to use its nuclear weapons. For example, this might involve retaliatory use against a conventional or nuclear attack against Iran. In such a model Iranian nuclear weapons would be dispersed and concealed in order to enhance their survival potential and to discourage preemptive attacks against them. Although it would be inherently defensive, this Iranian nuclear capability could, nevertheless, feature an Iranian first use of nuclear weapons to protect vital national interests or a launch-under-attack scenario in keeping with a "use them or lose them" mentality.

Model II: An Aggressive Iran postulates a situation in which Iran, backed by its nuclear weapons, aspires to a greater leadership role in the wider Middle East. Nuclear weapons would embolden Iran to pursue a more active foreign policy in and beyond the Middle East. This would include the establishment of a nuclear umbrella over an ally such as Syria or over a nonstate armed group such as Hezbollah, giving these actors greater freedom in certain contingencies. The United States would have greater difficulty deterring Iranian conventional or unconventional operations if Iran possessed nuclear weapons. Under this model Iran would gain unprecedented freedom of action in the Persian Gulf and the Strait of Hormuz, including especially maritime operations and possibly even military operations against its Gulf neighbors. An Aggressive Iran model would also lead Teheran to place great emphasis on a more robust and diversified nuclear weapons capability than in the first model, and it would embolden Iran in its dealings with neighbors such as Iraq and Saudi Arabia. This model would also have major consequences for security guarantees extended by the United States and could encourage additional powers to consider their own nuclear weapons options.

Model III: An Unstable Iran is defined by state collapse and the prospect of loose nukes. One faction or another might gain control of Iran's nuclear weapons, raising questions about technology and materials transfers as well as command and control of Iran's nuclear weapons. In this model, too, Iran's nuclear weapons might be taken out of the country to keep them from being seized by an opposing faction, or they might be transferred to IRGC elements seeking control of Iran's government. This model poses the greatest proliferation threat because the world's most dangerous weapons might fall into the hands of the world's most dangerous actors. Deterring regime elements in possession of nuclear weapons from transferring them or even using them would become an important planning focus for the United States.

As suggested earlier, a nuclear-armed Iran would pose essentially three types of operational planning challenges for the United States. To varying degrees they are present in each of the models: deterring or countering the potential for actual use of Iranian nuclear weapons against allies, U.S. forces in the region, allies outside the region, and the United States itself; countering the use of Iranian conventional forces under the protection of Iran's nuclear umbrella; and countering the transfer of nuclear weapons to terrorist groups and their possible use by such groups. In later chapters, with reference to our three models, we address the following overarching questions, recognizing that the three models provide the basis for different answers to each and the fact that there is incomplete information on which to base such answers:

- Based on what we know about Iran's nuclear, missile, and associated development programs, what would an initial Iranian nuclear posture look like? How might it evolve over time? What does this suggest about the ability of the United States and other external powers and agencies (e.g., the IAEA, the Nuclear Suppliers Group [NSG], and the Proliferation Security Initiative [PSI]) to influence the scale and future evolution of an Iranian nuclear weapons program?
- How would Iran likely deploy and use its nuclear weapons as a deterrent, a tool for geopolitical leverage, and a war-fighting asset (either in their own right or as an enabler for conventional force operations)? In that context, what kind of nuclear doctrine might Iran espouse, and how would it influence Iranian decision making with respect to future force composition and deployment or in the context of signaling (i.e., strategic communications), crisis management and bargaining, or even a limited nuclear weapons use?
- How, and to what degree, would an explicit nuclear status embolden Iran or its proxies to pursue more disruptive policies within the region and beyond? Where and how could we expect a nuclear Iran to flex its broader strategic reach? What are the likely consequences for U.S. interests and for those of its regional allies and friends?
- How might a nuclear Iran proliferate to other regimes or terrorists? How might it trigger broader regional proliferation? What are the likeliest scenarios in both circumstances? What is least likely?
- Finally, in light of analysis based on the models we have postulated, how can the United States best deter, contain, and, if need be, defeat a nuclear Iran, either unilaterally or in concert with allies and other partner states? What is the optimal set of capabilities for the likeliest scenario of a nuclear Iran? What specific sets of U.S. and allied/partner capabilities could be most effectively leveraged to counter and dampen the ambitions of a nuclear Iran? To what extent can diplomatic and other nonmilitary measures provide vital reinforcing leverage?

With the three models as the framework for analysis, we provide an assessment of the strategic, political, and operational planning implications of Iran as a nuclear weapons state. Chapter 2 examines the deterrence dynamics related to an Iran with nuclear weapons. Chapter 3 focuses on Iran's nuclear ambitions as they relate to its foreign policy objectives, domestic political considerations, and role in the Islamic world. Chapter 4 explores the possible ways in which Iran might operationalize a nuclear weapons capability, and chapter 5 assesses the implications of Iran's nuclear development for U.S. strategic and operational planning. Chapter 6 lays out specific options for updating U.S. defense and deterrence planning, and chapter 7 examines the more explicit implications of Iran's nuclear development for hybrid warfare and deterrence of nonstate and rogue actors. Finally, we offer some concluding observations and recommendations for U.S. policy.

2
The Deterrence Dynamics of an Iran with Nuclear Weapons

How Iran crosses the nuclear threshold, together with the levels and types of nuclear forces that it chooses to deploy become important factors in considering how to deter or contain a nuclear Iran. In the event that Iran chooses a covert weapons deployment (the Israeli model) or opts to maintain a "threshold" capability (the Japan model), the international response is likely to be more restrained than in the case of an overt Iranian nuclear deployment (the North Korean model). It is logical to assume that there would be less of an international outcry because of the strategic ambiguity surrounding Iran's nuclear weapons status and because Iran could continue to adhere to the fiction that it was abiding by its obligations as a nonnuclear signatory of the NPT while also maintaining that its nuclear development programs were for civilian purposes only. Nevertheless, even short of weaponization, Iran's nuclear activities would be and indeed are cause for concern, especially in Israel, which would continue to worry about an Iranian "breakout" capability. They would also raise apprehension in Iran's smaller Persian Gulf neighbors such as Bahrain and Kuwait,[1] which have substantial Shi'ite populations, and in the United Arab Emirates (UAE), which has a territorial dispute with Iran over control of three small islands in the Persian Gulf.[2] For Saudi Arabia, the largest of the Gulf Cooperation Council (GCC) states, and Iran's nuclear activities, even short of a decision to weaponize, have raised serious questions about allied and partner reassurance and engendered new thinking about security options, including Saudi Arabia's own nuclear development. This situation also has the potential to induce greater caution on the part of the smaller Arab Gulf states, contributing to the "Finlandization" of the Arabian Gulf region.[3] With nuclear weapons,

Iran's capacity to intimidate its weaker Gulf neighbors is certain to grow. Thus, even in anticipation of a nuclear Iran, it becomes essential to shore up U.S. defense and deterrence options for allied/partner reassurance. This would be even more pressing if Iran became a nuclear weapons state given the implications for proliferation—or nuclear cascading— and for regional stability and U.S. homeland defense.

If Iran decides to showcase a nuclear weapons capability (as opposed to adopting the Israeli model of ambiguity or of stopping at the threshold of weaponization as Japan has done), the United States will have to be much more active in updating its approach to defense and deterrence planning. Under each of our models there will be a need to strengthen U.S. extended security guarantees in the Persian Gulf region.[4] This could include the establishment of a more formal alliance framework with one or several nations in the region, as well as the enhancement of missile defenses located in the region and the incorporation of cyberwarfare into a new deterrence paradigm. It might also require a more concerted effort to strengthen the U.S. force presence in the region—something that will not be easy in light of defense budget cuts and competing pressures for sustained force presence in the Asia-Pacific area.[5] While the United States already maintains sizeable forces in the Persian Gulf region, with the headquarters of the U.S. Navy's Fifth Fleet located in Bahrain and the forward headquarters of U.S. Central Command (CENTCOM) situated in Qatar, in addition to conditional access to bases in the UAE and Kuwait, a nuclear Iran might necessitate an increased carrier battle group presence and offshore U.S. Marine Corps deployments to bolster our commitment to the region and to U.S. partners faced with a nuclear Iran. Moreover, for the United States the strategic importance of Iraq and of a post-Assad Syria would increase with a nuclear Iran that was flexing its muscles in the region and extending its influence from Lebanon to Syria and in Afghanistan. In neighboring Iraq, Iran is trying to influence the succession of Grand Ayatollah Ali al-Sistani, the leader of Iraq's Shia community, contributing to concerns that Iran is trying to transplant its Islamic Revolution to Iraq and destroy the country's fragile democracy.[6] In short, a nuclear Iran would make it necessary for the United States to provide greater reassurance and extended deterrence.

A nuclear Iran would likewise pose numerous challenges for U.S. thinking and assumptions about crisis management and escalation. Especially in Models II and III, Iran would probably conclude that nuclear weapons conferred additional escalation options that included greater latitude to use nonnuclear forces and support for nonstate armed groups without fear of U.S. retaliation. Although the United States might believe that it still controlled the escalation process in a crisis with Iran, a nuclear Iran might believe that it could successfully challenge the United States, which would be deterred from acting against a nuclear-armed Iran for fear of nuclear retaliation against U.S. interests in the region or even against the United States itself. In other words, the United States would be more likely to be deterred than would Iran. According to such logic, Iran would be prepared to escalate to the nuclear level because it operates in a region close to its own territory. In contrast, the United States would be less likely to escalate to the nuclear level because its interests in the region were not seen as vital to its security. Of course, such reasoning might also be the basis for miscalculation on the part of Iran, especially in our Model II. Moreover, in this context as well, the United States could not be confident that Iranian leaders would be deterred from using nuclear weapons first in a crisis. In the absence of transparency about Iranian nuclear decision making and how an Iranian leadership would view nuclear weapons, we can only speculate about the circumstances under which Iran would resort to nuclear weapons. Our use of models represents a means of engaging in such speculative analysis.

Iranian decision making about nuclear weapons use may depend on a number of factors, several of which could be at odds with prevalent Western conceptions of nuclear planning and the assumptions that underlie such weapons. Here it is useful to recall Amitai Etzioni's suggestion that Iran's leaders could act "non-rationally," that is, "in response to deeply held beliefs that cannot be proven or disproven; for instance, their sense that God commanded them to act in a particular manner."[7] This could encourage Iran's leaders to exaggerate the significance of, or attach greater importance to, issues that we may perceive as lying beyond the core interest of national survival for which we might be prepared to use nuclear weapons. With respect to the delineation of our three models, we posit that Iran's willingness to threaten, or actually use, nuclear weapons is greater in our second (Aggressive Iran) and third (Unstable Iran) models, than in our first model (Defensive Iran), which condones nuclear weapons use only on behalf of the core national interest of regime or territorial survival. However, having an Iranian leadership that understands U.S. red lines is an essential component of deterrence planning if we seek strategic certainty in place of strategic ambiguity. Communicating with clarity those red lines is an important aspect of the deterrence dynamic in each of the models, as is having an accurate assessment of what the Iranian leadership, elites, and public value; what interests they will protect; and the priorities they attach to those interests. If it wishes to do so, Iran can probably gain considerable insight into how the United States might respond. As an open society, the United States publishes or reveals extensive information and strategy about itself, including its nuclear posture. The same cannot be said for Iran, which has little published information about such issues as deterrence and defense policy in general. There is a vast asymmetry between Iran and the United States with respect to issues of nuclear doctrine and nuclear use. This could hardly be otherwise because Iran has consistently denied that it is actually developing nuclear weapons and, of course, there is no established Iranian literature on nuclear matters comparable to what has been published in the United States. Even in the Soviet Union during the Cold War there were classified studies that became available to Western strategic analysts. There were also numerous conferences and negotiations with Soviet officials and other contacts that often provided a basis for strategic-military information and insights into Soviet thinking about nuclear issues.

Transparency with respect to Iranian thinking about nuclear issues is therefore limited. Iran's current regime has turned aside U.S. overtures to discuss nuclear questions while adopting a hard line on U.S. threat-reduction initiatives, including the Obama administration's decision to reduce the role of nuclear weapons in U.S. strategy, as set forth in the Nuclear Posture Review (NPR),[8] which is available to anyone in Tehran able to visit the U.S. Department of Defense website. More troubling still is that Iran's leadership hierarchy has limited knowledge about the world beyond Iran, traveling outside of the country infrequently and engaging only those with sympathetic perspectives. When they do travel abroad and participate in forums on nuclear matters, Iranian officials and academics tend to espouse ideas obtained from academic literature of the 1960s or 1970s on nuclear deterrence, thereby limiting our ability to understand precisely Iranian interests and red lines. As a result, the potential for misunderstanding and miscalculation in a crisis is very great. This could lead to a precipitous decision to resort to nuclear weapons. The danger of miscalculation is an enduring feature in each of our models and the state of relations between the United States and Iran today. Nevertheless, over time, and in Model I: A Defensive Iran a future Iranian leadership might embrace the need for greater nuclear transparency as part of a more normal relationship with the United States.

Short of a fundamental change in the U.S.-Iranian relationship and with a regime that is not projected to alter its perspectives, Iran's leaders appear to believe that nuclear weapons have a unique quality that confers strategic advantage on their possessor, especially against a larger power such as the United States. This contrasts starkly with Western nuclear-abolitionist notions of a world without nuclear weapons and the dawning of a "post-nuclear age."[9] In fact, the greater the U.S. emphasis on nonnuclear options, the greater the interest in nuclear weapons is likely to be among states such as Iran, which can never hope to match the United States in conventional capabilities. Facing a conventionally superior enemy (Iraq) that also used asymmetric tactics (missiles targeted on cities) during the Iran-Iraq war in the 1980s, Iran was unable to deter such attacks with conventional weapons. However, faced with nuclear weapons, even the most determined adversary might be deterred. This is a lesson that the Iranian regime seems to have taken to heart. At a minimum, nuclear weapons are probably perceived as capable of deterring a larger adversary from attacking Iranian interests. As with North Korea, nuclear weapons also may be seen as the means of ensuring regime survival, as posited in Model I: A Defensive Iran.

Iranian leaders may also believe that nuclear weapons will serve other purposes beyond deterrence. These include the goals of enhancing the country's influence regionally and in the wider Muslim world while augmenting its power and prestige on the global stage. Nuclear weapons would form an important element of national power in support of specific regime objectives. As postulated in Model II: An Aggressive Iran, they would be seen as furnishing a tool to support an expansionist foreign policy agenda. The political shadow that is cast by military power—in this case, nuclear weapons—provides a means of influencing and shaping the policies of other states. Deterring or containing an Aggressive Iran may be more difficult than deterring the Soviet Union was, although such a judgment about the Soviet Union is more easily formulated after the Cold War than it was during it. The United States and the Soviet Union developed a substantial understanding of each other over more than two generations of the Cold War. We faced a dyadic relationship in which a principal focus of each superpower was the other's strategic nuclear forces. Instead, an Aggressive Iran may be immune to such a risk calculus. Such an Iran may have different ideas about the meaning of "victory" in a crisis engagement. An Aggressive Iran, or even an Unstable Iran (Model III), might conclude that it had more to gain by using nuclear weapons than by refraining from nuclear escalation. War avoidance, the core of the Western conception of nuclear deterrence, would not be the principal objective of Iran in these models. In the words of Keith Payne, reflecting on an approach to nuclear weapons starkly different from that of the United States:

Some opponents, however, may place highest priority on intangible, transcendent values, including those that cannot obviously be put at risk by the U.S. threat to destroy physical targets no matter how lethal the threat. Worse yet from a deterrence perspective, as in the past some contemporary opponents may hold in highest regard transcendent values and goals that they believe can be advanced only through high-risk actions and the destruction of physical, tangible targets. If intangible or transcendent goals and values are at the center of conflict with the United States, we should not expect that the opponent's decision making will be compatible with the balance of terror tenets which place the protection of tangible targets as the ultimate priority in decision making.[10]

This is not to suggest that the Iranian leadership would be necessarily motivated to act "irrationally" to protect Iran's interests. Instead, it is meant as a cautionary warning about gaps in American intelligence about what Iran's leadership actually values and the risks that it may be willing to accept in order to achieve its goals. Therefore, how Iran's leadership might assess the nuclear risk/gain calculus as well as the broader problems that a nuclear Iran would pose for the United States and the international community becomes essential, especially because of potentially wide differences between Iranian and U.S. views of nuclear weapons and their place in national security strategy. If Iran is in the process of acquiring nuclear weapons, undoubtedly it means that Tehran attaches substantial value to such capabilities and therefore is prepared to devote the resources needed for their development and deployment. While nuclear weapons may be increasing in importance for Iran, they are seen as having diminishing utility to national security from the U.S. perspective to judge by trends in American nuclear strategy and force structure. Thus, there appears to be a growing divergence between Iranian and U.S. views on nuclear weapons.

Only in Model I does it seem realistic to think that nuclear weapons would have a strictly defensive role in Iran's national security strategy limited to the deterrence of an attack on Iranian territory. In our Aggressive Iran model, such strategic stability would not be Iran's principal objective in deploying nuclear weapons. Our Model II includes the possibility that religious zealotry or other deeply ingrained beliefs may prompt people to act in ways that we might think irrational but, in fact, are not irrational if viewed through Iranian religious or ideological lenses. Thus, as Amitai Etzioni has suggested, "a religious fanatic Iranian leader may well believe that God commands him to wipe out Tel Aviv, may calculate whether to use missiles or bombs, and what season to attack, but not whether or not to heed God's command to kill the infidels."[11] As alien as it seems to the Western strategic analyst accustomed to carefully calculated risk/gain assessments as the basis for designing nuclear deterrence forces, use of nuclear weapons could be seen instead as a means of hastening the appearance of the "Hidden Imam," a crucial aspect of Shia so-called Twelver religious thought.[12] With such disparate notions of nuclear weapons use, given this apparent disregard for the mass casualties that a nuclear detonation would induce, deterring a nuclear Iran could perhaps be far more difficult and complex than deterring states or regimes that value their own survival above all else, together with the integrity of territory or regime stability.[13] Such considerations increase the importance of what form an Iranian nuclear capability will take. For example, if Iran adopts the "Israeli model" and its strategic ambiguity (neither denying nor declaring that it possesses nuclear weapons), such an approach is compatible with a Defensive Iran (Model I), which seeks a deterrent capability rather than an offensive nuclear force. By adopting this approach to nuclear development, Iran would confound the international community and likely encourage divisions about how to respond to the ambiguity of the situation in which Iran might already have crossed the nuclear threshold. The Iranian leadership may hope that over time the international community would come to accept Iran's nuclear status as a fait accompli, much as it did with respect to India and Pakistan after their attainment of nuclear status. Iran probably would face fewer international consequences in the form of crippling sanctions than would be the case with an overt capability. However, if Iran adopts the "North Korean model," the chances for coordinating a more coherent set of international responses would perhaps become more promising. At the same time, Iran could reap political/diplomatic benefits from the possession of nuclear weapons. The Iranians may have figured this out. As pointed out by one analyst: "The fact is that an Iranian bomb would enable Tehran to fulfill the goals of the revolution without using it."[14]

The United States has few good options when facing the challenges posed by a nuclear Iran. Military responses could be considered, as described in greater detail in chapter 6. However, none of them would be cost-free or easy to implement, especially in an era of fiscal restraint in defense spending. This reality lends new urgency to deterrence and containment for dealing with a nuclear Iran at a time when nuclear weapons are assuming greater legitimacy in other parts of the world while their utility to U.S. and Western security is challenged by nuclear abolitionists, emboldened by the Obama administration's "global zero" initiative.[15] Unfortunately, as North Korea and China's nuclear-modernization programs attest, nuclear weapons are perceived as important instruments of power and prestige. In many instances they may be deemed essential to building domestic support for the ruling regime. In Iran's case, both considerations may be at play, given the efforts of Iran's government to direct public attention from its domestic failures. Nuclear weapons would not only be intended to deter an attack against Iran but also to prevent regime change in Iran, and, in the Aggressive Iran model, nuclear weapons would form the basis of an expansionist foreign policy.

In each of our three models, the maintenance of strategic stability in the Middle East would continue to rest largely with the United States. This includes both the capacity to defend against and mitigate the consequences of a threatened or an actual attack as well as efforts to shape adversary thinking about the utility of nuclear deployments to achieve specific strategic goals. Persuading an adversary leadership of the risks and costs associated with nuclear weapons use has long been an aspect of U.S. non-, and counter-proliferation planning, but as suggested in a recent study of dissuasion, not all actors view the world in the same way or "share the same model of rationality."[16] If states do not share the same model of rationality, it follows that what may deter one actor will not necessarily deter others. Unlike deterrence, the focus of dissuasion is not the threat of military retaliation. Instead, dissuasion may be defined as those actions taken to shape or influence an actor's perceptions of the anticipated costs or benefits from a particular action (e.g., crossing the nuclear threshold) or military capacity (e.g., nuclear weapons). It may entail a wide variety of diplomatic, economic, and military instruments designed to prevent, or dissuade, the acquisition of a nuclear capability by would-be nuclear states. Dissuasion may be considered a precursor to deterrence planning, which depends on capabilities in place and the will to use force to protect vital interests. In certain circumstances, the perceived willingness to use force and the mere existence of a credible military posture could be dissuasive in and of itself. Even short of an actual nuclear acquisition, a country's efforts to obtain or develop nuclear technologies might be enough to influence decision making in neighboring states. The mere possession of nuclear-relevant capabilities, together with the belief that nuclear weapons might actually be used once they had been acquired, could have dissuasive implications for other states, allowing the possessor to shape the perceived options of potential adversaries. In other words, the political shadow that is cast by nuclear weapons remains a potent force in international relations.

It is uncertain that even a comprehensive strategic approach that used all available tools based on a focused, "whole-of-government" approach by the United States and other nations would dissuade Iran. As suggested earlier, there is widespread support in Iran today for that country's civilian nuclear development. The sanctions imposed on Iran have had a major effect on Iran's economy. However, they appear to have slowed but not halted Iran's ability to develop indigenous technologies for uranium enrichment and plutonium production. Sanctions have not prevented Iran from completing construction, with

Russian help, of its Bushehr nuclear reactor.[17] From this perspective, international sanctions to prevent Iran from acquiring a nuclear weapons capability seem doomed to failure, as Iran has found the means to lessen their impact and continue with its nuclear development.[18] In addition to Iran's development of an indigenous technology base to sustain its nuclear ambitions, Tehran has circumvented Western counter-proliferation measures through the creation of cutout companies to import banned technologies and to create an intricate network of shell companies to thwart Western efforts to enforce Proliferation Security Initiatives activities.[19] Iran also has benefited from the unwillingness of some countries, notably Turkey, China, and Russia, to halt trade with Iran, especially in energy. Russia is already on record as opposing additional sanctions, arguing that the fourth round of UN sanctions was based on a consensus that should not be challenged by individual nations seeking to tighten the noose around Iran. Thus, even though sanctions may indeed damage Iran's fragile domestic economy, there is no reason to assume that they will alter leadership ambitions to develop a latent or actual nuclear weapons capability.

DOES THE NATURE OF THE REGIME MATTER?

It is important to address the question of whether regime change would affect Iran's nuclear ambitions, and if so, how? For example, would the emergence of a government based on democratic principles that inherited a nuclear weapons capability become a Defensive Iran in keeping with Model I? Or might it give them up altogether? More than one analyst has suggested that regime change is a key to containing Iran's nuclear ambitions. For example, Geoffrey Kemp has argued that a moderate Iranian regime that withdraws from the NPT and crosses the nuclear threshold openly would "be easier to tolerate" than a nuclear regime that espoused a radical ideology.[20] Democracies are said to be more responsible and transparent custodians of nuclear weapons, regarding them as weapons of last resort to be used only if supreme national interests are at stake—in other words, as defensive deterrents in keeping with Model I. In democracies nuclear weapons are held under civilian control by governments responsible to their respective electorates. As the world's largest democracy in terms of population, India with nuclear weapons arouses less fear than a nuclear Iran or North Korea. In India's case, facing both a nuclear China and a nuclear Pakistan, development of a nuclear weapons capability has become a central aspect of defense and security. From New Delhi's perspective, nuclear weapons not only confer on India a special political status but also represent a deterrent against China. In the case of Israel, nuclear weapons are viewed as essential to ensuring the survival of the state, although Israel's nuclear programs have proceeded with great secrecy. Therefore, it may be assumed that Israel has developed operational plans for their use if it should face the imminent prospect of destruction. In the United States, neither India nor Israel is seen as a threat because of nuclear weapons. If democracies are less to be feared with nuclear weapons, it follows that regime change in Iran might produce a leadership more amenable to stopping short of nuclear weaponization, as the Japanese have done, or result in the deployment of a nuclear force posture that is clearly defensive in nature along the lines of the British and French nuclear forces, sharply contrasted to a nuclear force that supports an aggressive foreign policy, as set forth in our Aggressive Iran model.

Arguments along these lines imply the need to think about regime change in Iran as a policy priority in the United States. To do so will not be easy as long as our understanding of the political forces within Iran remains limited. Identifying a center of gravity for leading domestic opposition to the regime is made difficult by inadequate intelligence and by the regime's ongoing, active repression of regime opponents. In other words, choosing regime change as a means of stopping Iran's breakout from the NPT, or of influencing the way in which it weaponizes, may be theoretically attractive, but in reality it faces many uncertainties. The cultivation of opposition groups is difficult under the best of circumstances. In any event, it takes extensive planning and time, which may not be available before Iran crosses the nuclear threshold.

Moreover, Pakistan may be the exceptional case in this regard that could provide a template either for a "democratic" Iran or for the Unstable Iran depicted in our Model III, depending of the evolution of Iran's government and its strategic objectives, worldview, and sociocultural moorings. Although a democracy, Pakistan's civilian government is weak, and control of its nuclear weapons effectively lies with the military, the strongest institution in the country. In recent years, Pakistan's politics have become increasingly polarized, and the emergence of radical Islamist sentiments within Pakistani society has been pronounced, despite recent efforts to "tame" Pakistan's northwestern provinces, which border Afghanistan. Osama bin Laden was tracked down in Pakistan. Elements of Afghanistan's Taliban are situated in Pakistan. In fact, the Taliban was created in part by Pakistan's Inter-Services Intelligence (ISI) directorate to oust Soviet forces from Afghanistan. Even after the Taliban formed a Pakistan movement, whose purpose is the overthrow of Pakistan's secular democratic government, support for the Taliban (mostly the Afghani Taliban) remains high among a large percentage of Pakistan's population because of its potential to undermine India's influence in Kashmir, along the "Line of Control" between the two countries, and in the broader South and Central Asian regions, including Kabul. Moreover, a growing number of Pakistanis harbor anti-American sentiments, in part as a result of U.S. drone attacks against targets in Pakistan and in part because U.S. forces were seen as having violated Pakistan's sovereignty in the raid to get bin Laden. They also are skeptical of American intentions, especially the U.S. relationship with arch-enemy India, perceiving a tilt toward New Delhi on issues of importance to Pakistan—despite significant changes in U.S. policy toward Pakistan, including the lifting of sanctions imposed after Pakistan's 1998 nuclear tests and enhanced security cooperation since the 9/11 attacks. Because of the potential for Pakistan to become a "failed state," there is fear that terrorists could gain access to nuclear materials, despite Pakistani assurances that its nuclear stockpile is safe, secure, and under tight control. The same might happen in Iran, especially an Iran in chaos, as described in Model III.

Or it might not, if the nature of the regime matters, as has been argued by several Iran analysts. From their perspective, a democratic Iran would pose fewer dangers than an authoritarian regime imbued with radical ideology. If democratization came to characterize a nuclear Iran, which would behave essentially in accordance with our Model I, elite opinion in Iran, more likely than not, would view Iran's development of nuclear weapons as a defensive deterrent. Nuclear weapons would form an important tool of political and strategic leverage to contain U.S. regional influence and to deter the United States or Israel from attacking Iran.

This would contrast with an Iran that seeks to exert greater influence over its more vulnerable neighbors and pursues a more active foreign policy, as developed in Model II.

However, neither in Model I nor in Model II, is Iran's leadership likely to be dissuaded from its pursuit of civilian nuclear-energy develop-ment. Moreover, this is a path that is widely supported by most Iranians. For this reason, proposals to allow some civilian nuclear development, based on a tight inspections regime, strict oversight, and acquiescence to the safeguards protocols (to the NPT) that the United Nations has stipulated have been rejected out of hand by Iran. Pre-dictably, the Iranian reaction has been highly critical of any effort to impose constraints on Iranian reprocessing activities, characterizing them as "discriminatory." In any event, concerns remain that even if Iran were to agree to reprocessing constraints, the country would con-tinue to accumulate the knowledge and experience needed to build nuclear weapons in the future while keeping in operation its second path toward nuclear development, namely, plutonium reprocessing using its Arak heavy-water reactor. In Ahmadinejad's words, "some powerful states practice a discriminatory approach against access of NPT members to material, equipment, and peaceful nuclear technol-ogy, and by doing so, intend to impose a nuclear apartheid." He also stated: "Today, the most serious challenge is that the culprits are arro-gating to themselves the role of the prosecutor. Even more danger-ous is that certain parties are relying on their power and wealth to try to impose a climate of intimidation and injustice over the world, while through their huge media resources they portray themselves as defenders of freedom, democracy, and human rights."[21]

In order to understand precisely the implications of a nuclear Iran for U.S. and allied/partner security planning, it is necessary to consider carefully the possible motivations underlying Iran's nuclear "breakout," as well as the assumptions that might shape Iran's nuclear posture. In this way, we can more usefully explore options for U.S. strategic and operational planning, including extended deterrence considerations and innovative ideas for containing Iran's ability to use its newfound nuclear status to influence regional power dynamics and strategic interactions with the United States. Thus, what follows is an in-depth description of our three models of a nuclear Iran, with an assessment of how they might relate to Iran's existing and projected strategic objectives and foreign policy goals.

MODEL I: A DEFENSIVE IRAN

As described in chapter 1, this model might provide a more democratic Iran with an "existential" deterrent capability to protect the country from invasion, a threatened conventional attack, or the use of nuclear weapons—or other weapons of mass destruction—by an adversary state. However, this model might also have relevance to Iran's current situation in which the regime in Tehran seeks nuclear weapons to deter the United States from attempting regime change or to deter Israel from attacking Iran with either conventional or nuclear weapons. On this basis, in theory, a Defensive Iran would be less concerned about operational strategies and more inclined to view its nuclear weapons as an "existential" capability, not fundamentally different from how countries such as Pakistan and India perceive nuclear weapons.[22] The Defensive Iran model is based on the assumption that Iran is more a nation-state than a revolutionary cause, to paraphrase Henry Kissinger's distinction between status quo and revolutionary powers.[23] In other words, in the Defensive Iran model, contrasted with the Aggressive Iran model (II), nuclear weapons would not be used as war-fighting capabilities but instead only as instruments of last resort to prevent national annihilation.

In this model Iran would have essentially two options. It could either adopt a policy of "strategic ambiguity," neither denying nor confirming that it had nuclear weapons, as Israel has done, or it could demonstrate its nuclear capability by openly testing a nuclear device as India, Pakistan, and North Korea did. In this regard, it could signal that it had successfully crossed the nuclear threshold either by means of an official announcement or by displaying its capabilities via a highly choreographed public setting such as a military parade as was done frequently in the Soviet Union. For Iran, providing demonstrable proof that it had crossed the nuclear threshold and had an operational nuclear weapons capability would offer several benefits. Above all, it would send the message that an attack upon Iran would be met by the potential for escalation to nuclear weapons use, reinforcing the defensive nature of Iran's nuclear capability. The purpose would be to raise the stakes for an adversary and allow the regime to feel confident that its survival could not be threatened by outside powers, especially the United States. Once Iran actually crossed the nuclear threshold, initial concerns about the country's isolation (which might well be one result) would likely be replaced by the pride that many Iranians would feel as a result of Iran's technological achievement, and this would (in the eyes of many Iranians) oblige the rest of the world to treat Iran with the deference and respect that many Iranians perceive is due Iran today. Iranian officials, pointing to India and Pakistan's nuclear tests, seem to have drawn the lesson that even if Iran is initially ostracized for its nuclear activities, the global need for energy would force energy-dependent states (and developing nations) to resume normal trading relations after a "decent" interval in order to have access to Iranian oil and not upset the world energy market.

Because of concerns about international isolation, Iran might conclude that its best option lies in concealing its nuclear programs for as long as possible, preferring to operate in the twilight as Israel currently does, to create ambiguity about Iranian nuclear weapons and to inject greater uncertainty into the regional power equation. With imperfect information about Iran's possession of nuclear weapons, potential adversaries would find it necessary to engage in worst-case planning. At a minimum, they would deal cautiously with Iran. Therefore, Iran would have the benefit of having induced greater caution from its adversaries without having actually deployed nuclear weapons. Such an approach might reduce or postpone the negative consequences of an overt nuclear weapons capability. The regime would gain a degree of flexibility as it maneuvered around NPT seams to minimize the ability of the international community to make Tehran accountable for past actions while possibly reducing suspicions about its current programs. Iran could conceal its nuclear weapons activities and even deny the existence of such programs in order to buy time for its strategic stockpile to grow from a small number of weapons to the more substantial number needed for a more reliable deterrence policy.

Rumors and speculation about the Iranian nuclear program might have as great an effect on regional perceptions as an official unveiling of a specific weapons system. In other words, at least initially, Iran might not have to deploy nuclear weapons overtly in order to create uncertainty in the minds of its immediate neighbors as well as the United States and Israel. If, for example, the regime's objective was to create a situation of ambiguity in which it was not possible to verify that Iran had deployed an operational weapons capability, then Iran could decide to use deception and other tactics to create the impression that it had a nuclear weapons capability when in fact it did not. This approach is fraught with potential pitfalls. Saddam Hussein apparently tried such a strategy with WMD, but ultimately not only did he not deter a U.S. attack but instead may even have increased the U.S. determination to destroy whatever WMD capability it erroneously assumed that Iraq possessed. The Soviet leadership failed also at the time of the Cuban missile crisis to intimidate the United States into acquiescing in the installation of nuclear missiles under Moscow's control in Cuba, which ended instead in the withdrawal of Soviet missiles from Cuba and included a nuclear escalatory threat against the Soviet Union from the United States if Soviet nuclear missiles were to be launched against any Western Hemisphere country from Cuba.[24]

The Defensive Iran model assumes not only a commitment to a minimum deterrence posture but also that Iran chooses overt deployment instead of nuclear ambiguity. Such a force would be small but reliable, its sole objective being deterrence of a direct attack. Therefore, Iran's strategy under this model is likely to be accompanied by a declaratory policy that specifies the conditions under which Iran would use or threaten to use nuclear weapons. Under this model, the Iranian leadership might declare or otherwise signal that Iranian nuclear weapons would only be employed in retaliation against a conventional or a nuclear attack against Iran. Iran could thus be the first to use nuclear weapons, but only after Iranian territory had been attacked. Because Iran's nuclear weapons would be used only in extreme circumstances, according to the assumptions of this model, and in response to an enemy attack, the priority would be to convey publicly the defensive nature of its deterrent posture. Declaratory policy would be important with respect to making red lines clear and specifying the conditions under which nuclear weapons would be used in response to an attack on Iran.

Under the Defensive Iran model, Tehran would be likely to deploy a nuclear force that was dispersed and concealed so as to enhance its chances of surviving a preemptive attack under the assumption that nuclear weapons are intended to deter an attack on Iran, as discussed at greater length in chapter 4. However, the Defensive Iran model would raise for Iran's leadership the need to consider options for launch-on-warning (LOW) or launch-under-attack (LUA), both of which would require a sophisticated command and control and intelligence network. To attain a credible LOW or LUA capability, Iran would need to enhance its intelligence, surveillance, and reconnaissance (ISR) capabilities to detect an adversary attack and at the same time develop or acquire more advanced defensive technologies to protect high-value targets such as delivery vehicles and storage sites. Iran has been attempting to obtain the Russian S-300 surface-to-air missile system for years, presumably to protect nuclear weapon facilities as well as ballistic missile launchers and other high-value assets. According to the Congressional Research Service, in December 2007 Russia agreed to sell the S-300 air defense system to Iran for $800 million. Delivery was due by March 2009, but strong U.S. opposition forced the Russians to reconsider the sale. Accordingly, in September 2010, three months after the imposition of the fourth round of UN sanctions on Iran (UNSC Resolution 1929), Russia formally banned the sale of S-300 air defense missile systems to Tehran.[25] A year after Russia suspended the deal, Iranian officials claimed that they had produced and deployed a domestic version of the S-300.[26]

Although Iran with a defensive deterrent force (Model I) would not resort to nuclear weapons use unless it was the object of a first-strike attack, a nuclear posture along these lines would still cast a long political shadow over Iran's relations with other states in the Middle East, Europe, and (possibly) Asia, confronting the United States with the need to reassure allies and to protect them from intimidation and Iranian efforts to shape the political agendas of its Gulf neighbors at a time when allies or coalition partners might not agree about or even understand the nature and extent of the threat from a Defensive Iran. As with the second model—an Aggressive Iran—the United States would find it necessary to update its extended deterrence and security commitments and place greater emphasis on active defenses, including missile defense. A Defensive Iran would still generate outside uncertainty about the extent of the Iranian threat. Under this model, strategic stability would rest on an assumption that Iran would deploy a relatively small nuclear force that would not require sophisticated targeting strategies. However, such a force would need to be survivable if it was to provide deterrence against preemption. While the Aggressive Iran model could also be based on a small nuclear force structure, it is more likely that it would rely on a more robust and survivable set of capabilities with retaliation potential.

MODEL II: AN AGGRESSIVE IRAN

An Aggressive Iran with nuclear weapons increases the prospect for crisis confrontation and miscalculation, as well as protracted strategic instability in the Middle East. An expansive Iranian strategy would be underwritten by nuclear weapons, and the regime in Tehran would likely rely on their nuclear weapons to inform and shape Iran's interactions with neighbors in the Middle East and with powers outside the region, especially the United States. Iranian foreign policy goals, presumably, would include (1) expanding Tehran's influence over other Persian Gulf states and reclaiming sovereignty over disputed territories and waters; (2) strengthening the influence of Persian nationalism among dissident tribes and provinces within and bordering Iranian territory; (3) controlling the flow of Persian Gulf oil and its pricing; (4) isolating the United States and undermining its influence in the region; and (5) bolstering Iran's credentials as leader of all Muslims, including those in the Arab world. Permutations of these objectives exist, but they embody the primary influences on Iranian policy formation and the setting within which our Aggressive Iran model was developed. This portends a dangerous situation as an Aggressive Iran would likely harbor misperceptions about the United States and its willingness to use force in the post–Iraq War era to protect American interests, allies, and coalition partners.

In the Aggressive Iran model, nuclear weapons would enhance Iran's international influence and bargaining power and empower it in dealings with regional neighbors, including Turkey, also potentially a nuclear state; Russia, which has been a nuclear benefactor to Iran; India, a once and future partner; a nuclear Pakistan, which looms as a possible rival; and Afghanistan, which, together with Iraq before the withdrawal of U.S. forces from Iraq and the announced end of combat operations in Afghanistan by the end of 2014, was perceived to be essential to a U.S. plan to encircle Iran. The dynamics of deterrence for an Aggressive Iran vary in relation to each of these possible security challenges. Iran's possession of nuclear weapons, whether or not it adds to Iranian security, would put an Aggressive Iran on a more or less equal footing with prospective adversaries. It also has the potential to provide Tehran with a more cost-effective alternative to a conventional force build-up. In a crisis, nuclear weapons may be regarded as a "great equalizer" to compensate for deficiencies in other Iranian military capabilities such as airpower, which has not had extensive modernization since the fall of the shah in 1979.

An Aggressive Iran aspiring to leadership in the wider Middle East would seek to neutralize the deterrent effect of Israel's conventional and nuclear power and ensure that Iran has the capacity to shape escalation in a confrontation with the United States. Against Israel, Iran can employ missiles and asymmetric attacks, creating the potential to implement "compound escalation," or the manipulation of seemingly unrelated issues or use of disparate capabilities to raise the stakes for an adversary. For example, Iran would have the possibility of using proxy forces to terrorize the civilian populations. Against the United States, Iran might perceive that it could disrupt oil flows through the Strait of Hormuz. Iran is developing a variety of asymmetric tactics, for example, the use of small, high-speed attack boats employing swarm tactics to surround U.S. and allied navies operating in the Gulf.[27] It would also be capable of unleashing Hezbollah or even Hamas against U.S. and allied/coalition partner high-value targets in the region. Presumably, the leadership of an Aggressive Iran would emphasize the development of new capabilities to threaten the United States directly, such as intercontinental ballistic missile (ICBM), antisatellite (ASAT), or EMP capability, as was already mentioned and will be discussed at greater length in chapter 4. An Aggressive Iran would present the United States with multiple and complex challenges, including the need to think about deterrence in a multilateral context.[28] According to Paul Bracken, this second nuclear age differs from the Cold War in several respects. According to Bracken:

> The Cold War was a struggle waged with the icy rationality and cool logic that characterized the two superpowers' approach to nuclear weapons, There was no place for hysteria; indeed, one striking feature of even the most dangerous nuclear issues was that

the two sides never really got angry at each other. . . . But the second nuclear age is driven by national insecurities incomprehensible to outsiders whose security is no longer endangered. In the West, the politics of rage had no role in foreign policy. This cannot be said for the disputes in Asia between Pakistan and India, the two Koreas, or the Arab states and Israel.[29]

The "politics of rage" certainly applies as well to Iran and its disputes with Israel and the United States. Rage and "non-rationality" have the potential to upend the fundamentals of traditional deterrence planning and threaten to create a new paradigm for the use of force that includes nuclear weapons use. As Bracken points out, during the Cold War the nuclear calculus rested with the United States and the Soviet Union. The "road to nuclear war always went through Washington and Moscow because they controlled the triggers."[30] With the emergence of a world where multiple states have nuclear weapons, this is no longer the case. In the Middle East, South Asia, and East Asia there are newer or emerging nuclear powers, and this leads to rising danger of nuclear escalation that will be not easily controlled by the United States. Accordingly, we are entering a dangerous age, a perspective that is starkly at odds with that of Kenneth Waltz, which holds that proliferation may in fact be a stabilizing phenomenon. Which is the correct view may well be revealed in the context of Iran's nuclear weapons development. The best that may be hoped for is that this comes about as a defensive deterrent and not as part of a comprehensive Aggressive Iran model.

Another important factor enters into the deterrence discussion: the close link presumed to exist between deterrence and rationality. Deterrence is based on expectations about how "rational" opponents behave toward one another. Rationality presumes that actors can be deterred, whether by threatening the objects that they most value (deterrence by punishment) or by making it difficult if not impossible to destroy the intended target (deterrence by denial). In either case, deterrence would be achieved by the deterrer's ability to communicate credibly the futility of the action. However, what constitutes rationality as a basis for deterrence presents numerous problems. Some leaders are likely to be more accepting of risk than others based on perceived threats, losses, gains, and interests at stake. What one side views as unacceptable stakes for the other may turn out to be wrong. Opponents may misread each other as a result of cultural differences. Psychological factors also enter into the rationality calculus. In a quest for cognitive balance or consistency, decision makers may filter out of their minds information or advice that does not conform to their existing perception or worldview. As Amatzia Baram points out in a study of Iraqi documents, Saddam Hussein acted "rationally" in accordance with a "coherent set of self-interested preferences" that turned out to fatally wrong for him when it came to judging what the United States would do both in response to Iraq's invasion of Kuwait in 2000 and in the U.S. invasion of Iraq in 2003. Baram concludes: "This was because the Iraqi leader tended to ignore inconvenient facts and unpleasant information. He would repeatedly construct convoluted scenarios that allowed him to believe events would play out in a way that he wanted, even though others could see that such outcomes were highly unlikely." Rationality may be bounded by the decision maker's own cognitive processes and limitations, together with the tendency of at least some advisors to reinforce mistaken beliefs, perhaps to curry favor. Such rationality limitations may have profound implications for deterrence in each of our models, but especially in Models II and III.[31]

An Aggressive Iran represents a worst-case scenario for the United States. With nuclear weapons, an Aggressive Iran increases the potential for confrontation and hence miscalculation, as Iranian misperceptions and potential to overreach inform and shape the leadership's foreign policy calculations. An Aggressive Iran with nuclear weapons could also become problematic for Pakistan. It may have to contend with the possible proliferation consequences for such foreign rivals as Saudi Arabia or Egypt. Pakistan and Iran are competitors for influence in the Middle East. Iran's recent efforts to court India and both the government in Kabul and the Taliban should certainly be seen in that light. Notably, Iran has expressed concerns about the growing radical Salafist influence in Pakistan and what this might portend for regional stability.[32] There may be Iranian concern about the extent to which extremist elements in Pakistan might reinforce and shape Taliban influence in Afghanistan after international forces are withdrawn. This may help to explain why Iran decided to engage the government in Kabul while hedging its bets with support to the Taliban and at the same time to enhance efforts to influence decision making in New Delhi with inducements of energy at affordable prices in rupees, the Indian currency. Looking to the future, Iran has considered creating what essentially would be an anti-American alliance network in the region. Ideally, from Iran's perspective, such an alliance would be composed of Afghanistan, India, Russia, and possibly even the Central Asian states and China, essentially the nations that are already members of, or have observer status in, the Shanghai Cooperation Organization (SCO). An Aggressive Iran could be expected to support and leverage such a competing anti-U.S. coalition for its own purposes, including containing or deterring a failed state in Pakistan in the face of a military coup or other change of government.

Iranian concerns about the stability of Pakistan's government have increased since the 2007 assassination of Benazir Bhutto and President Pervez Musharraf's forced resignation in 2008. In addition to the rise of radical jihadist elements that could be the catalyst for a failed state or a military coup, Iranian leaders have expressed concerns about Baluch separatism, which is identified as another prospective security challenge for Iran.[33] Other challenges include the weakness of Afghanistan's Pashtun government,[34] especially its inability to control the drug trade across Iranian borders, and ethnic unrest in Tajikistan (the one Central Asian state that is predominantly Persian-speaking and Shia). Furthermore, there is the potential for crisis and conflict between Iran and Pakistan or among Iran, Pakistan, and Afghanistan (into which the United States conceivably could be drawn). According to one analysis, the "inter-regional linkages between theaters of conflict" may reinforce for Iran the case for nuclear weapons because the military dimension of major-power relations in the Middle East/Central Asian region sets the tone for political partnerships and alignments.[35] Possession of nuclear weapons may be viewed in Tehran as essential to deter Pakistan, as compensation for Iran's inadequate conventional forces, and as an increasingly important diplomatic tool for intimidating weaker neighbors. However, nuclear weapons do *not* necessarily guarantee deterrence between their possessors, even if one side is weaker than the other, as the 1999 Kargil crisis between India and Pakistan illustrates.[36] Pakistan with nuclear weapons was prepared to confront a superior conventionally armed India that also possessed nuclear weapons. Nevertheless, nuclear weapons proved to be a threshold that neither side was prepared to cross. India may have been deterred from conventional escalation that would have triggered a

Pakistan nuclear response. To infer from the Kargil crisis, a nuclear Iran confronted with nuclear-armed neighbors might be prepared to engage in conventional escalation. However, Tehran could not be certain that a nuclear-armed neighbor would not escalate to the nuclear level if it feared the defeat of its conventional forces by Iran. On this basis, and under our Aggressive Iran model, a nuclear Iran would strive to develop a more robust nuclear force posture (compared to our Defensive Iran model), but it also might continue to develop more capable conventional forces to gain greater control over the escalation dynamic and to have a range of options, including asymmetric options, for use in limited warfare contingencies.

In the post-Saddam era, Iran unquestionably perceives itself to be the preeminent power in the region. Especially in our Aggressive Iran model, nuclear weapons would be deemed critical to the perpetuation and further consolidation of that status. Nuclear weapons would promote Iran's political and economic interests and reinforce its claim to regional dominance. However, their deployment would likely be accompanied by conventional-force modernization. As part of a multidimensional, so-called whole-of-government approach to national security planning, Iran could be expected to place a greater priority on diplomacy, backed by its military modernization and nuclear weapons, to secure its desired objectives. Thus, we can expect that Iran, under Model II, would intensify its efforts to engage Sunni Arab leaders (such as the Saudi leadership) to marginalize the United States and those Arab leaders (for example, the al-Khalifa family in Bahrain and the bin Zayed dynasty in the United Arab Emirates) whose legitimacy Iranian leaders do not accept. This strategy is not without pitfalls, and, as events in Iraq continue to illustrate, Iran's support for Iraq's Shi'ite militias and for sectarian violence in Iraq has come at the expense of that country's Sunni population—a fact that is not lost on the Saudi and Jordanian leaderships. It is also a strategy that threatens to irritate Iraq's secular leadership, especially if the prospects for reconciliation within Iraq improve over time and Iraqi nationalism grows, even among Shi'ites in the south, who increasingly have shown signs of alienation from Iranian efforts to influence Iraq's domestic politics. An Iran with nuclear weapons might either subdue a restive Iraq, now that U.S. combat forces have been withdrawn or, in extremis, it could even lead to reconsideration in Baghdad of Iraq's own nuclear (or other WMD) options. In either case, a nuclear Iran under our Aggressive Iran model can be expected to take the initiative in promoting Iranian interests, even if this risks crisis or confrontation with weaker neighbors.

In other words, with this model, Iran would also likely make clear its willingness to use nuclear weapons not only if vital Iranian interests were at risk but also to support an increasingly bold foreign policy that would include pressure on Iraq. Nuclear weapons would be integrated into broader strategic-military planning. For this reason, an Aggressive Iran would have no interest in depending on a virtual (nuclear-deployment) model for its security. Strategic ambiguity would be incompatible with the rationale for going nuclear in the first place. An Aggressive Iran would be more likely to demonstrate its nuclear capability with a larger and more diversified force posture. It could conceivably seek to field a first-strike capability and create redundancy by developing an air- or sea-launched nuclear capability. An Aggressive Iran might arm cruise missiles with nuclear warheads and deploy nuclear mines in Persian Gulf waters. This model also envisages the possible use of asymmetric tactics and capabilities such as dirty bombs by Hezbollah, for example, against U.S. facilities in the Gulf, or to inflict damage on allied/coalition partner territories (such as Israel or Saudi Arabia), or economic infrastructure (although a nuclear weapon would not be necessary to destroy offshore oil platforms or natural-gas pipelines). Under this model, Iran would also be likely to pursue more advanced collateral technologies (satellite guidance or warhead miniaturization, for example) to enhance its nuclear power.

Motivated by aspirations to regional leadership, an Aggressive Iran may be unwilling to transfer weapons, components, or know-how to an ally (e.g., Syria) or even to proxy forces (e.g., Hezbollah). Conceivably, it might be willing to help a country outside the region, such as Venezuela, develop its own nuclear weapons, although it is more likely that under our Aggressive Iran model, Iran would transfer ballistic-missile systems to an outside country while keeping to itself the critical warhead technologies. By virtue of their close relationship, Iran could offer Venezuela an extended deterrence guarantee. There are reports that Iran proposed establishment of a joint military facility in Venezuela to be manned by Iranian personnel from the Revolutionary Guards and Venezuelan missile officers. Such a facility has the potential to increase the deterrent power of Iran against the United States, much as the Soviet Union attempted to do with its gambit to place nuclear weapons in Cuba.[37] It can only be assumed that in an Aggressive Iran Model, Tehran would take bold steps to underwrite Venezuela's security and to find ways to embolden Hezbollah operations in the Americas to keep the United States off balance and preoccupied with its security to the south. However, especially if it could do so without timely detection, an Aggressive Iran might be prepared to transfer materials for a dirty bomb to a proxy. Yet nuclear weapons transfers or trafficking are more likely in an Unstable Iran (Model III).

An Aggressive Iran might extend a deterrence umbrella over selected partners, Syria or Venezuela, for example, or perhaps even Hezbollah, as a means of empowering their actions in situations where Iranian interests might be served. Operational control of Iranian weapons would still reside with Iran's leadership. One exception, as noted above, might be the provision of radioactive materials to proxy forces for the manufacture of a dirty bomb, but this would most likely occur only if Iran was confident that its role would not be discovered. An Aggressive Iran would be prepared to make such materials available in the belief that it could do so without fear of retaliation from the United States. In our Unstable Iran model under a fractured regime, ultranationalists, Islamist elements, or rogue military commanders might gain control over Iran's nuclear weapons and decide to transfer them or their components to proxy forces outside Iran. The threatened or actual use of nuclear weapons to settle old scores, notably the creation of Israel and its territorial gains since the 1967 Six Day War, is conceivable in a setting rife with fanatics who believe that they derive spiritual power from the Mahdi. As described by one senior Israeli analyst:

> The rhetoric sounded by President Ahmadinejad with regard to the annihilation of Israel and his denial of the Holocaust highlights the problem. Ahmadinejad represents a group of politicians who rose to power through the ranks of the Revolutionary Guards and nationalist radicals who want to return to the core values of the revolution, and who endorse confrontation with the West and hatred towards Israel. . . . Leaders of his type at the helm of the

Iranian regime are liable to take unforeseen, reckless steps that defy accepted logic, and such conduct will also hamper the cultivation of stable deterrent relations with a nuclear-enabled Iran.[38]

This "insider problem" has potentially serious implications for a nuclear Iran, particularly in light of the growing role of Iran's Revolutionary Guards Corps in national security decision making.[39]

MODEL III: AN UNSTABLE IRAN

Regime stability based on challenges to its legitimacy could become an issue in the years ahead. Fissures among elites are widening; popular expectations about economic reform are not being met; and structural problems relating to Iran's economy appear to be getting worse. Continuing dissatisfaction with the June 2009 elections and subsequently with the way in which the regime handled the protests lingers in Iran, especially among educated elites and the business community. Moreover, the cumulative effect of international sanctions has had an impact on Iran's economy, exacerbating the results of the leadership's disastrous economic policies. For example, the 2012 U.S. and EU sanctions on Iran have restricted Tehran's access to the global financial system and are affecting the country's ability to export oil more rapidly than predicted, in large measure because oil shippers are having increasing difficulty insuring their vessels, according to a U.S. State Department official.[40] In addition, Iran has experienced an enormous flight of capital, with thousands of businesses relocating to Dubai alone. Inflation rates are skyrocketing, and unemployment is estimated by the CIA to be over 15 percent in 2011, which includes a 23–30 percent unemployment level for people between the ages of fifteen and twenty-four. There is speculation that the real figure is much higher. Iran's youth bulge is a significant factor, even though the vast majority of Iranian young people were not politically active until June 2009 election, which resulted in a contested outcome and the arrest of popular opposition leaders. For this reason, and since then, many of Iran's younger generation are choosing to emigrate rather than face imprisonment or worse for their political activities.

This is the domestic setting in which Supreme Leader Ayatollah Khamenei, who was appointed in 1989 as the country's highest authority, has attempted to consolidate his power, working through members of the Guardian Council, the powerful body that decides who may run for office in Iran and what bills may become law. Increasingly, in Iran's fractured and highly personalized political culture, the relationship between the Supreme Leader and the president has soured, largely over Ahmadinejad's rather inept handling of domestic discontent. This was reinforced by the outcome of the May 2012 parliamentary elections, which resulted in a decline in representation for the faction supporting Iran's president. However, it is important to keep in mind that in Iran, the president essentially serves at the pleasure of the clerical community, which, along with the military, controls the essential levers of power from the Guardian Council (which vets candidates, laws, and political parties) to the Assembly of Experts (which appoints the Supreme Leader) and the Supreme Council for National Security (SCNS)—which until October 2007 boasted the participation of former nuclear negotiator Ali Larijani as the Supreme Leader's representative. Larijani, like Ahmadinejad, was an IRGC Commander and has become a force in Iranian politics, together with his four brothers. After resigning as chief nuclear negotiator and later becoming speaker of parliament, he has emerged as the leader of the so-called principalists, an anti-Ahmadinejad faction in parliament that advocates allegiance to the Supreme Leader and the Islamic establishment.[41] The March 2012 parliamentary elections resulted in a landslide win for Larijani and his faction. The election also strengthened Ayatollah Khamenei's power vis-à-vis that of Ahmadinejad, with the Supreme Leader's supporters winning over 75 percent of the seats. This trend was reinforced with the victory of Hassan Rouhani in the 2013 presidential election. While perceived in the West as a pragmatist, he is actually a hardliner on nuclear issues.

Without question, the results of Iran's March 2012 parliamentary elections were a victory for the hard-line conservative supporters of Supreme Leader Ayatollah Khamenei, reinforcing the power and position of the Supreme Leader, including on nuclear issues. With opposition parties mostly banned or refusing to participate and reformist candidates (such as members of the Green Movement) barred from running, the election process in Iran has basically come down to a contest between rival conservative factions. Khamenei supporters in two parties, the United Principlist Front and the Stability Front, took over 75 percent of seats in the parliament in the March 2012 election. The United Principlist Front, founded in response to Ayatollah Khamenei's appeal for unity following the 2009 election and subsequent protests, is led by Ayatollah Mohammad Reza Mahdavi Kani, secretary general of the Militant Clergy Association. Ayatollah Mesbah-Yazdi, the former spiritual adviser to President Ahmadinejad, having withdrawn his support of the president, heads the Stability Front. The question still remains what impact, if any, will these personalities and the fractured nature of Iran's politics have on Iran's nuclear weapons program and international efforts to forestall it.

On the nuclear issue, differences between Iran's competing factions are principally about how the regime should present itself to the West, and not whether nuclear development programs should be retained and move forward to give Iran a "breakout" nuclear weapons capability. In many respects, as Shahram Chubin observes, the nuclear debate in Iran is a "surrogate for the country's future."[42] Increasingly, Iran's competing factions differ on the fundamentals of governance, which is based on Ayatollah Khomeini's concept of *Velayat-e-Faqih*, or the idea that the Supreme Leader, as the representative of the Twelfth Imam on Earth, has specific powers and constitutional responsibilities, melding church and state. Thus, while among Iran's clerics and government leaders there is no official support for returning to a secular government, there appears to be considerable nongovernmental elite support for the creation of a less authoritarian government that distances religion from political considerations. Some have referred to this as the "Turkish" model. Others, however, especially some younger clerics, members of the reformist movement, have begun to speak out in support of adopting a "China model" for Iran's economy,[43] which suggests that the desire for change cuts across Iranian society.[44] Indeed, the events of recent years, from the election protests to the defection of some Iranian scientists and diplomats, indicate that real fissures exist in Iran that cannot simply be papered over or ignored by an unpopular regime. Whether such divisions are severe enough to create openings for effective exploitation by democratic forces remains to be seen. The emergence of a more democratic Iranian regime, of course, would be entirely compatible with our

Model I: A Defensive Iran, whereas the breakdown of governance in Iran could set the stage for considerations inherent in our Model III.

Command and control of Iran's nuclear weapons and related delivery systems would emerge as a central concern, especially in Model III. For example, in a state-collapse scenario, rogue elements of the IRGC and its Qods Force could seek to empower one faction over another by seizing control of Iran's nuclear weapons. They might also attempt to use Iran's nuclear weapons to support the radical Islamist agenda and transfer nuclear materials or know-how outright to Hezbollah, Hamas, or al-Qaeda, using the Qods Force network (for terrorist training and support) that is already in place. Or as posited in Model II, leadership elements might use Iran's nuclear weapons to divert popular attention away from domestic problems by brandishing them at long-standing adversaries—Saudi Arabia comes to mind—to demonstrate Shia dominance in the region and to undermine Saudi security, especially in Saudi Arabia's eastern provinces, which have large Shia majorities. Indeed, some in Iran might welcome armed conflict with the United States so long as it was limited and produced low collateral damage, as a U.S. surgical strike might do. This could galvanize public support for the regime and undermine the voices of pragmatists, such as former president Akbar Hashemi Rafsanjani[45] and Mohammad Khatami, who at one time had argued for a grand bargain with the United States as a means of appeasing Western concerns about Iran's nuclear activities and ensuring that crippling sanctions could not be enacted by the United Nations.[46]

If developments inside Iran destabilize the regime in coming years, the need for cutting-edge "hedging" policies and strategies will grow. Deterring regime elements or nonstate armed groups requires a different mix of capabilities than deterring another state. It also necessitates an interagency, whole-of-government approach, using nonmilitary as well as military tools—hard power and soft power. A dedicated intelligence effort aimed at identifying Iranian elites and future leaders as early as possible is especially important, together with enhanced and focused activities to trace and disrupt the networks that support IRGC/Qods Force operations. Because proliferation, in this case "loose nukes," is a grave concern in the Unstable Iran model, activities under the Proliferation Security Initiative and the Global Initiative to Combat Nuclear Terrorism (GICNT) also would take on greater importance.[47]

Increased attention and resources should be devoted to nuclear forensics to enhance the prospects for tracing the origin of nuclear weapons and their components if, for example, nuclear weapons from an Unstable Iran were used elsewhere in the world, having fallen into terrorist hands. The problem that would arise, of course, would be what to do even after attribution had been established. Against whom, how, and to what effect would retaliation be ordered and executed? At a minimum, such issues should be addressed as part of our effort to understand the implications of a nuclear Iran for U.S. security planning. Regional security initiatives should likewise be expanded to include greater international maritime collaboration (similar to what has been developed in the Mediterranean by the U.S. Navy's Sixth Fleet and NATO's Maritime Headquarters) and broader investment in the U.S.-Gulf Security Dialogue. The Unstable Iran model would increase the need for a sophisticated campaign using a range of political, military, and economic capabilities to help shape the domestic Iranian setting in ways that minimize the grave threats arising from the disintegration of a regime with nuclear weapons. Presumably, this would also include unconventional warfare (UW) conducted clandestinely inside Iran.[48]

3
Considerations Influencing Iran's Nuclear Emergence

Iran's efforts to develop nuclear technologies are based on several inter-related motivations and considerations, which in turn will influence the scope and nature of Iran's nuclear posture if the decision is made to cross the nuclear threshold. According to Iranian officials, and as demonstrated in the preceding chapters of this book, domestic economic factors are among the primary drivers behind Iran's pursuit of nuclear-power technologies, but this is not the entire story by any means. It is clear that many Iranians equate nuclear energy with technological progress and with power and influence at the international level. There is an underlying premise that nuclear energy is essential to enable Iran to meet future domestic energy needs. Nuclear weapons may also provide a less costly alternative to conventional military forces as they do for Pakistan, which is confronted by a vastly more conventionally powerful India. Nuclear weapons may also be viewed as a means to ensure regime survival against enemies international and domestic. Obviously, this rationale has its limits; in Model III: An Unstable Iran, we postulate the disintegration of an Iran that possesses nuclear weapons. The possession of a vast nuclear arsenal did not prevent the collapse of the Soviet Union. Concerns have been raised about the disposition and control of North Korea's nuclear weapons if the regime were to disintegrate. Still, as a means of regional survival, possession of nuclear weapons is seen as vitally important. This leads us to speculate further about Iran's motivations for crossing the nuclear threshold.

While repeatedly insisting that its nuclear programs will serve only peaceful purposes, Iran nevertheless maintains that it has the inherent right to develop nuclear weapons technologies. Western efforts to constrain such technologies or to impose sanctions are often characterized in Iran as a poorly disguised attempt to maintain nuclear hegemony in the hands of the United States and other nuclear weapons states. International forums such as the G-8 and the United Nations Security Council are said to favor disproportionately the most technologically advanced nations, who have an interest in thwarting Iran's nuclear aspirations. Many in Iran feel that their country is being discriminated against by powers that have an interest in containing Iran's nuclear aspirations. After all, they contend, Israel is a de facto nuclear power that still enjoys U.S. support despite having crossed the nuclear threshold. The same is perceived to be true with respect to India. Again, as viewed in Tehran, India defied the international community by testing and deploying nuclear weapons in 1998 but still benefits from good relations with the United States, including a civilian nuclear-power deal, approved by the U.S. Congress in 2008.[1] Beyond these friends of the West, North Korea, which made nuclear-related technologies available to Syria, including the reactor that Israel disabled in 2007, crossed the nuclear threshold and continues to leverage its nuclear program to extract, or attempt to extract, aid, trade, and international recognition and legitimacy from the United States and other countries. At the same time, it has used its nuclear capabilities to intimidate South Korea and Japan, for example, with nuclear tests, to deter efforts at regime change or to shape the decision calculus in a crisis between Pyongyang and Seoul or Tokyo.

As discussed in the preceding chapters and depicted in box 3.1, "Iran's Presumed Strategic and Operational Goals," nuclear weapons may be seen as promoting a range of strategic and operational objectives. Depending on the context within which they are developed and the force structure they are meant to support, nuclear weapons might be viewed as instruments of prestige to bolster Iran's international and regional power aspirations, as posited under Model II: An Aggressive Iran, or they could be considered as essential elements of military policy, either to deter enemy aggression against Iran or to gain the initiative in escalation calculations, or both, as suggested in Model I: A Defensive Iran.

Box 3.1. Iran's Presumed Strategic and Operational Goals

STRATEGIC GOALS

- Expand Iranian influence over the Persian Gulf Arabs and reclaim sovereignty over disputed waters/territories
- Consolidate the influence of Persian nationalism over dissident tribes and provinces within and bordering Iranian territory
- Control the flow and pricing of Gulf oil
- Isolate the United States and eliminate its influence in the region
- Establish Iran as leader of the Muslim world

OPERATIONAL GOALS

- Implement a strategic deterrence strategy to deter a U.S. or Israeli attack on Iran and to change the power equation in the Middle East/Central and South Asian regions
- Keep Afghanistan in turmoil after 2014
- Use terror as a tool and proxies to strike at "soft" or asymmetric targets (e.g., Hezbollah and Hamas)
- Master nuclear technologies before or in connection with engaging with the West and diversify infrastructure

---

In the case of Iran, however, a further consideration—ideological/ religious matters—plays a role and must be factored into an understanding of nuclear decision making. Even in Model I, ideology and religion may be important in the Iranian decision calculus; perhaps they would drive Shi'ite Iran to deploy nuclear weapons in order not to be overshadowed by Sunni Pakistan. Here we have a combination of political (prestige and status) and military considerations. Even more worrisome, Iran's orthodox Shi'ite ideology is imbued with an apocalyptic vision associated with the return of the Twelfth Imam, or Mahdi, which may be a more important motivating factor behind Iran's nuclear ambitions. Nuclear weapons use in support of religious principles has already been ruled as acceptable under Islam.[2] In 2006, Iran's spiritual leaders produced a fatwa, or holy order, sanctioning the use of nuclear weapons against Iran's enemies. It was issued by Mohsen Gharavian, who is a disciple of Ayatollah Mohammad Taghi Mesbah-Yazdi and a member of the influential Guardian Council, which interprets the constitution and vets political candidates. In a speech in Qom, Gharavian reportedly observed that "when the entire world is armed with nuclear weapons, it is permissible to use those weapons as a countermeasure."[3] This line of thought dovetails with Ayatollah Yazdi's previous contention that the use of suicide bombers against the "enemies of Islam" is justified. Given these and similar reports, we may assume that at least one faction in Tehran's clerical community appears to view Iran's pursuit of nuclear weapons as essential to the country's defense and deterrence planning.

Religious motivations may also reinforce Iranian or Persian nationalism. They might even provide insights into the operations and strategy that Iran's nuclear weapons might be called on to support. The greater the religious zealotry within Iran's leadership, for example, the greater might be the propensity to brandish nuclear weapons on behalf of an Aggressive Iran (Model II). Conversely, if religious motivations were not in the forefront of Iran's nuclear development, the greater the likelihood that nuclear weapons would play a defensive-deterrent role (Model I). Such contending conceptions of religion as a factor in Iran's nuclear development, in turn, have implications for its preferred nuclear doctrine and specific force-structure choices. Before addressing such factors, it is useful to set forth several fundamental factors directly related to Iran's nuclear development.

First, the Iran-Iraq war was the formative and integrating event for the generation of Iranians now in charge; it provided the military leadership with actual battle experience that shaped subsequent Iranian thinking about weapons of mass destruction. Iraq's use of chemical weapons, together with its missile strikes in the "war of the cities," contributed two major insights into contemporary Iranian military planning. The first is that exclusive reliance on conventional forces may be inadequate for deterrence purposes if an opponent possesses WMD (in this case chemical weapons). Nuclear weapons may be the only weapons that can deter WMD use and keep a conventionally armed adversary from attacking Iran in the first place. The second is the importance of asymmetric strategies to keep an adversary off guard and to gain strategic and psychological advantage. From this perspective, nuclear weapons can be viewed as the ultimate asymmetric weapon. This implies a willingness to use nuclear weapons if circumstances dictate their employment and raises questions about Iranian conceptions of deterrence, escalation management, and crisis de-escalation.

Second, Iranian paranoia about the United States and what it perceives as American policies to outflank Iran feeds the mindset of Iranians who believe that Iran is the center of the universe. At a minimum, this could foster overconfidence leading to miscalculation in Iran's ability to deal with the United States and other countries. Both phenomena, that is, Iranian paranoia about the United States and an ethnocentrism that perceives Iran as the focal point of U.S. strategy, could be important factors driving Iran toward crossing the nuclear threshold, and each presents a difficult planning challenge for the United States. While the Tehran regime is convinced that the United States has had plans to attack Iran, there is also the somewhat contradictory perception that the United States has been so overextended, first in Iraq and now in Afghanistan, that it would be hard pressed and therefore unlikely to take direct military action against Iran, especially after having withdrawn its military forces from both countries. Far from diminishing Iranian paranoia about the United States, the retrenchment of U.S. power in the wake of the withdrawal of combat forces from Iraq and Afghanistan (at the end of 2014), may actually embolden Iran to take a more active role in and beyond the Gulf, in keeping with Model II, as they have done in Syria and, increasingly, in neighboring Iraq and with respect to the government in Kabul.

The regime in Tehran is not risk adverse, and its level of confidence could well be increased after Iran crosses the nuclear threshold, especially if radical Shi'ite theology and Persian nationalism are considered in the decision-making mix. Such factors may yield a sense of "manifest destiny" among a generation of Iranians who know little of the outside world except from Internet activities when they are not censored. This is a challenge to Western efforts to influence a nonnuclear Iran today, much less a nuclear Iran tomorrow. At the very least, it could lead to Iranian miscalculation in a crisis based on an overestimation of the value of nuclear capabilities to Iran and an underestimation of the resolve of the United States and its allies to counter a nuclear Iran. Getting inside and shaping the Iranian mindset thus emerges as a strategic imperative and intelligence necessity for the United States and its partners.

Iranian aspirations to lead the Muslim world are well documented. In recent years, especially since the Iran-Iraq war, this has included creation of Hezbollah and support to Sunni terrorist groups, including Hamas, as a means of creating ambiguity and taking the worldwide struggle for

Islam to its enemies in asymmetric fashion. Indeed, Iran's emphasis on irregular warfare is an important component of its operational planning, and, with Iran's messianic vision, there is no telling how far an Iranian regime may go to attain its objectives. Of course, much will depend in this regard on the nature of the regime in control of Iran, its threat perceptions, and, most important, how it views the United States. However, the willingness of the current regime to use terror as an instrument of policy suggests an analogy with respect to nuclear weapons, especially in Model II: An Aggressive Iran. Iran's embrace of irregular warfare includes the reliance on proxy forces and nonstate armed groups, such as Hezbollah and Hamas, to achieve its objectives. With nuclear weapons, Iran will have attained the ultimate asymmetric tool to support an aggressive foreign policy agenda.

Over the last several years, Iran has pursued a more active foreign policy based, presumably, on a calculation that the United States is becoming a "sunset" power while Iran's regional and global influence is on the rise, for example, with its outreach to Venezuela and its efforts to expand its influence over the Shia community in Iraq. During the Iraqi insurgency, Iran also provided refuge for elements of the Sadr Organization, including its leader, Moqtada al-Sadr, and supplied weapons and explosively formed projectiles to Shi'ite insurgents in Iraq. Within its immediate neighborhood, Iran has the potential to stoke sectarian antipathy in Iraq and to sow dissent among Shi'ite minorities in Bahrain, Kuwait, and Saudi Arabia. It also has the capacity to thwart the UAE's efforts to impose sovereignty on the disputed islands of Abu Musa and the Greater and Lesser Tunbs. Because of its financial stake in the economy of Dubai, it has the potential to shape and influence the strategic perspectives of Dubai's Rashid family, potentially undermining Crown Prince Mohammed bin Zayed's more pro-U.S. and pro-Western stance on Iranian issues.

Iranian perceptions about the United States as a declining superpower will only be strengthened and reinforced by the U.S. military withdrawals from Iraq and Afghanistan. As nations reconsider their own security options in the changed political landscape of the wider Middle East, Iran can be expected to push even harder to exert its influence, based upon a "zero-sum" calculation that America's losses are Iran's gains. Already, Iran has adopted an active role in support of Shia populations in the

Arab Gulf states, and it is stepping up its engagement with Afghanistan and Pakistan to outflank the United States in the volatile Central and South Asian regions. Iran's observer status in the Shanghai Cooperation Organization (SCO) should be seen in this light as it establishes a security forum in the region that excludes the participation of the United States. Additionally, Iran's efforts to court the Karzai government in Afghanistan and to strengthen its support for Iraq's Shi'ite community reflect a "balance of power" approach to regional and stability planning.

With these considerations in mind, Iran's emergence as a nuclear weapons state portends important and far-reaching implications for regional stability and its interactions with the United States. Just how Iran's weaponization will evolve and for what purposes carry implications for the way in which U.S. defense and deterrence planning should proceed. As the following analysis suggests, Iran's nuclear weapons could support a defensive-deterrent stance, or they could reinforce a more aggressive foreign policy, depending on the assumptions that its leadership makes about doctrine and the force posture it intends to develop.

A DEFENSIVE IRAN'S NUCLEAR POSTURE, DOCTRINAL PRIORITIES, AND FORCE POSTURE (MODEL I)

Iran's nuclear programs were begun not by the radical Iranian leadership that came to power after the overthrow of Mohammad Reza Shah Pahlavi but instead by the shah himself, with the aid of the U.S. Atoms for Peace program.[4] While speculation abounds as to whether the shah really wanted to use Iran's civilian nuclear reactors as the basis for a weapons-development program, his commissioning of Akbar Etemard to build the Atomic Energy Organization of Iran (AEOI) seems to confirm this view. Etemard was the scientist who oversaw Iranian efforts to construct a dual-track program aimed at uranium enrichment and plutonium production. After the Iranian revolution in 1979 and the shah's ouster, Iran's clerical leadership shelved Iran's nuclear programs to concentrate on more immediate concerns. It was not until the Iran-Iraq war of 1981–88 that Iran's nuclear ambitions were revived, primarily as the result of Iraq's use of chemical weapons against Iranian forces. From that point on, evidence suggests that Iran began to consider seriously the nuclear option, first, as a deterrent to offset Iraq's own efforts to develop nuclear weapons and, later, to deter the United States from attempting regime change in Tehran. However, we simply do not know how and even whether U.S. strategies and policies have motivated Iran to acquire nuclear weapons. For example, it has been argued that the removal of Saddam Hussein's regime in Iraq instilled fear in Tehran that Iran might be next in line for such treatment, leading to the halting of certain parts of Iran's nuclear program as noted in the controversial 2007 National Intelligence Estimate on Iran.[5] According to another line of strategic reasoning, U.S. military operations in the Gulf and especially in Iraq and Afghanistan represented a de facto encirclement of Iran, causing its leadership to regard development of nuclear weapons as essential to national security and regime survival. However, according to this logic, the withdrawal of U.S. forces from Iraq and Afghanistan should have had the effect of lessening Tehran's incentive to go nuclear. This does not seem to be the case.

If suspicions about U.S. intentions constitute a key factor in the regime's decision making, nuclear weapons arguably would provide a means to deter the use of force by the United States against Iran. According to this strategic logic, the United States possesses superior conventional forces that no other nation can match. Therefore, the only way for a conventionally inferior nation such as Iran to deter the United States would be by acquiring nuclear weapons. Presumably, a decision by the United States to deemphasize nuclear weapons in its own force posture should provide the basis for dissuading Iran from acquiring nuclear weapons, but this also has not been the case. The ratification of the New START Treaty in 2010 by the U.S. Senate and in 2011 by the Russian parliament reduced significantly the number of strategic nuclear launchers and warheads. Together with the 2010 U.S. Nuclear Posture Review, which reaffirmed that the United States will refrain from the "first use" of nuclear weapons against nonnuclear states in compliance with its obligations under the Nuclear Non-Proliferation Treaty, the New START Treaty opened the door to deep reductions in the American nuclear arsenal and has given rise to further discussion of another round of cuts, either unilaterally or in follow-on negotiations with the Russians. From an Iranian perspective, however, this apparently has not been good enough to curtail its nuclear programs. It is more than likely that American's vast conventional arsenal, which could be used against

Iran in lieu of nuclear weapons, also provides an important motivation for Iran's nuclear weapons development. Because the United States is viewed as prepared to use superior conventional force, Iran's leadership may have concluded that its best option is to continue with its nuclear programs in order to deter any attack—conventional or nuclear—by either the United States or Israel. In other words, Iran's nuclear weapons development would be based on Model I: A Defensive Iran.

As a defensive deterrent, Iran's nuclear posture under Model I need not be overly complicated, although force protection or force survivability would weigh heavily, especially with respect to command and control. This deterrence model, as described briefly earlier, could also include a launch-under-attack policy directed against U.S. regional partners and allies (Israel and NATO Europe). Under the LUA policy, Iran would use its Shahab family of ballistic missiles in an effort to intimidate NATO-European nations and in so doing undermine the U.S.-NATO partnership, potentially by creating political and logistical support difficulties for U.S. operations in a crisis or conflict involving Iran.[6] One of the main objectives of any Iranian deterrence strategy may be to reduce the credibility of the U.S. extended-deterrence concept by sowing doubts in the minds of allied and coalition partners about America's willingness to defend countries under threat of attack from a nuclear-armed Iran. By planting these doubts, Iranian leaders may hope to erode allied/coalition support for the United States, including with respect to potential participation in a military operation against Iran but also by constraining U.S. access to bases and facilities in the region and denying over-flight rights for U.S. and allied/coalition partner forces operating against Iran.

More importantly, from a U.S. defense perspective, a regime seeking nuclear weapons for defensive purposes alone might be content to rely on a minimal force structure, whereby a dozen or several more weapons, rather than hundreds, would be deemed sufficient for deterrence purposes. If indeed this was the main motivation for the regime's nuclear weapons programs, then it follows that, as in Pakistan, Iran would probably choose to arm its Shahab-family ballistic missiles with rudimentary nuclear warheads or perhaps use the solid-fueled but shorter-range Sajjil missile (to target regional and European sites), being less concerned, for example, about precision targeting or lowering collateral damage and more interested in creating a psychological effect on neighbors and potential adversaries. Emblematic of this mindset are the 2001 remarks of former Iranian president Akbar Hashemi Rafsanjani, who claimed that while "even a single bomb on Israel would destroy everything . . . such a bomb would only cause marginal damage to the Muslim world."[7] If the main purpose of an Iranian weapons program was to telegraph to potential enemies Iran's capacity to retaliate with devastating consequences, then it is likely that the regime would choose to display its nuclear weapons in such settings as military parades, as the Soviet Union did during the Cold War, in order to communicate to a global audience that Iran is now a nuclear power with commensurate international status. Iran would be signaling to the United States that it could inflict devastating damage on its enemies in the region. In the event of a U.S. attack, Iran would have the option of striking Israel and targeting the Arab Gulf states as well. A Defensive Iran would probably refrain from targeting U.S. military facilities in the Gulf region with nuclear weapons, which would be primarily, if not exclusively, deployed for use in the event of an attack against Iranian territory. The expectation would be that a nuclear Iran could deter the United States from attacking Iran. At the same time, by demonstrating its nuclear capability, either through testing or some less overt means, Iran would also be sending a signal that it had assumed the mantle of leadership within the Islamic world.

Another goal of an overt display of Iranian nuclear weapons capability would be to demonstrate to the Western world, and to the United States in particular, that Tehran would never again be subject to Western domination. Whether a more democratic regime could be dissuaded from crossing the nuclear threshold or, if not, whether such a government would be more likely to slow Iran's nuclear weapons program is a worthy topic for speculation, as was discussed in chapter 2. If this is the case, the nature of the regime could determine the shape of the Iranian nuclear force and its likely role. However, given the rapid pace of the Iranian nuclear program, it is likely that Iran will reach nuclear weapons status long before a democratic government could be established. We posit that a democratic, transparent nuclear Iran would deploy a smaller nuclear force in keeping with Model I: A Defensive Iran. By the same token, an authoritarian regime would be more likely to build a nuclear capability in support of a more active, expansionist foreign policy in keeping with Model II: An Aggressive Iran.

Box 3.2. A Snapshot of Selected Iranian Missile Capabilities

SHAHAB-1, 2
Two Scud variants, with ranges between 300 and 500 kilometers. Both are indigenously produced.

SHAHAB-3
A derivative of North Korea's No Dong-1 ballistic missile, this is a single-stage, liquid-propelled missile with a range of 1,000–1,500 kilometers. In 2005, Iran claimed to have successfully tested a solid-fueled Shahab-3. Sometimes referred to as the Zelzal-3 ballistic missile.

SHAHAB-3B, 4, BM-25
The Shahab-3B, Shahab-4, and the BM-25 are all derived from Shahab-3 technologies. Each is said to have a range between 1,500 and 3,000 kilometers, allowing the targeting of the Gulf Cooperation Council (GCC) nations, Turkey, and southern Europe. Some may be operational, such as the Shahab-4, which is thought to be a two-stage, liquid-propelled missile with a 2,200-km range. Other improvements to the Shahab-3B include a new guidance system, an improved reentry vehicle, and greater maneuverability.

SHAHAB-6
Thought to be in the development stage, this missile is believed to be a three-stage ICBM with a target range of 5,500 to 6,200 kilometers, with a 1,000-, 750-, or 500-kilogram warhead depending on the number of stages used in its launch. The Shahab-6 is often referred to as the Kosar and reports indicate that it is based on North Korea's Taepo Dong-2 technology. Its development has also benefited from Russian help, with the incorporation of SS-4 and SS-5 IRBM technologies.

GHADR-1
Declared in September 2007 as a new 2,500–3,000 kilometer range, solid-fuel missile; independent experts believe the Ghadr-1 is a redesigned Shahab-3 and not a new missile.

KH-55
Ukraine surreptitiously exported twelve 3,000-kilometer cruise missiles to Iran. Though nuclear-capable, the missiles are believed to be in poor condition.

THAQEB
Iran's first and only submarine-launched missile; some analysts claim the 2006 demonstration of the Thaqeb was a hoax and Iran cannot launch missiles from underwater, only torpedoes.

Box 3.2. (*continued*)

KOWSAR
Iran's newest antiship missile; a cruise missile allegedly capable of speeds of 300 miles per hour, traveling ten feet above the water's surface.

NOUR
Air-launched cruise missile with a 200-kilometer range.

SS-N-26
Iran may have access to this Russian-developed sea-launched cruise missile via a sale from Syria.

AN AGGRESSIVE IRAN THAT FLEXES ITS MUSCLES (MODEL II)

If Iran pursues nuclear weapons to support a more aggressive foreign policy, rather than for strictly defensive purposes, its deterrence posture would look different and be based on different planning assumptions. With the Iran-Iraq war as the defining experience for much of the population, Iranian elites would likely have concluded that a nuclear weapons capability would embolden Iran's foreign policy positions and raise Iran's international profile. It would also provide the essential capability for deterring potential U.S. efforts at regime change, especially if much of Iran's nuclear force and infrastructure is buried in tunnels or otherwise protected, as already is the case.[8] Against Israel, a nuclear Iran would gain the potential to deter nuclear use in a crisis, notwithstanding Israeli efforts to take the necessary steps to assure that its own nuclear force was not vulnerable to preemption. Because Israel falls within range of Iran's ballistic missiles, we can expect it to modernize and diversify its nuclear posture and to develop redundant retaliatory capabilities. However, it would be a mistake to focus on Israel alone as the principal variable in Iranian foreign policy and nuclear calculations. Other considerations also likely shape Iranian thinking. A perceived requirement to take into account India's nuclear capability and to counter a nuclear Pakistan has been cited by Iranian officials as important in their thinking about nuclear weapons. Coupled with considerations of Persian pride and ambition, these factors may provide additional incentives to risk international condemnation as part of the price to be paid for Iran's crossing the nuclear threshold.

With nuclear weapons Iran could enhance its influence over the smaller states in the region. A nuclear Iran has the potential to change the political dynamics in the Middle East. In Model II: An Aggressive Iran, an Iran with nuclear weapons might be emboldened to occupy Bahrain, solidify control over Abu Musa or the Tunbs, and move to secure access to the vast natural-gas reserves that lie in the offshore North Field adjacent to Qatar as well as the pipeline through which natural gas is sent to a large export facility and storage terminal that the UAE has established in Fujairah on the Gulf of Oman. It has been widely assumed that Iran would take military action to close the Strait of Hormuz only if it was attacked by the United States or Israel. A nuclear Iran might be a game changer; namely, a nuclear Iran (Model II) might be emboldened to attempt to seize the strait and to extend its control over the UAE and other GCC countries. Under its nuclear umbrella Iran might be tempted to occupy UAE and Oman territories, giving Tehran land control on both sides of the Strait of Hormuz. Iran might also extend its deterrence protection to Syria as a means of cementing its alliance against Israel and possibly deterring future Israeli military action against Syria. This is made more likely with the signing of a defense agreement between Iran and Syria in December 2009. The predominately Shi'ite Iran has a long history of mutual interest and collaboration with Syria, which is dominated by members of the Alawite sect, a branch of Shi'ite Islam. Their mutual strategic goals have bound the two nations for three decades. Together they have supported Hezbollah, Hamas, Palestinian Islamic Jihad, and other radical Palestinian groups, in part to neutralize Israeli capabilities and thwart American influence in the region.

Iran has continued to support Syria in this period of growing political instability and to support the efforts of the Bashar al-Assad regime to retain its tenuous grip on political power, which include using brutal suppression tactics and its military to kill civilian protesters. Tehran has also been positioning itself to retain major influence in Syria in the post-Assad era. Our analysis is premised on the assumption that Syria will remain a strategic asset for Iran. Tehran will do what it can to shore up the embattled al-Assad regime, but it will also do what it needs to do to establish inroads with any successor regime. This includes efforts to protect Syria from possible Israeli military action while seeing Syria as a strategic springboard for operations against Israel, including, for example, for Hezbollah in Lebanon. Conceivably, in the Aggressive Iran model, Iran could threaten to use nuclear weapons against Israel to deter an Israeli strike against Syria—in effect providing an Iranian extended-deterrence guarantee for Syria.

Beyond providing a deterrence shield for Syria, a nuclear Iran could also extend a deterrent umbrella over Hezbollah. In our Aggressive Iran model, Iran would seek to retain control over its nuclear weapons and refrain from transferring nuclear weapons systems or technologies to Syria. However, Iran might choose to provide Hezbollah, or some other terrorist organization, with nuclear materials (for a radiological device or dirty bomb), especially if Iran's role could be obfuscated. Our Model III: An Unstable Iran speculates that regime elements in a disintegrating Iran are likely to transfer nuclear weapons, as well as know-how or materials, to their allies or that loose nukes might fall into the hands of groups prepared to use them against enemies such as the United States. This might well include Hezbollah.

AN UNSTABLE IRAN AND THE DETERRENCE OF ROGUE ELEMENTS AND NONSTATE ACTORS (MODEL III)

The "Divine Victory" operation against Israel in the summer of 2006 demonstrated a tight connection between Hezbollah and Iran. This included Iranian construction of a fiber-optic "backbone" in Lebanon for Hezbollah. Qods Force elements of the Iranian Revolutionary Guard Corps have reportedly been integrated into every level of Hezbollah's operations and have transferred advanced equipment, including unmanned aerial vehicles, missiles (C-802s), and electronic warfare capabilities to jam Israeli equipment.[9] This reinforces our contention that in Model III: An Unstable Iran, the tottering regime might decide to transfer nuclear assets out of Iran either to ensure IRGC control or to protect them for use (or threatened use) to further the cause of the Islamic revolution.[10] Although both contingencies obviously are speculative, they need to be addressed in U.S. operational planning, as discussed more extensively in chapters 6 and 7.

Given Iran's relationship with Hezbollah, it is useful to speculate as well about the possible effect on U.S. (and Israeli) deterrence planning if Iran were to transfer fissile materials to extremist organizations or if they were seized by radical elements of the military and transferred to Hezbollah for use in a Lebanese or other scenario. Deterrence as a construct may have applicability to nonstate actors and armed groups if it is adapted to take account of fundamental differences between requirements for deterring states and deterring nonstate armed groups. It can be applied to such groups only with careful thought about the personalities of their leaders, their support and financial structures and networks, and the entities used to further their objectives. In other words, the ability to deter nonstate armed groups depends on the extent to which their support structure, including middlemen, can be put at risk of destruction.

Tailoring a deterrence strategy to focus on networks and actors other than states is a far more daunting task than holding accountable a sovereign state and its leadership clearly identifiable as the nuclear perpetrator.[11] The attribution problem is magnified because of uncertainties in tracing the origins of such weapons in the case of nonstate armed groups. However, it is increasingly clear that the IRCG plays the critical operational role in the control of Iran's ballistic missiles. Therefore, its leadership probably has a major voice in Iran's nuclear policy that is likely to grow as weapons come online. According to one Iranian dissident, twenty-one IRGC commanders are top scientists in Iran's nuclear programs.[12] Moreover, the Mujahedin-e Khalq (MeK) has identified specific individuals thought to be associated with Iran's nuclear weapons development, and their identification with the IRGC underscores the extent to which Iran's Revolutionary Guard is an active participant in the country's nuclear programs.

Model II presents important challenges for established deterrence theorizing. It has been suggested that Iran, even without having deployed nuclear weapons, had already attained a "sloppy, asymmetrical" form of deterrence.[13] According to Thomas Schelling, whose ideas shaped much of Cold War thinking about deterrence, the logic of deterrence holds that states have too much to lose from the use of nuclear weapons and thus will refrain from their use because of the assured-destruction threat that was central to deterrence thinking in the last century. Schelling's thesis suggests that a nuclear Iran would not be any different.[14] However, this assumes a state-centric Iran that would not risk the country's destruction for a religious principle or in support of an extreme conception of Islamic jihad. Such assumptions about deterrence are most compatible with our Defensive Iran model. Nuclear weapons could induce greater caution if states with such capabilities seek to avoid the possibility that armed conflicts will escalate to the nuclear level. This assumption is central to the argument put forward by Kenneth Waltz, as noted in chapter 1.[15] Waltz contends that states with nuclear weapons are deterred from using such capabilities against other nuclear-armed states. In our Aggressive or Unstable Iran models, however, this may not be the case. As suggested by one observer of the Iranian scene, "an Iran with nuclear weapons might behave as other nuclear powers have, but there are reasons to fear it would not."[16] Instead, as in our Model II, a nuclear Iran would become an increasingly destabilizing influence in and beyond the Middle East.

Prominent among the reasons an Iran with nuclear weapons might threaten to use them as part of an aggressive foreign policy are Persian nationalism, religious fervor, and a martyrdom mentality. If an Iranian leadership entertained an apocalyptic vision, it might be inclined to see nuclear weapons as useable instruments in an effort to alter the course of history. Such an Iranian leadership would have rejected the "balance of terror" Cold War deterrence concept. Under such circumstances, the United States might be deterred by Iranian nuclear weapons, and not the other way around. The perceived willingness of Iran to use nuclear weapons would be expected to have a restraining influence on the United States, which might seek to avoid nuclear escalation. This is a situation that is likely to be exacerbated if Iran fractured along ethnic or religious lines or if the country became embroiled in a civil war between the reformers and the regime. It is less clear that nuclear weapons would be used by one faction against another in an Iranian civil war than perhaps that they would be seen as a deterrent against outside intervention. The collapse of the Soviet Union in 1991 offers some insight into this issue. Here was a nuclear superpower that did not descend into nuclear civil war. However, if there had been outside military intervention in the Soviet Union to take advantage of the unrest that accompanied the collapse of communism, there might well have been a nuclear confrontation. Another example that comes to mind is China, which was well on the way to becoming a nuclear power after its first nuclear test in October 1964. As the Chinese nuclear force developed, China passed through its Cultural Revolution without intervention from other states. Under such circumstances, assumptions about assured destruction in Western deterrence theories may not hold up, especially if the Iranian regime were to find itself in a power struggle and facing intervention from abroad in support of insurgent forces.

Our Model III also addresses the question of whether, in an Iran in chaos, nuclear weapons might fall into the hands of opposition elements or groups prepared to make them available to terrorists or others outside Iran. Neither the assured-destruction deterrence paradigm from the Cold War nor more recent efforts to update U.S. planning to focus on tailored responses would necessarily be sufficient to deter such groups. Iran could be "undeterrable" by retaliatory threats. For example, rogue elements of the IRGC, seeking to retain their domestic power base or to occupy other territory, might not be deterred if they concluded that the United States was not able or willing to escalate conventionally or with nuclear weapons. If Iran's leadership were incorrect in this assumption, such miscalculation in itself could lead either to nuclear escalation or to Iran's use of nuclear weapons in a conflict in which its opponents escalated to massive conventional strikes. If Iranian nuclear thought is shaped by "shi'ism, with its cult of suffering and martyrdom dating to the murder of Iman Husayn—the Sayyed al-Shuhada, or Prince of Martyrs—in Karbala in the seventh century," such use becomes plausible.[17] Iran's use of children, some as young as ten, to clear minefields during the Iran-Iraq war lends further credence to the possibility that Iran, in our Model III, would be prepared to sacrifice human life on a substantial scale. Iran's martyrdom complex becomes worrisome in light of the rise in importance within Iran's political circles of an ultraconservative sect led by Ayatollah Mesbah-Yazdi, who once was considered to be Ahmadinejad's spiritual inspiration.

Thus, there is a scenario in which a religious fanatic, perhaps even operating alone, sanctions the transfer of radioactive material (for use in manufacturing a dirty bomb) to one or more suicide bombers.[18] This scenario provides a basis for speculation, despite the fact that "we have so tamed and, in a sense, marginalized religion in the West that we have consistently underestimated its ferocity and strength."[19] Much remains unknown about the control of Iran's nuclear materials, although the chain of command is not entirely opaque. The Supreme Leader holds ultimate authority over Iran's nuclear policies. Iran's military, specifically the Iranian Revolutionary Guards, plays a role in Iran's weapons development and most likely also in their operational control. The role of Iran's president is debated, although many have speculated that if his views did not correspond generally to those of the Supreme Leader he would not be allowed to make public pronouncements on foreign and security policy, much less on nuclear issues. However, both belong to Iran's Committee for Special Operations, which, as far as can be discerned, operates independently from the Supreme National Security Council, whose membership includes the chief of the general staff, and, depending on the topic, specific ministers of government and informal counselors. In recent years, both organizations have espoused a hard-line view, with increased representation by former military men and protégées of Ayatollah Mesbah-Yazdi.[20] Many observers contend that Mesbah-Yazdi stopped supporting Mahmoud Ahmadinejad because he aspires to succeed Supreme Leader Ayatollah Khamenei, with whom Ahmadinejad had been engaged in a power struggle, which in 2012 broke out in public over the culpability for Iran's declining economic status, the result of the sanctions and the government's approach to handling the nuclear issue. By all accounts, Mesbah-Yazdi holds more conservative social views than the Supreme Leader, and he advocates greater social, cultural, and political restrictions on Iran's population. As the first senior figure explicitly to endorse Iran's nuclear programs, Mesbah-Yazdi has also worked to undermine the position of former president Rafsanjani, who, despite his past role in supporting Iran's nuclear efforts, is now viewed with disdain by hard-line regime elements because of his support for the Green Movement. As a result, a sophisticated and continuing effort is necessary to identify key actors, understand more precisely technology-transfer networks, and, above all, discern the nature of the relationships among major personalities involved in Iran's nuclear enterprise. This presumably is being done within the various intelligence communities and others who monitor Iranian nuclear issues. Such information and insight have important implications for understanding how Iran might view the utility of nuclear weapons.

4 Nuclear Weapons Operationalization: What Type of Nuclear Force?

The nature of any nuclear weapons capability that Iran might deploy will rest on how the leadership views the role of nuclear weapons and their relationship to defensive and offensive strategic calculations and objectives. If those goals are strictly limited to deterring an attack on Iran or to regime survival, a small nuclear force would be sufficient—one that could retaliate against an enemy nuclear or conventional attack. A "use them or lose them" mentality might also apply if Iran were invaded. Deterrence, under Model I: A Defensive Iran, presumes that an opponent would thus be dissuaded from interfering in Iran's domestic affairs out of fear that an endangered Iranian government would be prepared to resort to nuclear weapons in a last-ditch effort to prevent its removal. In any such contingency, under the Defensive Iran model, it is likely that Iran would adhere to a limited nuclear force posture, with just enough nuclear weapons in the Iranian inventory to lend credence to this type of deterrence threat.

However, even under the Defensive Iran model, Iran could conceivably develop, over time, a larger and more diversified force structure to enhance the survivability of Iran's deterrence posture. This could include longer-range ballistic-missile capabilities to target Western Europe or the United States directly. It might also include the development of air-launched weapons or sea-based nuclear systems to inject an element of redundancy in Iran's force posture. Such capabilities, which are already under development in Iran, could pose a direct threat to the United States, as well as to U.S. forces stationed in the Persian Gulf region and to allies and partners of the United States in the Middle East and Europe, making Tehran's capacity for threatening nuclear retaliation all the more credible. The implicit threat of escalation to nuclear weapons use should Iran's interests be directly challenged could cause the United States to rethink the wisdom of intervention in Persian Gulf or Iranian affairs, especially if vital U.S. interests were not at stake.

At the same time, Iranian nuclear weapons would exist alongside asymmetric nonnuclear capabilities that could be launched against U.S. targets in and outside the Middle East (and against Israel) to make the point that Iran has a number of options even before considering nuclear weapons. Iran could use asymmetric tactics against U.S. forces as well as allies and coalition partners to dissuade them from either actively supporting U.S. operations or allowing the United States use of facilities on their territories. Another option open to Iran would be closure of the Strait of Hormuz to commercial traffic, although in doing so Iran risks bringing harm to its own economy, together with a U.S. response designed quickly to reopen the vitally important waterway and the loss of support from other countries, such as China, that have important energy-related trading relationships with Tehran.[1] Conventionally armed ballistic and cruise missiles and mines in Gulf waters, for example, could be employed to target U.S. naval forces operating in the region, reinforcing the implicit threat of escalation in an Iranian contingency. Finally, the regime could intensify efforts to interdict gas and oil flows throughout the region by targeting off-shore platforms and other energy infrastructure. A nuclear Iran might be emboldened to undertake such operations based upon a strategic calculation that the response from the United States and others would be restrained precisely because of Iran's capacity for nuclear escalation.

If Iran's motivations for obtaining nuclear weapons are strictly related to deterrence, as Model I: Defensive Iran postulates, nuclear weapons would be considered weapons of last resort and its force posture would be based on a minimum deterrence construct. However, if the predominant rationale for an Iranian nuclear force is to support an aggressive foreign policy, then the Iranian leadership might seek a larger nuclear force based on a diversified capability to include various types of ballistic missiles as delivery systems and the offensive, first use of nuclear weapons might be considered in certain circumstances (in contrast to a defensive nuclear retaliation). Iran is already developing long-range ballistic missiles, and it may be testing satellite guidance technologies, allowing for heavier payloads and greater accuracy, perhaps to attain limited coun-terforce capabilities.[2] In addition to an intercontinental ballistic missile (ICBM), Iran is experimenting with multiple independently targeted reentry vehicles (MIRVs), using its space-launch program as the basis for such development. According to one official U.S. government esti-mate, Iran will obtain ICBM capability by 2015 or so. If Iran has benefited from Pakistan's warhead-miniaturization designs, as suggested in chap-ter 1, it may be able to field a credible deterrent force relatively quickly.[3] In so doing, Iran may hope to deploy an assured-destruction capability explicitly to hold U.S. or Israeli cities hostage or to threaten U.S. conven-tional forces with catastrophic attacks. Even without an ICBM capability, Iran has the option to threaten the United States by deploying a con-tainer ship with nuclear-tipped cruise missiles off the U.S. coast. Used to threaten targets in the United States, this type of "strategic" capability would have devastating effects that would have to be taken into account by U.S. defense planners in their deterrence and escalation calcula-tions. To this point, the head of Iran's navy, Rear Admiral Habibollah Sayyari, made the startling assertion in September 2011 that the navy could operate near U.S. "maritime borders." According to the Iranian press, "top Iranian officials" later more specifically clarified this claim to include ships that may go as far as the Gulf of Mexico. White House and Pentagon spokesmen have been skeptical of these Iranian claims, but they should not be summarily dismissed. At the very least, because such a strike with even one nuclear warhead against a U.S. naval port city such as Norfolk would result in vast devastation, the United States would be forced to rethink its homeland defense plans while putting greater effort into designing options for missile defense and critical infrastruc-ture protection, which are discussed at greater length in chapter 6.

Both the 1998 Rumsfeld Commission Report on the ballistic-missile threat to the United States and the Commission to Assess the Threat to the United States from Electromagnetic Pulse Attack suggested that Iran was developing capabilities to threaten the U.S. homeland directly, potentially with nuclear-armed missiles. Specifically, the EMP Com-mission noted that Iran had launched a ballistic missile from a vessel in the Caspian Sea and "triggered" it in a way that might indicate that it intended to detonate a nuclear weapon at altitudes of up to 400 kilome-ters to simulate an EMP attack that could have devastating, long-lasting effects over a large area if not the entire United States, depending on the size and point of detonation of an EMP device. Iran may be developing an EMP weapon, which would be based on a nuclear warhead launched and detonated at an altitude to destroy or disable not only command and control and intelligence networks, but also U.S. civilian infrastructure, including electricity-generating capacity, transportation systems, financial and banking infrastructure, and communication systems.[4] The United States could suffer catastrophic damage from which recovery would be difficult, protracted, and potentially impossible in light of the cascading effects and consequences of such an EMP attack.[5]

Iran's ballistic-missile development programs are aiming to provide the country with a capability to target the United States directly. Iran is also developing an intermediate ballistic-missile capability to target NATO Europe and the Middle East. With Kilo-class submarines acquired from Russia, Iran might develop a sea-based nuclear capability. Iran's development of the Thaqeb (Saturn) submarine-launched ballistic missile (SLBM) suggests a desire to move in this direction. Speculation about an air-delivery capability focuses on Iran's aging fighter/bomber fleet, purchased from France and more recently from Russia, together with Iran's own developing indigenous technology base.[6] Any of these capabilities could be configured to carry nuclear weapons, although this would be easier with some than with others, either using gravity bombs or carrying air-launched cruise missiles. To maximize delivery redundancy or create options for irregular warfare, Iran could also develop asymmetric delivery options for use by IRGC/Qods Force elements. Tehran's preoccupation with strategic surprise and escalation dominance enhances the possibility that Iran will seek to develop nuclear-armed mines and small bombs for possible suicide missions, to be delivered by small boats or even in container ships and freighters. Iran might also consider the use of a dirty bomb to disable off-shore platforms in the Persian Gulf. Because this type of capability is easier to achieve than the weaponization of missiles and aircraft, Iran might conclude that a nuclear mine or a dirty bomb would not provoke a U.S. nuclear response because U.S. actions against Iran would be constrained out of fear of nuclear escalation. In this case, a nuclear Iran would have deterred U.S. nuclear use, although the United States would retain a number of non-nuclear escalatory-response options.

A Defensive Iran and an Aggressive Iran (Models I and II) presume an Iran that remains intact as a state. In Model III: An Unstable Iran, the regime has lost control over large parts, if not all, of its population, territory, and military capabilities. This would include Iran's nuclear weapons and infrastructure. Nuclear weapons or their components could fall into the hands of dissident elements within Iran or be diverted to external groups, replicating the long-feared loose-nukes scenario in which nonstate actors gain access to weapons of mass destruction. With this as context, a closer examination of how Iran's nuclear weaponization might evolve in each of the three models is warranted.

MODEL I: A DEFENSIVE DETERRENT

Because the major purpose of Iran's nuclear weapons would be to deter a U.S. conventional attack or an Israeli preemptive strike, Iran's leaders would likely regard nuclear weapons primarily as defensive tools against a would-be attacker rather than as part of an offensive strategy to coerce potential enemies or shape strategic outcomes. Under the Defensive Iran Model, the leadership in Tehran would deliberately threaten nuclear escalation in order to raise the stakes for an aggressor. As a basis for deterrence, Iran would likely rely on a declaratory policy calling for rapid escalation to nuclear weapons use if Iran were attacked with conventional or nuclear weapons or invaded. This declaratory policy would, in turn, inform Iran's nuclear development, which would have to rely only on a minimal force structure based on imprecise, "countervalue" weapons.[7] In reality, because of the relatively less sophisticated nature of Iran's command-and-control systems, this declaratory policy would conform to the reality that Iran's weapons might be put on a "hair-trigger" alert to compensate for command-and-control vulnerabilities.[8]

As the ultimate line of the country's defense, Iranian nuclear capabilities under this model would not have to be precise enough to target enemy military forces, just sufficiently effective to instill fear at the thought of their use against the civilian populations of the opposing country or third-party actor. Accuracy and low collateral-damage rates would be essentially irrelevant to an Iranian defensive deterrent. Iran's ongoing activities in the areas of ballistic-missile development and warhead miniaturization would be compatible with this model's minimal deterrence purposes. The number of weapons required would not be high, although the requirement for survivability would be great. This might generate a research and development effort in force protection, including passive measures and development of a more diversified nuclear force structure that included a submarine-launched ballistic missile or nuclear-armed air-delivered cruise missiles.

To deter Israel or to intimidate its neighbors, Iran would not need to develop longer-range systems. Because such systems would be necessary to influence Europe and to shape the U.S. deterrence decision-making calculus, it may be assumed that Iran has such goals in mind and will continue to invest in developing longer-range ballistic missiles. However, as suggested earlier, even short-range systems, targeted on the territory of U.S. allies or against U.S. forward-based forces, might be sufficient to influence American strategic and operational planning. For example, they would allow Iran to threaten important (but not vital) U.S. interests in the expectation that America would not escalate to nuclear weapons unless its own territory was threatened. In the case of Israel, because of its small geographic size, Iran could mount a nuclear attack with vastly more devastating consequences. Unless Israel itself develops a survivable second-strike capability—which it appears to be doing—Iran might be able to obtain escalation dominance over Israel if it were able not only to threaten the Israeli population but also to target its land-based deterrent weapons. This would require sophisticated guidance technologies beyond those that exist today in the Shahab missile. However, a Defensive Iran presumably would limit its ambitions in this regard, preferring instead to concentrate on the protection and concealment of its nuclear forces to deter attacks intended to coerce Iran or provoke a change in its leadership.

As with France, however, and French strategic doctrine, which in the 1970s and into the 1980s, provided for a possible "prestrategic" use of nuclear weapons to demonstrate escalatory resolve, a Defensive Iran might conclude that a single nuclear "test" detonation would be important to signal Iran's willingness to escalate to use of nuclear weapons in order to halt an enemy attack. This path might be attractive if Tehran believed that the United States, in a conflict with Iran, could be deterred from further military action after an Iranian "test" first use, signaling

Iran's escalatory intent should hostilities continue. Such action presumes an Iranian nuclear weapons stockpile sufficient to afford the use of one warhead for this purpose while retaining sufficient numbers of nuclear weapons for strategic deterrence purposes.

In this connection, as well, we should also consider the possibility, as one analyst has put it, "that [since] the strategic culture of rogue states might not be so amenable to the otherwise persuasive logic of Western deterrence [theories], the possibility of deterrence failure— even a 'bolt-out-of-the-blue attack'—cannot be discounted."[9] By this strategic logic Iran would be prepared to resort to nuclear weapons earlier rather than later in a conflict. Western notions of damage limitation would not be a major factor in Iranian decision making. It is more probable that an Iran bent on deterring war in the first place, or on terminating further action, would seek precisely the opposite. The regime would place a premium on inflicting as much damage as early as possible against U.S. forces, partners, and allies, notably Israel and NATO. If Iran hoped to play to an international audience, to get the United Nations, for example, to prevail upon the United States, its leaders might forgo targeting Israel and NATO allies. Instead, the focus of Iranian military action, including nuclear threats, might well be limited to the targeting of Iran's Arab neighbors. The goal would be to signal Iran's determination and capability for further escalation without placing at direct risk any permanent member of the UN Security Council. As noted elsewhere, Iran could also conduct asymmetrical terrorist attacks against the Arab Gulf states or use conventional cruise and ballistic missiles to intimidate GCC leaders, employing a strategy of compound escalation.

MODEL II: AN OFFENSIVE DETERRENT FOR AN AGGRESSIVE IRAN

As an offensive deterrent, Iran's nuclear weapons would be foreign policy tools, providing the basis for an expansionist foreign policy designed to facilitate Iran's attainment of regional hegemonic goals. According to the logic of Model II, Iran would be expected to deploy larger numbers of nuclear weapons than in the defensive Model I. Nuclear forces would provide not only an escalatory option in a protracted crisis but also the

Table 4.1 Essential Elements of the Three Models for Iran's Nuclear Operationalization

	DEFENSIVE IRAN	AGGRESSIVE IRAN	UNSTABLE IRAN
Objectives	Status-quo oriented; prevent enemy aggression "Security insurance"	Anti-status-quo oriented Punish and coerce	Preserve revolution and deny Western capacity to exploit regime instability
Deterrence Concepts	"Existential deterrent" as in India Ambiguity about capability, like Israel Deception and concealment	Operational planning like Pakistan Escalation-ominance considerations MAD Dispersed and survivable force Augmented command and control Possible "prestrategic" use Extended deterrence over Syria and Hezbollah	Secure assured-destruction capability Possible "use it or lose it" mentality Shi'ite apocalyptic vision could inform use Extended deterrence for Syria, Hezbollah, and Sunni extremists possible
Nuclear Posture	Minimum deterrent Precision not required Numbers limited Mobility, but not necessarily platform diversity	Larger and diversified posture Ballistic and cruise missiles and Kilo platforms Warhead precision as satellite guidance evolves, but not necessary Target neighbors, Israel, U.S. bases, NATO, and eventually CONUS	"Small but sufficient capacity" IRGC/Qods elements command and control Dispersion outside of Iran possibly to support regime factions or a religious cause or to secure strategic assets

Table continued next page

Table 4.1 (*continued*)

	DEFENSIVE IRAN	AGGRESSIVE IRAN	UNSTABLE IRAN
Operational Concepts	"Defensive first use" Survivable capability Launch under attack (LUA) No transfers to Hezbollah or Syria	Reject "no first use" Hone first-strike capability and create viable follow-on strike options for Israeli and U.S. contingencies Asymmetric/ disruptive options to include ASAT and EMP options Use on behalf of Hezbollah through Qods if control resides in IRGC	Asymmetric targeting and terror "Dirty-bomb" and improvised nuclear device use Focus on Israel, GCC, and U.S. forces in theater Transfer of assets outside of Iran possible

basis for deterring retaliation against Iran in the event of Iranian use of nonnuclear forces. In other words, nuclear weapons would be seen as enhancing Iran's ability to engage in conventional or asymmetric warfare without necessarily incurring retaliation, even by another nuclear power such as the United States. A combination of capabilities (e.g., missiles, mines, and air-delivered weapons) could be deployed to safeguard Iran's territorial security, backed by a survivable nuclear capability as well as flexible options to facilitate operations across the warfare spectrum. Under this model, escalation-dominance considerations would loom large, and the need for a diversified force posture, based on variants of the Shahab ballistic missile as well as a sea-launched system and perhaps even a nuclear cruise missile, would drive Iranian development efforts.

In our Aggressive Iran model, Iran's leadership would be prepared to test U.S. resolve and to take greater risks. Iran might facilitate or support al-Qaeda or Hezbollah by covertly providing (under Qods Force control) dirty-bomb materials as a means of promoting shared interests. In doing so, however, plausible deniability would be the preferred Iranian approach. Qods Force operatives would retain control over Iran's nuclear materials and manage the process by which nuclear weapons materials, technologies, and know-how were provided to nonstate armed groups. In this instance, Iran would be taking a calculated risk that the U.S. ability to trace the origin of nuclear materials is not adequate, leaving room for doubt about where the nuclear components came from or how they had fallen into terrorist hands. In other words, in the absence of such certainty on the part of the United States, Iran could believe that its role could be obfuscated and the likelihood of U.S. retaliation against Iran minimized. Iran would have reason to conclude that a nuclear strike by a nonstate actor against U.S. interests in the Middle East might not result in retaliation against Iran. Notable in this regard would be the questions that inevitably would arise about whether the United States had sufficient intelligence to assign attribution and whether U.S. leadership was prepared (i.e., had the political will) to retaliate against civilian populations who had had little or nothing to do with the transfer of nuclear weapons parts to a terrorist organization.

Under the Aggressive Iran model, Tehran would likely seek to develop long-range strike capabilities to target NATO Europe and the United States directly as a means of minimizing the likelihood of an escalatory response. Iran would endeavor to develop an assured-destruction capability that could target the U.S. homeland directly in order to influence U.S. decision-making calculations, similar to what the Chinese have done with their nuclear-modernization programs that are being designed to provide Beijing with a mutual-assured-destruction capability in relation to the United States. In the case of Europe, Iran presumably hopes to separate NATO Europe from the United States in a crisis, undermining alliance cohesion. The ability to strike targets in Europe would be seen in Tehran as a deterrent against European NATO countries joining with the United States to oppose Iran. Europe would be deeply divided about whether or how to respond. Iranian officials would probably concede that the American public would not tolerate another resource-intensive operation in the volatile Middle East, especially in the absence of NATO participation. Such reluctance might also be strengthened if the United States became increasingly vulnerable to an Iranian missile or nuclear attack. Some, but perhaps not all, members might be prepared to invoke NATO's Article 5 collective-defense commitment that an attack on one is an attack on all. However, in the current strategic setting, such NATO collective action would not be assured. Much might depend on which ally or allies Tehran had targeted and the level of damage threatened or anticipated. Even the potential to strike Europe would probably be sufficient to inhibit a robust response, especially if Europe is not protected by a missile defense or if it comes to doubt the credibility of the U.S. extended-deterrence guarantee.[10] In this way, Iran may hope to divide the transatlantic allies from mounting a coherent and unified response to a threatened Iranian action.

A major aspect of Iranian strategy would be to undermine U.S. extended deterrence by creating doubts about U.S. security guarantees in Europe and the broader Persian Gulf region. This could have one of two effects: either U.S. allies would become intimidated and increasingly bend to Iran's will or they would begin to consider seriously their own nuclear weapons options. With respect to the first, Iran's emergence as a nuclear power would enhance its political clout in the Persian Gulf region, especially if the smaller GCC states began to doubt the credibility of U.S. security guarantees. This might become the case if differences over human rights, for example, lead to congressional action restricting U.S. weapons sales to the region and this, in turn, causes regime leaderships to consider diversification of their security options. Or this might result from the perception of a U.S. "pivot" to the Asia-Pacific area, which posits that America's most important interests lie there and that is where its defense resources should be concentrated. The U.S. pivot to Asia could also provide a catalyst for other Middle East states to consider their own nuclear weapons options. Countries that once relied on the United States for their security would move toward nuclear weapons status themselves. This is reminiscent of French and British arguments after World War II and during the Cold War that led to their development of nuclear weapons.[11] Turkey, Saudi Arabia, and Egypt have often been cited in this regard, although even the UAE has begun to put in place programs for the creation of a civilian nuclear power program, which could be adapted to weapons development with the right incentive and access to relevant technologies. Their principal goal would be to deter an Iranian nuclear attack or to minimize the political influence that might come from Iran's nuclear weapons status. Short of developing nuclear weapons themselves, Saudi Arabia or the UAE might try to strike a deal with Pakistan to provide weapons capabilities or a nuclear guarantee.[12] In either instance, Iran might find itself facing multiple nuclear weapons challenges beyond those posed by Israel and the United States.

However, in a world where multiple states have nuclear weapons, Iran has other options that undoubtedly would form part of its strategy in the Aggressive Iran model. Notably, it could attempt to restrict access to the Gulf in an effort to harm the economies of countries friendly to the United States. However, because Iran's interests would also be damaged, this is an option that Tehran would probably implement selectively and most likely only for a limited time, depending on the positioning of U.S. forces. In the event that U.S. naval assets were deployed outside the Strait of Hormuz, they would be forced to fight their way back into the Gulf. Once inside the Gulf, they would likely be subjected to small-boat swarm attacks and mine threats, creating hazards for military operations. Although not an impossible situation for the U.S. Navy, platform vulnerability would become an important issue, placing increased emphasis on the need for fleet self-defense capabilities (against missiles), the capacity to deal with swarm attacks and mines in the strait and in Persian Gulf waterways, and the ability to take out land targets and Iran's air defense network.[13] In the case of a nuclear-armed Iran, U.S. forces would also be tasked with interdiction of Iran's nuclear forces to forestall their use in a contingency, and this would require the deployment of earth-penetrating weapons to get at concealed targets.

From the Iranian perspective, deterrence under the Aggressive Iran Model might also be enhanced by the possibility of asymmetric Iranian use of nuclear weapons and other WMD. For example, this might include a suitcase-type bomb in a suicide attack or a dirty bomb detonated in the vicinity of a major U.S. base, against maritime platforms operating in the Persian Gulf, or against one or more civilian targets in states friendly to the United States. Recalling Iraq's use of chemical weapons against Iran in the 1980s, an Aggressive Iran might resort to biological or chemical weapons to target coalition-partner cities or U.S. bases in the region. It might believe that such action could be undertaken with less likelihood of retaliation if it also possessed nuclear weapons. In other words, an Iranian nuclear force would provide the security umbrella under which operations extending from chemical warfare to conventional warfare could be undertaken. In so doing, an Aggressive Iran might calculate that one of the results would be to divide regional allies from the United

States and coerce them into denying the United States access to facilities and forces located on their territory.

An Aggressive Iran might also aim at confounding American retaliatory calculations on the assumption that the United States would not want to be the first to use nuclear weapons in any contingency, but especially in response to Iran's use of nonnuclear WMD. Indeed, the distinctions set forth in the Obama administration's nuclear strategy may not have been lost on Tehran. According to the 2010 NPR, the United States will refrain from using nuclear weapons against non-nuclear WMD threats, including those from Iran, although a specific declaratory statement to this effect was left out of the NPR apparently because of internal debate over its wording.[14] In any event, Tehran may hope that by putting the burden for first use on the United States, American decision makers would be deterred from resorting to nuclear weapons in these circumstances. In this way, Iran might very well use nonnuclear WMD to attain its objectives without great concern that the United States would retaliate with nuclear weapons. In either instance, an Aggressive Iran may try to achieve a strategy of "triangular or indirect deterrence." As described by Robert Harkavy, triangular or indirect deterrence comes about when

> a weaker power lacking the capability to deter a stronger and (importantly) distant power might choose to threaten a nuclear (or chemical or biological, or also conventional) riposte against a smaller, closer or contiguous state, usually but perhaps not always one allied to the larger tormentor or to one of its clients (or providing them base access in a crisis), but perhaps also a neutral state, one with no real political connection to the ongoing conflict.[15]

By this strategic logic, the center of gravity for disrupting a U.S. strike would be to target countries that supported such operations. By undermining the security of U.S. coalition partners, Iran could achieve its deterrence objectives without having to target the U.S. homeland directly or without necessarily using nuclear weapons. This assumes, of course, that the United States could be deterred from such escalation by the fact that its coalition partners or allies would be targeted by a nuclear Iran but its homeland would be immune from attack.

As an extraregional power, United States relies on forward basing or over-flight rights for military operations. This would mean that countries from which such U.S. operations might be mounted would become vulnerable to Iranian attack. Deprived of forward bases, the United States would retain the option to use long-range airpower or to launch an attack from the sea. In this case U.S. Global Strike and navy assets (i.e., carrier-based air and Tomahawk cruise missiles) would form the centerpiece of American operations.[16] This scenario would entail a certain amount of risk for U.S. carriers, especially those deployed in or near the Strait of Hormuz, where the threat of enemy mining, swarming speedboats, and missile operations would be present. Depending on the timeframe, Iran might seek to deter such U.S. operations by deployment of an intercontinental ballistic missile to target the continental United States directly. It is also possible that a more confident adversary, as an Aggressive Iran is likely to be, would seek to develop increasingly sophisticated attack options—for example, space-oriented capabilities to disrupt or destroy U.S. command-and-control networks or even critical infrastructure in the United States itself. Thus, in Model II: An Aggressive Iran, escalation control and war termination would emerge as important considerations in U.S. strategic thinking, and they might also become central aspects of Iranian operational strategy. The deterrence goals of an Aggressive Iran would likely be not only to deter a U.S. attack in the first instance but also to prevent the United States from exercising more limited conventional options, such as blockading Iran or seizing control of off-shore oil platforms. Understanding U.S. "red lines" and leveraging them to Iran's benefit become imperative in this context, particularly with respect to neutralizing the ability of the United States to control the escalatory chain in a warfare contingency.

MODEL III: AN UNSTABLE IRAN AND THE NEED TO DETER REGIME ELEMENTS

In our Unstable Iran model, Iran is in the midst of chaos in which opposing forces are attempting to gain governmental control. In these circumstances, there would be a struggle to seize Iran's nuclear weapons. Depending on the specific circumstances in which such a contingency unfolds, elements of the IRGC might attempt to wrest control of Iran's government, or the government might find itself fighting an insurgency created out of the unification of opposition forces. In either contingency, those in control of Iran's nuclear weapons might conclude that it was necessary to transfer elements of its nuclear arsenal to an allied group, either within the military, the Qods Force, for example, or to another country, Syria perhaps, to protect these assets and possibly to build a power base to be used inside Iran if the factionalism continued and internal conditions deteriorated. This would be an Iran whose regime would have little interest in established nuclear doctrine, particularly if threats from within were perceived to be more serious than threats from abroad. In fact, as is often the case with unstable regimes, certain elements could seek to use external threats as a means of regaining domestic support. In this case, elements of the IRGC, in an effort to reassert control within Iran, could transfer weapons or materials to groups outside Iran, possibly to create incidents that would heighten the sense of external danger to the Iranian people. Alternatively, if democratic forces within Iran were seen to be making advances, IRGC elements or Qods Force members could try to sustain their hold on power or support for their objectives by transferring or making available nuclear components, weapons, or materials to groups that share an interest in promoting fundamentalist objectives and anti-Western agendas, perhaps the Taliban or surviving remnants of al-Qaeda on the Arabian Peninsula (AQAP).

Iran already has in place an extensive network for importing nuclear materials and nuclear-relevant or -oriented technologies. Its relationship with North Korea in this regard is well documented. Less readily appreciated is its creation of a network, reportedly more extensive than the A. Q. Khan network, that could be used to facilitate a "proliferation in reverse" system of getting nuclear materials, components, or know-how to transnational actors or rogue-state allies were it determined that in doing so specific Iranian or Islamist objectives could be met. From all appearances, the IRGC and its Qods Force element would be central to such a network. Funding for IRGC and Qods Force operations is obtained primarily through business enterprises that have been established for that purpose.[17] Presumably, they would also provide an important conduit for nuclear sales and technology transfers were a decision made to embark on such a course. Iran works with numerous groups abroad. Such proxies are described in box 4.1.

Box 4.1: Iran's Potential to Support Proxies

In the event of a U.S. or Israeli military operation against Iran, the Islamic Republic has the potential to call upon proxy forces to implement asymmetric operations. Among its options, Iran or elements within Iran could operate in:

1. Iraq: By increasing its support to Shi'ite militias or by adopting a higher profile in support of foreign (Sunni) fighters if it appeared that political reconciliation was succeeding, particularly at the expense of Iran's political influence in the south and over the government in Baghdad.

2. Hezbollah: By providing longer-range missiles to target Israeli cities, strike shipping in the wider Gulf region, and increase its activities in Lebanon.

3. Insurgent forces in Afghanistan: Iran has great potential to destabilize the Afghan government and create chaos in the western provinces of Afghanistan.

4. South America: Iranian-supported Hezbollah cells could be used in terror attacks, as they were in 1994 with the bombing of a Jewish facility in Buenos Aires. The Hezbollah presence in the Tri-Border area gives Iran a reach into South America.

5. Europe: European intelligence agencies have identified thousands of Hezbollah members living in European Union countries. Members of Hezbollah and sympathetic individuals could be organized to conduct terror operations on the continent and in the UK.

6. Shi'ite cells in Gulf: Iran has extensive intelligence networks throughout the Shi'ite populations in GCC states. Using sympathetic populations to stir political unrest or engage in violent attacks, Iran has the potential to undermine allied governments and to destroy bases and infrastructure support for U.S. forces.

7. Israel/Jordan/Gaza: Following Hamas's seizure of Gaza, Iran has become its largest financial backer. The Iran/Syria/Hezbollah "alliance" is responsible for training and enabling terrorists in Lebanon and Syria.

8. United States: Iranian-backed Hezbollah cells have been monitored in the United States since the 1980s for their fund-raising activities. This nonviolent presence could be activated to initiate terrorist action in the United States in a crisis.

Also important is Iran's intelligence network, whose operations include infiltration of businesses in countries outside Iran. Under certain circumstances, Qods Force elements could probably carry out a weapons transfer. To do so, however, they would likely have to rely on leaders within the IRGC to gain access to an operational weapon, but given the tight relationship that Qods leaders enjoy with the IRGC, this is possible and certainly a contingency that offers elements in Iran the option of altering the "correlation of forces" either domestically or in the broader regional setting. For example, a radiological weapon (a dirty bomb) would be sufficient for asymmetric-warfare purposes. In this case, the objective would be to incite terror among the populations of the United States and its allies. Implementation of such asymmetric tactics using nuclear capabilities would also place the onus for further escalation on the United States. Given the aversion to nuclear weapons that shapes much of Western strategic thinking, nuclear retaliation by the United States cannot be the assumed response, and Iran may believe that the United States would be "self-deterred."

However, Iran may discount the escalation potential and dynamics of this particular situation. While America's nuclear posture is built around the idea that use of nuclear weapons might be considered in retaliation for an adversary's use, or in the face of a devastating conventional attack by a nuclear power, in this instance two qualifying factors are likely to influence the U.S. debate. First, the use of a dirty bomb would not necessarily be regarded as qualitatively equivalent to the employment of nuclear weapons. While its effects may cause major disruptions and instill terror, the consequences of such use would be far less devastating than the detonation of an actual nuclear weapon. Second, the United States is in the midst of implementing a deterrence construct that emphasizes conventional precision strikes as well as missile defenses to deter an enemy attack or to mitigate its consequences. Under these circumstances, it would be unlikely that the United States would order a nuclear strike if the most vital U.S. interests were not at stake and if American territory had not been attacked. Threshold issues would continue to play a critical role in shaping U.S. decision making in any but the more direct case of an all-out attack against the territory of the United States. Thus, in the regional setting, U.S. adversaries might conclude that they had greater flexibility in launching an asymmetric WMD attack, even against U.S. operating forces, all the more so if attack attribution could not readily be assigned and the fear of U.S. nuclear retaliation further diminished.

In the Model III, as previously discussed, existing custody safeguards for nuclear weapons would have broken down, and nuclear weapons could become available to nonstate armed groups. This could come about in two ways. First, nuclear weapons could be seized by a regime faction seeking to oust its rivals and assert control over the levers of Iran's government. In one scenario, this could occur against the backdrop of an externally generated crisis, which would be used to heighten domestic fears of an external attack. Under Model III, IRGC elements might find themselves engaged in operations outside Iran, for example, in support of Hezbollah in the Americas. The result could be an escalating crisis with the United States. This, in turn, would likely generate domestic support for the IRGC, which could portray itself as the protector of Iranian interests in and outside Iran. In other words, the IRGC, now with Iran's nuclear weapons under its control, could consolidate its position (against the clerics or any other opposition faction) by concentrating domestic attention on the external threat to Iran's security. Iran's defense minister, Ahmad Vahidi, is a former IRGC commander who is wanted for his alleged part in the bombing of the Jewish community center in Buenos Aires in 1994. Extrapolating from this and other Iranian-inspired terrorist events, a situation might unfold to benefit the IRGC objective hypothesized in this contingency.

Iran's nuclear weapons or their components could be transferred to nonstate actors to support the objectives of one regime faction over another. For example, factions within the faltering regime could decide to transfer dirty-bomb materials to Sunni Arab groups, notably Hamas, the Palestinian Islamic Jihad (PIJ), or AQAP. It must be recalled that al-Qaeda has proclaimed its intention to acquire nuclear weapons for use against the United States and its allies, and a prominent Saudi cleric has written a detailed rationale for using such weapons against Western nations.[18] Notwithstanding Bin Laden's demise, the possibility of IRGC or regime collaboration with al-Qaeda cannot be dismissed, particularly in a situation where regime elements thought they were furthering the cause of Islamist extremism. Iran is already known to have provided a safe haven for some al-Qaeda fighters, and precedents have been established with Iran's provision of training to al-Qaeda fighters; its transfer of weapons to Afghan militants, as was documented in the Defense Department's Report to Congress on Iran; and its apparent provision of explosively formed projectiles (EFPs) to Sunni insurgents in Iraq.[19] Collaboration with jihadi groups may be seen as a way to enhance the capacity of IRGC or regime elements to strike the United States directly, but, as with other transfer scenarios, it is unlikely that this would be done without giving considerable thought to U.S. retaliation options. The key question in this regard would be the perceived stakes for the IRGC or regime elements and the calculation on their part about the level and type of U.S. retaliation. Specifically, would pursuit of radical extremist objectives be deemed worthy of the price of Iran's destruction as a result of U.S. military retaliation? Would such (regime) elements conclude that pursuit of radical extremist objectives would provoke U.S. military retaliation resulting in Iran's destruction? Plausible deniability might in this instance enhance the willingness to attack U.S. interests, but the larger issue would be how far religious fanatics would be willing to go to promote their radical agenda. IRGC members or elements of the regime might conclude that Iran's territorial integrity was far more important than wounding the world's remaining superpower. In other words, they might be deterred from transferring nuclear materials to groups such as Hezbollah or al-Qaeda if they feared U.S. retaliation against Iran in the event that terrorist attacks by such groups against the United States could be traced back to nuclear weapons or components of such weapons supplied by Iran.

5
Implications for U.S. Strategic and Operational Planning

Iran's pursuit of nuclear weapons poses a serious challenge to U.S. defense and deterrence planning. It is made even more difficult by the possible effect of radical Islamic ideology on Iranian national security policy and use of nuclear weapons. This effect has been the object of debate and speculation. According to Michael Eisenstadt and Mehdi Khalaji, some students of Shia Islam downplay such concern; others attach greater importance to ideology in decision making.[1] Faced with an Iranian leadership imbued with an apocalyptic theology, the Western paradigm of deterrence by punishment, or retaliation, may have little practical utility when it comes to dealing with a nuclear Iran. Indeed, the possibility that such an approach to nuclear weapons could gain sway in Iran undermines the utility of a deterrence concept based on retaliation. Western deterrence theories that rely on Cold War–era assumptions about such factors as value structures, the level of violence a society is willing to endure, and the risk tolerance of a leadership considering the use of nuclear weapons may not be applicable in Model II: An Aggressive Iran or Model III: An Unstable Iran. For a nuclear Iran awaiting the Twelfth Imam and certain that the United States had been in Iraq in part to prevent his return, the nuclear calculus may be fundamentally different from that on which Western deterrence models have been based.

This apocalyptic perspective opposes the idea that an Islamic state such as Pakistan, already a nuclear power, or even Iran, would not act contrary to its national interests in deciding to use nuclear weapons. According to Michael Eisenstadt:

The perception, however, of Iran as an irrational, undeterrable state with a high pain threshold is both anachronistic and wrong. Within the context of a relatively activist foreign policy, Iranian decision-makers have generally sought to minimize risk by shunning direct confrontation and by acting through surrogates (such as the Lebanese Hezbollah) or by means of stealth (Iranian small boat and mine operations against shipping in the Gulf during the Iran-Iraq War) in order to preserve deniability and create ambiguity about their intentions. Such behavior is evidence of an ability to engage in rational calculation and to accurately assess power relationships.[2]

Indeed, a Defensive Iran (Model I) would act according to a logic that accords with Western conceptions of deterrence and identifies the use of nuclear weapons with national interests. Deterrence may be conceived as "existential" or as the ultimate means of ensuring national safety and regime survival in an uncertain world. In contrast, in a setting in which radical ideologies have been used as justification for violent political acts, it is possible to imagine a radicalized Iranian regime launching nuclear weapons. Mass civilian casualties, including Muslims, would be rationalized by the conviction of a just cause, especially in the case of the Aggressive Iran model, or as a way to preserve the regime, an objective of both the Defensive Iran and Aggressive Iran models, contrasted with the Unstable Iran model, in which the goal might be to restore the regime. However, Iran, with its educated and Western-oriented population, could be "deterrable" and its path to nuclear weaponization subject to influence. The objects of deterrence are numerous and diverse. Some segments of the Iranian population may be more deterrable than others. Among the less deterrable would be the Islamist extremists, and among the more deterrable would be the Westernized elites, for whom survival is an obvious value. Maximum attention to this variegated Iranian audience should be explicit in U.S. twenty-first-century deterrence thinking.

Updating U.S. strategic and operational planning for an Iranian contingency should be focused on four principal considerations: (1) implementing an operational strategy to achieve U.S. objectives in the face of the threatened use of nuclear weapons by Iran; (2) reassuring allies and coalition partners that extended deterrence remains viable in the face of Iran's development of nuclear weapons; (3) planning against and mitigating the effects of an Iranian first use of nuclear weapons or a dirty bomb; and (4) preventing the transfer of nuclear materials from Iran to other states or nonstate armed groups. Related to these objectives is the need to understand the escalation dynamics underlying contingency planning for Iran, especially with respect to intrawar deterrence and the implications of "catalytic warfare," where escalation control is out of U.S. hands as a result of actions taken by a third party.[3]

Reduced to its essentials, U.S. strategy for the Persian Gulf region would have as its basic goals containing a nuclear Iran, protecting U.S. coalition partners and allies, deterring nuclear and conventional attacks on U.S. forces and allied/coalition-partner territories, and mitigating the effects of an attack should one occur. In part because the United States and Iran have not had formal diplomatic relations since the hostage crisis of 1979, the danger of miscalculation is great. Washington has little knowledge about the conditions under which Iran would be willing to use force in pursuit of regime objectives, and Tehran could easily miscalculate U.S. resolve. This situation may worsen with a nuclear Iran. For that reason, crisis management and escalation control become crucial aspects of U.S. strategy. Iran already has a formidable capacity to leverage proxy forces, such as Hezbollah, using irregular warfare tactics. However, an Iran that was disposed to use nuclear weapons in support of proxy interests or to provide fissile materials or nuclear know-how and support to nonstate armed groups would pose escalatory challenges that would be difficult to anticipate. In either eventuality, the United States could find itself embroiled in a chain of events escalating to regionwide war.

Against this likelihood, and to contain and deter a nuclear Iran, the United States would face the need to reassure allies in the region with a variety of policies designed to counter a nuclear Iran. Deterring a nuclear Iran will present different strategic and operational challenges than those associated with efforts to dissuade the Iranian regime from weaponizing in the first place. In order to diminish the regional effects of Iran's possession of nuclear weapons, the United States must engage in a comprehensive effort to strengthen relationships with allies and coalition partners, build coalition-partner militaries, and create greater consequence-management capabilities, including the development of a layered missile defense over those partners and in defense of U.S. interests in and beyond the region.[4] Clear U.S. red lines would need to be set forth and backed by necessary capabilities in order to assure credibility. Strong signals through diplomatic initiatives and military deployments would need to be sent to show that the United States intends to remain fully engaged in the Middle East even after it withdraws combat forces from Afghanistan.

If Iran intended to use its nuclear programs to support a more aggressive foreign policy (Model II), then we might expect Tehran to develop a nuclear weapons posture that includes survivable second-strike forces for retaliation after an attack against Iran. Such a nuclear Iran would present a more complex deterrence problem for the United States than would reliance on a defensive-deterrent posture (Model I). As discussed earlier, an Aggressive Iran (Model II) could attempt to extend a nuclear umbrella over Syria or Hezbollah, creating new deterrence challenges for Israel and for U.S. Gulf partners. It could also make radioactive materials available to other states or to nonstate actors. This would not necessarily include the outright transfer of nuclear weapons to an ally or proxy force because of the need to preserve Iran's role as the dominant partner in its alliance relationships. The actual transfer of nuclear weapons would become a more likely prospect in a situation where regime stability in Iran (Model III) is in question and there is either a perceived need to get the systems out of harm's way or to move them in order to support a fanatical religious cause.

In all three models, the effect of Iranian policies on other nuclear aspirants, including Egypt, Syria, Saudi Arabia, and Turkey, could be substantial, producing a cascade effect upon other states in and beyond the Middle East. In this sense, it can be argued that Iran's breakout from the NPT would be potentially a more important development than North Korea's because of Iran's energy reserves, its regional power status, and its role in the Muslim world. North Korea, in contrast, is a poor, isolated country with few friends and little to offer the outside world beyond uranium deposits and nuclear "know-how." To be sure, North Korea's potential to become a failed state is of great concern, largely because of questions about the ultimate control of its nuclear weapons. However, an unstable Iran with nuclear weapons would increase the prospect that such capabilities would proliferate elsewhere in the Middle East. Unlike North Korea, Iran is situated in a region that, as a result of the 2011 Arab Spring, might face years of chaos as contending forces grapple for power.

Under these circumstances, a priority for the United States would be a concerted effort to gain control of as much of the Iranian nuclear stockpile as possible and to prevent its transfer to other parties. Even though the regional situation surrounding North Korea differs greatly from that of Iran, a collapsing North Korean regime nevertheless would confront the outside world, including the United States, with an urgent need to take control of Pyongyang's nuclear weapons in order to prevent them from falling into hostile hands.

In a sharply contrasting situation, Iran could choose not to reveal its nuclear weapons status. Tehran might see nuclear ambiguity as allowing greater flexibility in support of proxy operations.[5] Ambiguity might also calm global concerns. Nevertheless, under circumstances of ambiguity, a nuclear Iran might gain greater confidence in its ability to take risks in support of strategic objectives. With the U.S. withdrawal from Iraq and Afghanistan, together with a polarized U.S. domestic public, Iran's leadership could miscalculate American will. Statements by military leaders and the Supreme Leader give substance to this concern.[6] Perceiving the United States as a "sunset power," as it has often been described in the Iranian press, a nuclear Iran's leadership might be more willing to pursue its strategic objectives, raising the possibility of miscalculation.

From this perspective, the deterrence challenges arising from a nuclear Iran reside not so much in the regime's high threshold for pain but instead in its willingness to take risks and in its capacity for overreach in a crisis, both of which create dangers for U.S. operational planners.[7] A nuclear Iran might be emboldened to adopt a more confrontational posture in dealing with regional neighbors rather than trying to lull them into thinking that Iran's nuclear stature was not threatening. Similarly, an Iran in possession of nuclear weapons might be more willing to counter U.S. initiatives considered hostile or threatening to Iran. Iran could choose to demonstrate overtly to the world that it had a capability to raise the stakes in a crisis confrontation, either by threatening a missile strike against the United States or by using its conventional military forces against a regional U.S. ally.[8]

Alternatively, Iran could choose to be more nuanced about exercising its nuclear power, for example, by covertly mining the Persian Gulf while publicly declaring the creation of an exclusion zone to protect the country's vital economic interests.[9] The strategic ambiguity created by Iran's action and the uncertainty as to whether the mines were nuclear-capable and how and to what extent Iran's conventional capabilities would be backed up operationally by nuclear escalation might be sufficient to deter the Gulf states from taking action. Iran may also seek to deter the United States by arming a few of its growing arsenal of antiship missiles with nuclear warheads to target assets of the U.S. Navy Fifth Fleet, forward operating bases, and infrastructure—including perhaps mobile sea bases—and creating uncertainty among U.S. coalition partners by directly targeting their territories and by holding Europe hostage to the threat of a nuclear strike.

In essence, a nuclear-armed Iran would pose several distinct types of operational-planning challenges: terrorism and subversion, limited conventional options (under the protection of Iran's nuclear umbrella), and the actual use of nuclear weapons against U.S. forces operating in the Gulf region; against the territories of U.S. allies in Europe, Israel, and coalition partners in the GCC countries; and perhaps against the continental United States. To deal with these operational challenges, the United States would need to factor the Iranian nuclear dimension more systematically into its efforts to counter terrorism, defend forward-deployed forces and assets (such as facilities located in Bahrain, Qatar, the UAE, and Kuwait), enhance coalition-partner defenses and consequence-management capabilities (through an expanded and augmented U.S.-Gulf security strategic framework), and protect energy flows, infrastructure, and shipping in the Strait of Hormuz and the Gulf region.[10] As noted already with respect to nuclear-mine emplacement, nontraditional delivery systems for nuclear weapons cannot be discounted in U.S. operational planning, making early detection of gamma and neutron radiation a high priority. Contingency planning for Gulf-related operations must also consider unconventional methods of nuclear delivery, for example, a suitcase-bomb. Obviously, all of these planning challenges will require an even tighter coordination between the United States and its principal alliance and coalition partners in and beyond the Gulf region. As summarized in table 5.1, these challenges include the heightened need to dissuade other states from acquiring nuclear weapons; to deter Iran's use of nuclear weapons; to reassure allies and partners; and to deploy more robust active and passive defenses. The priorities include building security cooperation, strengthening consequence management, bolstering global strike, and expanding special operations forces and information warfare, gaining greater crisis escalation control, and augmenting nonkinetic operations. For each of these priorities, a series of policy initiatives is set forth in table 5.1.

Table 5.1 Iran's Nuclear Development: Strategic-Planning Challenges for the United States

STRATEGIC OBJECTIVES AND CHALLENGES	DISSUADE NUCLEAR ACQUISITION AND TECHNOLOGY TRANSFERS	DETER IRAN	REASSURE ALLIED PARTNERS AND PROVIDE SECURITY ASSURANCES NEGATIVE/ POSITIVE	DEPLOY ACTIVE/ PASSIVE DEFENSES, INCLUDING MISSILE DEFENSE
Build Security Cooperation	Influence and shape regional reactions and capabilities Augment and support local border control and sea lines of communication (SLOC) security efforts	Augment pace and scope of Proliferation Security Initiative (PSI) in the Gulf region Revisit declaratory policies Augment missile-defense assets in theater	Declaratory policy for Israel and Gulf Cooperation Council (GCC) states "Phase 0" activities with Israel/GCC states Maintain expeditionary strike group/ carrier strike group (CSG/ ESG) presence in the Gulf region	Consequence-management exercises Force-protection exercises PSI exercises Enhance Joint Combined Exchange Training (JCET) deployments
Strengthen Consequence Management	Enhance indigenous chemical, biological, radiological, nuclear, and explosive (CBRNE) defenses	Deploy chemical-biological incident response force (CBIRF)	Step up exercises with partners	Focused cooperation with Israel and GCC states

Table continued next page

Table 5.1 (*continued*)

STRATEGIC OBJECTIVES AND CHALLENGES	DISSUADE NUCLEAR ACQUISITION AND TECHNOLOGY TRANSFERS	DETER IRAN	REASSURE ALLIED PARTNERS AND PROVIDE SECURITY ASSURANCES NEGATIVE/ POSITIVE	DEPLOY ACTIVE/ PASSIVE DEFENSES, INCLUDING MISSILE DEFENSE
Bolster Global Strike	Reconfigure forces and alert status in the region Employ signaling and perception-management techniques to influence decision making in Tehran	Plan for preemptive option Develop targeting profile Dissuade independent Israeli action	Negotiate status of force agreements (SOFAs) and base-access agreements Prepare strike options and force packages	Upgrade missile-defense deployments Protect aerial port(s) of debarkation/ embarkation (APOD/Es) and seaport(s) of debarkation/ embarkation (SPOD/Es) in theater Enhance Strait of Hormuz patrolling and defenses
Expand Special Operations Forces (SOF) and Information Warfare (IW)	Develop comprehensive information operations (IO) and psychological operations (PSYOPS) campaign Proliferation Security Initiative (PSI) interdiction Targeted/focused options	Implement IO and PSYOPS campaign Support contingency plan (CONPLAN) for targeting, etc. Disable operational facilities and sites	Empower GCC SOF Work with Israeli SOF to counter Hezbollah	Implement render-safe options, as appropriate

STRATEGIC OBJECTIVES AND CHALLENGES	DISSUADE NUCLEAR ACQUISITION AND TECHNOLOGY TRANSFERS	DETER IRAN	REASSURE ALLIED PARTNERS AND PROVIDE SECURITY ASSURANCES NEGATIVE/ POSITIVE	DEPLOY ACTIVE/ PASSIVE DEFENSES, INCLUDING MISSILE DEFENSE
Gain Greater Crisis-Escalation Control	Activate options to influence strategic elites Employ special operations forces	Be clear about "red lines" Develop signaling mechanisms Deter independent Israeli action	Strengthen protection of Israel/GCC partners Coordinate allied and partner capabilities	Enhance CONUS protection Step-up consequence management (CM), collective protection (CP), and force protection activities in CENTCOM and EUCOM's AORs Include PSI and gross national income/global network initiative (GNI) in war plans
Augment Nonkinetic Operations	Employ PSYOPS and IO	Activate strategic communications plan	Hone public diplomacy with allies and partners	Table-top exercises Augment cyberdefenses and create cyberwarfare options

IRAN AS CATALYST FOR A NEW DETERRENCE DYNAMIC
AMONG NUCLEAR STATES

Iran's nuclear breakout threatens to affect regional nonnuclear states, including the Gulf Cooperation Council states, Jordan, Egypt, and Turkey, and their deliberations concerning security alternatives, especially, for Egypt, Turkey, and Saudi Arabia, consideration of the nuclear option. The cascading effect of a nuclear Iran will bring about new deterrence-planning challenges, which are addressed more fully in the next chapter.[11] If additional nations deploy nuclear weapons, the safety, security, and custody of nuclear stockpiles will become even more pressing issues than they are today. At the same time, a nuclear Iran creates a new set of deterrence dynamics between Tehran and other states also in possession of nuclear weapons. As a nuclear state, Iran would perceive that it now enjoyed greater international status. The result would be enhanced confidence in its diplomatic dealings with other nuclear states, including China, Russia, Pakistan, and India.

Leaving aside for the moment the deterrence relationships between the United States and a nuclear Iran, and between Israel and Iran, it is quite possible, especially in the Model II: An Aggressive Iran, that Tehran would be emboldened to take greater risks once it declared or demonstrated its nuclear weapons capability. In Model I: A Defensive Iran, we suggest that nuclear weapons might moderate Iranian behavior since the principal purpose of their deployment would be to deter an enemy attack. However, in the Aggressive Iran model, we assume that nuclear weapons have been deployed not only to deter an attack against Iran but also to underwrite an expansive foreign policy agenda and to "sanctuarize its homeland from reprisal." This would be an Iran that runs the risk of lowering the nuclear threshold.[12] It would also be an Iran that is prone to miscalculation in part because of the relative inexperience of its leadership in dealing with the outside world. As a Persian Shi'ite state surrounded by Arab Sunni neighbors, and with a view of the international setting (based on the need to exploit opportunities for Iran to expand its influence), Tehran in the Aggressive Iran model would likely regard nuclear weapons as a means to maximize its international status and underwrite a foreign policy designed to lead to regional hegemony. At the same time, Iran's leadership would be viewed as strengthening its domestic position and enhancing Iran's independence. From its experience in the Iran-Iraq War, Iran came to the view that it cannot rely on outside powers for its security. Therefore, this perspective would be not only a motivating factor leading to a nuclear Iran but also a factor reinforcing the importance of maximizing the benefits from its new status.

Iran's relationship with Russia would be no exception in this regard. A nuclear Iran, both in Model I and Model II, would probably seek to strengthen its relationship with Russia based on a shared desire to reduce U.S. power and influence in the Gulf and Central and South Asia. Similarly, a nuclear Iran could act more assertively in pursuing closer alignment options with China or even India as both provide lucrative markets for Iranian energy exports. However, at the same time, because energy remains an important aspect of Iranian diplomacy, this is an issue over which Iran and Russia could either compete or cooperate, depending on the politics and economics of "pipeline diplomacy." A new "great game" is being played out in Central and South Asia, with Iran hoping to benefit by its reemergence as the "unavoidable" junction on a new "silk road." In any event, a nuclear Iran would perceive that it had gained additional strength in energy diplomacy.

In addition to shared energy interests, Iran and Russia both seek to keep the lid on ethnic tensions in Azerbaijan (whose Azeri population spills over the border into Iran). Both are intent on developing the energy resources in the Caspian seabed. However, here, too, there are areas of discord. Iran and Russia still dispute the demarcation of their exclusive economic zones (EEZs). Moreover, while Iran's reliance on Russia for arms may have muted its inclination to intervene in Chechnya's separatist movement, simmering tensions throughout Central Asia among ethnic and religious factions could one day bring Iran and Russia into competition. A nuclear Iran might be emboldened to send military forces into Azerbaijan to quell ethnic violence spilling over into Iran. It is also conceivable that Russia, which opposes foreign intervention in the Caucasus, could challenge Iran's incursion, thus bringing the two nuclear-armed states into a confrontation in which Iran, lacking adequate conventional capabilities, would be prepared to threaten to escalate to limited nuclear weapons use as the alternative to backing down. There might also be a situation bearing some similarity to what occurred in August 2008, when Russian troops, to protect the Russian population of South Ossetia, crossed into Georgia. Such a scenario would also have the potential to embroil the United States in a Russo-Iranian confrontation over Azerbaijan, which is a NATO partner state.[13] As a result, three nuclear powers, each having important interests in the region, could find themselves facing off against one another, although, it must be emphasized, it is extremely unlikely that the United States would actively become engaged in a conflict in the Caucasus involving Iran and Russia. Iran lacks the extensive experience of interactions on nuclear issues with the United States that characterized the U.S.-Soviet Cold War relationship. This could lead Iran to miscalculate in a crisis, which would enhance the potential for escalation. Iran's behavior in a future crisis is dependent on the nature of its leadership as well as its role and interests in areas beyond its borders. Our Aggressive Iran model assumes that leadership and perceptions result in a propensity for greater rather than lesser action.

The leadership of an Aggressive Iran could be expected to view its relationship with the United States generally as a "zero-sum game."[14] Nevertheless, the prospects for "cooperative deterrence," or the construction of a deterrence relationship built around a shared conception of strategic stability would not be discounted, at least by the United States. In Iran, however, the response to U.S. efforts to promote such a nuclear relationship would not necessarily be positive. Iran's leaders would act under the zero-sum assumption that the United States seeks gains at Iran's expense. This is a situation that is a basis for miscalculation and crisis escalation. Escalation can result from three types of action: increasing violence, widening conflict, or introducing previously unrelated issues, also known as "compound escalation." An Aggressive Iran might be prepared to engage in escalatory behavior based on conventional and nuclear weapons. This could include the possible use of nuclear weapons on the battlefield as well as an expressed willingness to extend a nuclear umbrella over allies such as Syria and Hezbollah in order to enlist them more fully in Iran's strategies and policies.

Early in the nuclear era, nuclear planning presupposed that both the United States and the Soviet Union would be motivated to control the escalation chain because the other had deployed credible retaliatory forces that could destroy its adversary's cities and industrial base if it chose to do so. In other words, the perceived risks outweighed any likely gains. However, the introduction of more lethal and accurate non-nuclear munitions and delivery systems increased the importance of conventional deterrence for the United States, despite the development of nuclear weapons in countries such as India, Pakistan, and North Korea. Thus, in contrast to the United States, which sought to deemphasize nuclear weapons in its national security strategy, several other nations began to explore their nuclear options. Moreover, as the United States pushed nuclear deterrence to the periphery, it may have created doubts about whether a national command authority (NCA) would ever resort to nuclear weapons when other more "useable" weapons options had come into being. Largely on this basis, the notion of escalating a conflict to nuclear weapons use may be widely discounted in the United States—more so than in a nuclear weapon state such as the Iran depicted here.

Especially in the United States, the increased sophistication of non-nuclear systems, given their unprecedented lethality and accuracy, has served to diminish interest in developing a new generation of nuclear weapons. This was evident in the lack of support from the U.S. Congress for the Reliable Replacement Warhead (RRW) or for modernization initiatives associated with the 2010 Nuclear Posture Review and in connection with the ratification of the New START Treaty.[15] Even with respect to new, nonnuclear technologies, changing notions of the "acceptability" of using specific types of capabilities (such as cruise missiles armed with nuclear warheads) have obscured the message that was intended to be conveyed by a particular nuclear capability. This has led to confusion about intended signals—a problem that is only compounded by widely different cultures, ethnicities, and outlooks in countries such as Iran. For example, NATO leaders apparently believed that employment of conventionally armed cruise missiles in Bosnia would signal to the Serbs that the conflict was likely to escalate unless they ceased supporting the ethnic cleansing of Muslims in Bosnia. This failed to have its intended effect. In other situations, the employment of cruise missiles might not be expected to convey an escalatory message; in some cases, it might even be considered as an attempt to limit operations well below the nuclear threshold, given the precision accuracy of modern-day cruise-missile technologies. Controlling the escalation chain or deterring enemy escalation in a crisis or conflict is situation-specific. For example, Global Strike provides the United States with credible coercive options without imposing the need to cross the nuclear threshold. However, Global Strike critics contend that the use of nonnuclear weapons for strategic purposes could actually lower the nuclear threshold as prospective adversaries react to such strikes by escalating to the use of nuclear weapons. The rationale for such escalation would be that the United States possesses a level of conventional superiority that makes nuclear use necessary in order to have any hope of defeating the United States. Such a possibility should be factored into U.S. contingency planning for dealing with a nuclear Iran.

ISRAEL AND THE CHALLENGE OF CATALYTIC WARFARE

In the emerging security landscape, the potential for catalytic war is growing. Tehran's nuclear programs could provoke Israel into an attack to prevent Iran's emergence as a nuclear weapons state. Unlike the early post–World War II era, the contemporary security environment features third-party actors that have access to military capabilities and foreign policy and security considerations that are largely independent of great-power interactions. This is an issue that has long been debated in U.S. strategic circles, with seminal thinking done by Herman Kahn on catalytic war and crisis escalation. As described by Kahn, catalytic warfare refers to the "notion that some third party or nation might for its own reasons deliberately start a war between the two major powers." According to Kahn, "the widespread diffusion of nuclear weapons would make many nations able, and in some cases also create the pressure, to aggravate an on-going crisis, or even touch off a war between two other powers for purposes of their own."[16] Even though Kahn was writing about the U.S.-Soviet strategic rivalry, and his work centers on U.S. security planning, we can extrapolate this reasoning to the current setting in which Israel, perceiving an existential threat from Iran's nuclear development, initiates military strikes against Iran to degrade or halt Tehran's nuclear program and Iran retaliates not only against Israel but against the United States or against U.S. interests or forces overseas.

In Israel, few issues command greater attention, particularly given Iran's growing and higher-profile role in enabling Hezbollah and Hamas activities. From the Israeli perspective, a nuclear-armed Iran would pose an existential threat, no matter what the nature of Iran's nuclear deployment—i.e., defensive or aggressive. It may be viewed as so grave that Israel, *even short of an Iranian decision to weaponize*, may determine that it cannot live with the strategic ambiguity of the current situation. Many Israelis also contend that Iran would never be content with only a defensive deterrent. They foresee a situation in which a defensive deterrent is transformed to support Iran's more expansive foreign policy aspirations. In other words, an initial Iranian nuclear capability would constitute ample basis for evolution into the more robust nuclear force associated with Model II: An Aggressive Iran. For the Israelis, regime change in Iran, if the mullahs were ousted and some sort of "democratic" government were put into place, might make a difference in convincing them to live with a Defensive Iran, but few Israelis appear willing to gamble that Israel's security should be dependent on such Iranian goodwill.

The Israelis have contemplated unilateral military action against Iran's nuclear programs.[17] Israel would be most likely to take such a step if it perceived that the United States lacked the will to strike Iran, and if the international community was unable to come to agreement on the nature and urgency of the threat posed by a nuclear Iran. Israel has ample precedent for considering preventive action against Iran's nuclear infrastructure, having implemented two earlier preemptive strikes, one in 1981 against Iraq's Osirak reactor and the other in 2007 against a suspected reactor facility in Syria. However, the differences between those situations and a prospective attack on Iran's nuclear infrastructure and programs are vast.[18] For one, Iran appears to be building redundancy into its nuclear weapons development, and much of its uranium-based program is located at dispersed and concealed underground sites, according to U.S. intelligence and dissident reporting. This means that a strike on Iran's nuclear facilities would be extremely difficult. These facilities, such as those at Natanz or Fordow, tend to be sheltered deep underground with reinforced concrete, housed under a mountain, or protected by air defenses, and they may require several sorties to have high confidence of their destruction. For another thing, it cannot be determined conclusively if Tehran has been able to conceal any nuclear installations from Israeli/Western intelligence. The number of known sites identified as having a role in Iran's nuclear programs is more than twenty-five, but there could be more, some of which might even be more critical to Iran's nuclear development programs than those already identified.[19]

U.S. defense and intelligence officials have expressed doubts about the ability of Israel to carry out such an attack, citing the distance Israeli aircraft would have to travel and their need for refueling; the nature and number of targets that must be struck, including Iran's extensive air defense network; and Israel's limited inventory of bunker-busting ordinance. A strike of this nature would be far more complex and difficult than Israel's two previous preemptive attacks on Iran. Operationally, Israel would need to fly through unfriendly air space and conduct aerial refueling to get to potential targets in Iran, which are approximately 1,000 miles away and for the most part are defended by an extensive network of antiaircraft batteries. Moreover, U.S. officials are also skeptical about Israel's capacity for redundancy, which assumes that multiple strikes would be needed to ensure the destruction of high-value and protected targets. More fundamental than operational considerations, which include questions about the route that Israeli pilots would have to fly and their refueling capability, is that the effects of such a strike on Iran's nuclear weapons program remain unclear, although Israeli officials contend that an attack would delay Iran's nuclear program by three to five years. There are some who disagree with this assessment and maintain that the redundancy of Iran's nuclear infrastructure, its indigenous knowledge base, and an extensive program of deception, protection, and underground tunneling would limit the effectiveness of military action.[20]

The United States, unlike Israel, could undertake sustained air strikes using carrier-based air power and long-range bombers and cruise missiles. Moreover, an Israeli strike would have to over-fly Iraq, Jordan, or Turkey, and possibly Syria, creating additional political and possibly military challenges. Despite some evidence that the September 6, 2007, Israeli strike against the Syrian nuclear reactor was accomplished with at least Turkey's tacit approval for over-flight, using Turkish air space is probably no longer an option for Israel in light of rising tensions between the two countries in recent years.[21] (For that matter, it may also not be an option for the United States, to judge from recent U.S.-Turkish relations.) In any event, Israeli analysts contend that the strike against the Syrian facility was also intended to test the effectiveness of Syrian and Iranian air defenses in a future contingency against Israel and to demonstrate Israeli resolve to prevent the emergence of a nuclear Iran. The Israeli position is that it is prepared to do whatever it takes to eliminate Iran's existential threat to its survival, either on its own or in conjunction with the United States.[22] If Israel does strike before Iran can field a nuclear weapon, Iran could respond with asymmetric attacks against Israel as well as the United States as Israel's ally. Hezbollah sleeper cells in the United States could be activated to carry out such attacks, while attacks on Israel from Hezbollah positions in Lebanon or from Gaza using Hamas operatives could also be expected.

Indeed, Iran has the capacity to widen the scope of violence in a crisis or conflict with the United States by targeting U.S. coalition partners in the region, using proxy forces, or engaging in cyberwarfare. A nuclear Iran might use Hezbollah or Hamas against Israel or other U.S.-friendly targets. Iran might strive to widen the geographic area of conflict, deploying Hezbollah forces outside the Middle East to target NATO Europe or the United States. However, Israel also has its own options. For example, it could target known Hezbollah assets outside the Middle East or seek to engage the United States in Israeli military operations to destroy Iran's nuclear facilities. The Israelis have also considered the feasibility of NATO membership, an option that is extremely controversial and probably not acceptable to all NATO members. Nevertheless, the idea would be to provide Israel with a commitment guarantee like that in NATO's article 5 to deter Iran from threatening that state. However, there is no consensus for and even significant NATO opposition to enhancing relations with Israel, much less providing it with an extended deterrence guarantee. That option would fall to the United States, which is the only alliance member likely even to consider extending a greater security guarantee to Israel, with whom it shares a complicated relationship that already encompasses commitments that have been tangibly demonstrated since Israel's founding.

OF DYADS, TRIADS, AND THE NEED FOR A NEW DETERRENCE PARADIGM RELATING TO A NUCLEAR IRAN

The deterrence dynamic between Israel and Iran presents another formidable planning challenge for the United States: namely, the need to recognize that deterrence has moved beyond bilateral constructs to embrace a more complex dynamic comprising three nuclear actors. A deterrence triad is quite different from the bipolar U.S.-Soviet deterrence paradigm that preoccupied strategic planners during the Cold War. It is, however, emerging as the new norm, and much greater thought needs to be devoted to it and to the notion of catalytic warfare. In addition to a looming U.S.-Israeli-Iranian nuclear triangle, other three-way deterrence challenges are emerging. They include India-Pakistan-China, the Sino-American relationship vis-à-vis Taiwan, and the North Korea–South Korea relationship and Japan, although at this point Taiwan, Japan, and South Korea do not possess nuclear weapons. In the case of the U.S.-Israel-Iran triangle, Iran's fragmented decision-making structure, reinforced by a government that relies heavily on personal relationships, nepotism, and patronage, makes it difficult to identify the center of gravity beyond the Supreme Leader (who is notorious for not making difficult decisions) and, in turn, the various roles and relationships among institutional players, especially the Iranian military. This raises additional questions about U.S. ability to communicate intent in a crisis in order to influence Iranian behavior and deter Iran. Specifically, to whom should such messages be directed, and how, depending on the audience, should communications be nuanced? How would they be received? Would they be received? Questions about the chain of command further complicate U.S. efforts to interpret signals that an Iranian leadership may be sending and to devise strategic communications to influence and shape Iranian thinking about the use of force, including the role of nuclear weapons in a crisis.

If, for example, Iranian IRGC forces were to disperse Iran's mobile launchers in a crisis and bring what the United States assumes to be operational warheads to sites in proximity to the dispersed launchers, how should the United States interpret this behavior? Should one regard such moves as preparation for an Iranian nuclear strike? Whatever the reasons behind such Iranian moves, the effect might be to lead the United States or Israel to attempt preemptively to destroy such launchers. Although U.S. intelligence, surveillance, and reconnaissance (ISR) capabilities have improved greatly since Operation Desert Storm, the targeting of dispersed mobile assets remains a challenging and dangerous military mission, especially if mobile launchers are moved to tunnels or other camouflaged locations and if the Iranians rely on deception to mask their intentions, as they are already doing with respect to their nuclear-development programs.[23]

Western deterrence theories presume that, except in extreme circumstances, states will refrain from using nuclear weapons because the costs of doing so far outweigh any benefits to be derived. In other words, such deterrence theory relies on a presumption that states will be motivated to maintain territorial integrity and avoid catastrophic damage to their populations.[24] Western analysts widely attribute such motivations to Iran's leaders, but in doing so they fail to appreciate two factors that may figure heavily in the Iranian calculus regarding the use of nuclear weapons. The first, as discussed earlier, is the vision of Shia theology, which includes an apocalyptic end of the world and the revelation of the Twelfth Imam. The second is a scenario where Iran is in chaos (our Model III) and its leadership may consider that it has little to lose and much to gain (uniting the fractured population against an external aggressor) by using nuclear weapons first. The likelihood may be disproportionately higher if the regime considers itself to be at risk from an external force.

In other words, if the United States adhered to a regime-change policy and a crisis escalated to war, the impending doom of the Iranian leadership might only enhance its willingness to launch nuclear weapons both to destroy its enemy and to fulfill its apocalyptic vision. Even if the United States had backed away from discussion of regime change (or its more nuanced discussion of changing regime behavior), Tehran nevertheless would have attributed regime-change motives to the United States. Because the regime fears a "velvet revolution" supported from outside Iran, it would be prepared to resort to whatever actions it deemed necessary to destroy its opposition.[25] This may help to explain its clumsy handling and overreaction to the events of 2009, when the Green Movement for a time challenged the legitimacy of the government's authority. In a country that is convinced of its own vulnerability as well as its importance to the region and to the wider Muslim world, it would be difficult for almost any Iranian regime to give up any of the attributes of power, especially nuclear weapons. Thus, it seems improbable that Iran, whether Defensive or Aggressive, would be willing to forgo the nuclear option even in exchange for an explicit U.S. (negative) security guarantee that it would not attack Iran if it dismantled its nuclear weapons program and opened the country up to allow on-site inspection of all facilities of concern.

According to Model I: A Defensive Iran, deterrence could be maintained because Iran would care more about its own survival than pursuing expansionist objectives or fanatical religious causes, which are part of Model II: An Aggressive Iran. In this case, the challenges associated with maintaining strategic stability become more formidable, and the danger of overreach and miscalculation in a crisis is likely to grow. In the Persian Gulf region the United States has chosen to display its power through naval deployments and the creation of coalition partnerships with the Arab Gulf states, Jordan, Egypt, and Turkey. It has tried to establish strategic-partnership arrangements with Iraq and Pakistan, but that is proving to be problematic in both instances. It has negotiated such arrangements with India and Afghanistan (for after 2014), possibly creating the perception in Tehran of an encirclement to contain Iran. An Iran with nuclear weapons might seek to break out of this encirclement. With nuclear weapons, an Aggressive Iran might well be inclined to provoke a crisis in the hope (or expectation) that the United States would back down rather than risk a nuclear exchange.

In the face of Iran's nuclear development, the United States would need to think about regional deterrence and counterproliferation in innovative ways, especially with respect to an Aggressive Iran but also in the context of a Defensive Iran. With a nuclear Iran, the potential for wider proliferation in the Middle East would increase, especially in Models II and III. To begin to address these new operational and strategic challenges, at the very least, greater intelligence fusion and command-and-control interoperability are required with the Arab Gulf states. Adapting the NATO Active Endeavor model to a Gulf contingency may furnish a template, in that it provides for NATO and non-NATO partner integration, but much more needs to be done to incorporate missile defenses, cyberwarfare, and new-generation operational capabilities into deterrence planning for an Iranian contingency.[26] Essentially, this would demand much tighter collaboration among the GCC states, and with Jordan, Egypt, and possibly Iraq (although whether that is politically feasible is an open question given the consolidation of power by Shia elements in Iraq). Still, vestiges of Iraqi nationalism remain, and if

Iraq's interests were perceived as clashing with those of Iran, the potential exists for a reawakening of the historic Iranian-Iraqi enmity. Relying on the Active Endeavor model would also mean deployment of a U.S.-led naval force that would include Oman, Saudi Arabia, the UAE, and Bahrain to implement maritime surveillance, critical infrastructure protection (off-shore platforms, for example), and, if necessary, embargo interdiction operations. While Oman's participation could be problematic, that of the other GCC states would probably not be, although sectarian tensions in Bahrain could explode and result in either a Saudi "protectorate" or a new regime that was susceptible to Iran's influence. The following chapter explores the essential elements of twenty-first-century deterrence planning and their implications for key U.S. objectives, such as deterring or containing a nuclear Iran.

6
U.S. Deterrence Planning in the Event of an Iranian Nuclear Breakout

Iran's decision to develop and deploy nuclear weapons will have profound implications for regional stability, global nonproliferation objectives, and U.S. strategic and operational planning. In terms of regional stability and nonproliferation, it may not make a great difference if Iran develops a defensive-deterrent (Model I) or an aggressive posture (Model II) because states in the region will feel threatened by either and seek to bolster their security through a variety of measures. In the absence of new U.S. security assurances, nuclear weapons would become a more attractive option for some states in the region, especially if the United States is viewed as vulnerable to an Iranian nuclear threat, as posited in Model II: An Aggressive Iran. Thus ally/partner reassurance becomes an important element of twenty-first-century deterrence planning. However, extended deterrence must be based on credible options that heighten the modernization of U.S. nuclear forces to provide for "tailored deterrence" and new capabilities and options for cyberwarfare, missile defense, and consequence management to give greater credibility to U.S. defense and deterrence planning. Declaratory policy has always been a critical aspect of the deterrence dynamic, but with the emergence of new nuclear powers, some of which may reject Western deterrence assumptions, this aspect of U.S. strategy needs to be updated. The subsequent discussion highlights the principal elements of a twenty-first-century deterrence construct for the United States and identifies key challenges that must be addressed in U.S. strategic and operational planning.

DECLARATORY POLICY, ESCALATION CONTROL,
AND STRATEGIC COMMUNICATIONS

Clearly, declaratory policy remains an important aspect of deterrence planning under any circumstances. With the emergence of additional nuclear states, notably North Korea and Iran, this dimension of U.S. strategic planning needs to be enhanced to support clearly articulated policy objectives. Against a nuclear Iran, ambiguity is unlikely to serve our purposes. This means that the discussion of deterrence must leave little doubt about American interests and intentions. While there have been times when ambiguity has served us well, such as responding to nonnuclear WMD threats, countering a nuclear Iran requires that U.S. declaratory policy be clear and concise, leaving little room for misinterpretation, including our retaliatory stance if Iran used biological weapons. By the same token, U.S. declaratory policy must not be unrealistic. In other words, the United States must be careful not to promise something that it cannot or is unwilling to deliver. Thus, for example, in the present circumstances in which U.S. nuclear deterrence forces are built around Trident missiles, intercontinental prompt-response capabilities, and air-delivered munitions, the United States retains a diversified but limited capacity to tailor strikes and to contain collateral damage. In the absence of nuclear modernization initiatives, tailored deterrence may be difficult to achieve because the U.S. nuclear force was designed in an era of scenarios calling for a massive nuclear exchange with the Soviet Union as the basis for strategic deterrence.

A declaratory policy that affirms how the United States would respond to Iranian aggression—nuclear, other WMD, or conventional—arguably could stimulate debate within Iran about the relative costs and benefits of nuclear weapons. At the very least, it might have the effect of devaluing Iran's acquisition of nuclear weapons if the perceived price to be paid included an unacceptable level of risk to Iran. Without question, one of the biggest challenges that the United States faces is communicating with an Iranian regime that may not share our vision of deterrence. Lack of familiarity with Iran's value structures or with the perspectives of key leaders presents a daunting problem. Because there is no direct communication between Iran and the United States (or Israel) regarding the other's red lines, there is great danger of miscalculation and crisis escalation. For this reason, it will be necessary to assess specifically and systematically organizational structures in Iran and to identify key decision makers and their relationships with one another. It will also be necessary to scrutinize the writings and pronouncements of Iran's key decision makers to gain further insight into Iranian views of nuclear weapons and their uses. This will require more intensive and comprehensive human-terrain mapping and intelligence collaboration among U.S. agencies and with principal U.S. allies and partners concerned about developments in Iran.[1]

For deterrence planning against a nuclear Iran, it will also be essential to ensure that the messages and intentions conveyed by specific U.S. deployments or other activities are properly received and understood by those whom we seek to deter. This will entail at the minimum an understanding that strategic signaling has its place in deterrence strategy. The movement of forces to convey a message about U.S. intent, in line with declaratory policy, can play a role in reinforcing the credibility of America's deterrence posture and its extended deterrence guarantees. However, again, because the current generation of Iran's leadership has little experience with the West, this type of deterrence signaling may be misinterpreted and could result in an unwarranted crisis or conflict escalation. Thus, the United States must do whatever it can to be clear about its intentions and its interests. Previous instances of "moving U.S. red lines" in negotiations with North Korea and Iran, however, do not bode well in this regard as our adversaries may believe that the United States really does not mean what it says. Going forward, and with a nuclear Iran, it must be understood that words mean something and are supported by actions. Thus, U.S. deterrence policy must be considered part of a comprehensive whole-of-government effort of which military forces are but one essential component. Because strategic communications matter, we should develop messages that support and reinforce our preferred deterrence strategy.

The essence of nuclear deterrence theory is credibility and will: credibility based on a force posture that can do what it is supposed to do and the political will to use those forces if vital national interests are at risk. Unlike the Cold War, in which the United States and the Soviet Union deployed large nuclear arsenals to hold each other's populations, territories, and military forces at risk, the modern era calls for a much more differentiated strategy, tailored to meet a range of threats from the legacy challenge presented by Russia, to China's emergence as a peer competitor, to the deterrence of rogue states, such as North Korea, and, very likely, a nuclear Iran. As Keith Payne points out, this includes the need to understand a specific opponent's mindset as a basis for assessing risk taking and tolerance as well as perceived costs and benefits.[2] In tailoring deterrence, it is especially important to step outside one's own belief system and strategic culture in order to engage in deterrence planning for a twenty-first-century world with multiple nuclear players.

Unfortunately, the United States has not had great success in tailoring options, in part because the programs necessary to implement this construct have not been put in place. Public support for nuclear-deterrence strategy in general has declined since the end of the Cold War, despite the emergence of new nuclear powers and modernization programs in China, India, and Russia. It is incumbent upon us to gain a clearer understanding of the values, structures, actors, and capabilities possessed by these new nuclear weapons states if we are to have any success in developing tailored deterrence strategies to meet new threats (see table 6.1). In addition to the development of credible deterrence options, including strategic communications, for non-superpower competitors, it will also be necessary to understand more precisely the requirements for deterring nuclear proliferation. There is a potential nexus between state actors and nonstate armed groups. What is not so clear is how potential nuclear proliferators can be prevented from helping terrorists or other nonstate actors acquire nuclear weapons and, if such dissuasion fails, how newer possessors can be deterred from making such capabilities available to such actors.

OFFENSIVE-STRIKE OPTIONS AND PREVENTIVE PLANNING

American strategic planners have attempted to address twenty-first-century deterrence requirements based on changes in the global strategic setting and the effects of new technologies and ideas for tailoring forces for specific contingencies. Adapting deterrence, dissuasion, and assurance concepts in ways most appropriate to meet and mitigate new challenges while providing options for dealing with legacy threats requires

Table 6.1 Tailoring Deterrence to Meet Twenty-First-Century Threats

ESSENTIAL ELEMENTS OF A NEW DETERRENCE PARADIGM	LEGACY CHALLENGES AND NEAR-PEER COMPETITORS	ROGUE REGIMES AND THRESHOLD STATES	VIOLENT EXTREMISTS AND NONSTATE ACTORS
	Russia **China**	**North Korea** **Iran**	**Hezbollah** **al-Qaeda**
Reassurance	NATO Japan, South Korea, and Taiwan U.S. homeland defense Extended deterrence	Japan and South Korea Israel, NATO, Gulf Cooperation Council (GCC) U.S. homeland defense Extended deterrence	Israel, GCC U.S. homeland defense Updated security collaboration
Dissuasion and Deterrence	Dissuade antisatellite, EMP, and WMD acquisition and attacks Deter conventional attacks Discourage proliferation	Deter conventional and WMD use Transfer nuclear weapons and expertise Negative security guarantee Interagency and allied/partner nonkinetic initiatives (e.g., sanctions, blockade)	Dirty-bomb detonation Nonproliferation Asymmetric attacks WMD trafficking, state sponsorship, and establishment of sanctuaries (virtual and real)
Coercion and Compellence	Survivable second-strike forces "Prompt response" Global Strike, using nuclear and nonnuclear capabilities	Escalation control and dominance Human-terrain mapping Tailored forces for diverse scenarios Offshore strike assets Leverage coalition and partner assets	Value-chain interdiction Human-terrain mapping Identify support network

ESSENTIAL ELEMENTS OF A NEW DETERRENCE PARADIGM	LEGACY CHALLENGES AND NEAR-PEER COMPETITORS	ROGUE REGIMES AND THRESHOLD STATES	VIOLENT EXTREMISTS AND NONSTATE ACTORS
	Russia **China**	**North Korea** **Iran**	**Hezbollah** **al-Qaeda**
Defenses and Consequence Management	Space-based and -oriented assets Damage limitation and population protection Event mitigation Survivable command and control and ISR Infrastructure protection	Global missile-defense architecture Consequence management Enabling partner capacities Leverage U.S. allied security relationships	Consequence management Building partner capacity Military support to civil authorities "Render-safe" capabilities Enhance nuclear forensics and detection
Information Operations and Strategic Communications	Declaratory policy Influence and psychological operations	Declaratory policy Influence and psychological operations	Declaratory policy Influence and psychological operations

the integration of nonnuclear and nuclear options into a strategy that includes the deterrence of regional threats. As with planning for legacy challenges, deterrence of a nuclear Iran must include coercion and compellence options, such as those contained in the U.S. Strategic Command's (STRATCOM) Global Strike concept. As envisioned by U.S. strategic planners, Global Strike is intended to provide national command authorities with nuclear and nonnuclear options in times of crisis and war. Unfortunately, as noted by one former Pentagon official, "little progress has been made on plans to develop and field prompt, conventional Global Strike [capabilities] and to modernize the nuclear force." The United States has yet to address pressing nuclear-modernization decisions, such as development of new weapons and the future of NATO's dual-capable aircraft platforms in Europe.[3] If such questions continue to be deferred or are addressed without a clear understanding of their broader implications for deterrence, we risk the reduction of options for a future president to deter attack and protect and assure vital U.S. national interests.

Power-projection capabilities and expeditionary forces constitute major components of the U.S. capacity to deter regional threats. However, such operations face increasing challenges because of the proliferation of global anti-access/area-denial (A2/AD) and precision-weapon capabilities. Iran, by deploying ballistic and cruise missiles, antiship missiles, sea mines, and small speedboats using swarm tactics and relying on proxy forces to operate on its behalf, has already created an extremely challenging environment for U.S. and partner forces in a contingency involving the Strait of Hormuz. If Iran deploys nuclear weapons—what some regard as the ultimate anti-access assets—the ability of the United States to operate in this area would be even further constrained, especially if their threatened use caused regional states to refuse permission for the United States to operate from their territories. The problems presented by precision-guided weapons and anti-access/area-denial capabilities do not emanate solely from nation-states. Tehran may also use groups such as Hezbollah to conduct acts of terrorism in neighboring nations to deter them from allowing U.S. forces to operate from their territory during a conflict with Iran. For example, in the 2006 Lebanon war, Hezbollah (with substantial support from Iran and Syria) was able to launch more than 4,000 relatively inaccurate projectiles into Israel, which, while causing little physical damage, still brought northern Israel to a standstill and shut down its main port, refineries, and other strategic installations. In 2012 rockets launched into Israel from Gaza were countered by the Iron Dome system, which had a success rate approaching 85 percent and blunted the effect of these short-range rocket attacks. However, if only a small percentage of Hezbollah's inventory of rockets, artillery, mortars, and missiles—some reports say Hezbollah possesses more than 40,000—are upgraded with greater precision against key targets (and Iran has every incentive to make this happen), the threat to Israel, as well as to U.S. expeditionary forces, will increase significantly unless they can also be countered by an Israeli missile defense system. Hezbollah rocket attacks are expected to be one of the primary means of retaliation if Israel strikes Iran's nuclear facilities.

Because the ability to project military power will be essential to the preservation of alliance relationships and security partnerships, particularly in the Middle East, the United States will need either to degrade enemy anti-access capabilities or to abandon regions in which vital national interests are at stake. Given that the latter option is unacceptable, the United States has no choice but to develop strategies and capabilities to counter the anti-access efforts of Iran and other potential opponents to ensure that U.S. forward-deployed and power-projection forces remain capable of conducting forcible entry operations. In recent years, to counter and defeat anti-access threats, the U.S. Navy, in collaboration with the U.S. Air Force and U.S. Marine Corps, has developed and continues to enhance what they call Air-Sea Battle.[4] The Air-Sea Battle construct is based on the premise that combined maritime and air-and-space capabilities can address threats across the spectrum of operations, including against adversaries with advanced anti-access and area-denial capabilities.[5] In the future, however, Air-Sea Battle planning might have to embrace operations in a nuclear environment; for example, Iran in Model II might implement a nuclear attack against U.S. expeditionary forces, using nuclear-tipped mines or even ballistic or cruise missiles.

In our models, especially the second and third, the nuclear threshold is uncertain. The Cold War delineation of a threshold between nuclear weapons and conventional warfare may no longer be valid in case of irregular or hybrid warfare.[6] While a Defensive Iran might be prepared to use nuclear weapons only in the event of an attack against its territory or in a conflict in which other vital Iranian interests were judged to be at stake, an Aggressive Iran could threaten to use or actually employ nuclear weapons to attain a strategic goal such as the destruction of Israel. Of course, a key variable in any Iranian calculus to threaten or use nuclear weapons might be the extent to which the leadership or regime elements in control of nuclear weapons believed that the United States would be prepared to regard an Iranian attack on Israel as an attack requiring a full retaliatory strike against Iran.

Even if Iran doubted the extent of the U.S. commitment to Israel, no Iranian regime or leadership elements could conclude that Israel would not do all within its means to deter an Iranian nuclear attack or, if deterrence failed, to strike back. Iran would be concerned about nuclear retaliation by Israel, although Iranian officials may believe that Iran could survive an Israeli retaliatory strike. Nevertheless, given their sizes and demographics it is obvious that Iran, with its much larger population and territory, has far greater ability than Israel to absorb and survive a nuclear exchange between the two countries. Moreover, depending on the circumstances in which nuclear use was considered, the United States might not stand back, especially in a crisis where its forces deployed in the region were exposed to the threat of an Iranian attack and its regional partners faced annihilation. Dissuading Iran from getting to the point where it can launch an attack should remain central to U.S. strategy. Therefore, the option of preventive strikes should be retained in U.S. contingency planning.[7] Here the question is whether the ability of the United States to launch one or more preventive strikes, together with the clear willingness to do so, could dissuade Iran from actually deploying nuclear weapons.

Of course, preemption refers to the perceived imminence of use. Prevention is a form of dissuasion that includes steps to postpone or eliminate the possibility of acquiring or developing a certain capability. Preemption has to do with the destruction of capabilities that are about to be used. Prevention is related to acquisition or development while the purpose of preemption is to make it impossible to employ such systems. If, for example, we had substantial evidence that a nuclear Iran was about to launch a nuclear strike against Israel, we might preempt such action by attacking Iran's nuclear force before it could be launched. Preemption remains central to "anticipatory self-defense" against Iran's nuclear ambitions. Ideally, to be successful, a preemptive strategy would be able to identify and target crucial parts of Iran's nuclear programs and destroy them without great collateral damage. Optimally, this should be done before Iran operationalized and dispersed its nuclear weapons. However, preemption is limited by the fact that a country planning a nuclear strike or fearing that its nuclear force will be attacked is likely to disperse such capabilities to make them less vulnerable to preemption and more likely to survive any effort to destroy them. Because deception has long been an important aspect of Iranian military planning, with Iran having already embarked on a vast program to hide its nuclear facilities, the problems associated with locating hidden and dispersed launchers and warheads would be far more difficult than those encountered by Israel when it struck the Iraqi Osirak nuclear site in 1981.

Prevention and preemption are also politically controversial concepts and, as Colin S. Gray points out, often misunderstood. In relation to deterrence theory, preemption has been specifically associated with the launch-on-warning or launch-under-attack constructs and thus is intimately related to first-strike considerations. Prevention suggests action that is taken to forestall a specific act, such as the acquisition or development of nuclear weapons. For this reason, it has been considered a means of dealing with nuclear proliferation. In the early phase of the Cold War, preventive options were sometimes discussed in debates over whether the United States should strike the Soviet Union to forestall the growth of its nuclear arsenal. In the late 1960s, the United States warned the Soviet Union against attacking China's nuclear weapons program. However, in each of those instances, options for conducting preventive warfare were severely limited. In today's world, Global Strike opens additional options within a strategy that emphasizes nuclear and nonnuclear strike capabilities.

A crisis might arise in which the United States would find it necessary to counter a nuclear Iran that has the characteristics of our Model II. It would be essential to have military instruments available that would back a broader political strategy designed to deter Iran from escalating the crisis or to resolve the crisis on the best possible terms for the United States. These would include air and naval forces, supported by special operations forces (SOF) as well as targeting intelligence, reconnaissance, surveillance, and selected counter-WMD assets. In the event that SOF were used, they would be employed to conduct clandestine warfare well before a conventional strike was initiated. This might include efforts to strengthen opposition forces within Iran, together with other opponents of the regime.

Moreover, many of the targeted sites would be located deep inside Iran, some 2,000 miles from any border or coastline. The use of clandestine or covert (e.g., Central Intelligence Agency) forces would require a new generation of "enablers," including unmanned drones (Predators and Reapers), and dedicated intelligence, surveillance, and reconnaissance assets to support essential operations on the ground. Overflight of Turkey or the use of Turkish bases (or other European bases to which the United States has access via bilateral agreements) would be uncertain, especially in light of the deterioration in U.S.-Turkish relations in recent years and Ankara's more positive relationship with Tehran, which could be a "wildcard" in U.S. efforts to deter Iran or to defend allied/partner interests in the Eastern Mediterranean and Arabian Gulf regions. For this reason, and perhaps as a result of a reluctance on the part of Turkey and other neighbors of Iran to risk confrontation with a nuclear Iran, it is likely that the United States would be forced to rely on U.S.-based aircraft (B-2s) and other Global Strike capabilities (e.g., B-52s flying from Diego Garcia and ship- and air-launched Tomahawk cruise missiles) supported by tactical naval aviation.[8] Recently, however, there have been reports that the UK government has told U.S. officials that they "cannot rely on the use of British bases in Ascension Island, Cyprus, and Diego Garcia for an assault on Iran."[9] For this reason, among others, a long-range conventional ballistic missile capability would offer great potential.

Assuming that Iran will have taken considerable precautions to defend high-value nuclear and other WMD-related facilities, the United States could make use of B-2s armed with direct-attack weapons, strategic Tomahawks, and Prompt Global Strike systems,[10] when and if they become available, in the opening hours of a military campaign to degrade and destroy Iran's nuclear infrastructure and related delivery capabilities.[11] Once the B-2s had taken out key air-defense and communication nodes and cruise or conventional ballistic missiles and bombers had disrupted military units that may have fielded WMD weapons and minimized (with airfield attacks) the potential for Iranian air operations, carrier air and nonstealthy bombers could then follow up against lower-priority production and research and development sites. B-2s and additional Tomahawk and conventional strategic strikes could also be used in follow-up attacks against heavily fortified and larger-scale nuclear/WMD sites to ensure that normal operations would be brought to a halt.[12]

Whether the strike entailed substantial and consecutive raids or only one attack, the United States would be able to degrade Iran's nuclear inventory and infrastructure but probably could not achieve their complete destruction, given the Iranian practice of hiding and dispersing elements of its nuclear programs. The possibility of a U.S. attack aimed at destroying Iran's nuclear weapons and capacity for retaliation against Israel, the Gulf Arabs, and possibly even against targets in NATO Europe and the United States (using IEDs in major cities, for example) could prompt Iran's leadership to disperse its weapons and fissile material in advance of the attack. If there was little collateral damage to Iran resulting from such an attack, popular support might coalesce against the regime. However, it is more likely that the Iranian public would come together in support of Persian nationalism and the ruling regime. Escalation control would still remain a concern in this contingency, but the United States would have a means of responding to Iranian intimidation and taking the initiative to limit undesired escalation.

If the United States took preemptive military action against Iran, it could expect Iranian retaliation in each of the three models, at a minimum through proxy warfare and terrorism. In the case of Model II: An Aggressive Iran, the regime might consider nuclear retaliation against the United States directly, perhaps with the detonation of one or more dirty bombs on U.S. soil or a ship-borne attack using a nuclear cruise missile or a short-range ballistic missile. This could be an EMP attack that could inflict far-reaching and devastating damage on U.S. society. Another retaliatory option would be for Iran to encourage Hezbollah to strike targets in Israel or the United States and Western Europe. Focused terrorist attacks would likely emerge as an important aspect of an Iranian response to a U.S. attack against Iran's nuclear forces, as would small-boat swarm attacks against Gulf shipping. It is also likely that Iran would attempt to retaliate by closing down traffic in the Gulf and through the Strait of Hormuz. In doing so, Iran would face the overwhelming naval power of the United States. However, depending on the particular scenario, the U.S. Navy could find itself in the position of having to fight its way back into the Gulf, if it had repositioned American naval forces outside the Gulf to avoid Iranian swarm and missile attacks. Model II points up a range of anti-access/area-denial problems that the United States would face in and around the Gulf.

Although Iran is woefully lacking in military capabilities compared to the United States, it has considerable soft power based on influence over Shia minorities in the region, the ability to leverage anti-U.S. and anti-Israeli sentiment on the "Arab street," and the use of armed groups, including Hezbollah, Hamas, and even (when it suits their purposes) al-Qaeda and the Taliban. Irregular and hybrid warfare, therefore, would be of greater importance in U.S contingency planning, as discussed in chapter 7. This includes Iran's potential to use proxies to strike at soft and asymmetric targets and, once it has crossed the nuclear threshold, its willingness to transfer WMD components and systems to state and non-state allies (Syria and Hezbollah). Iran also has the option of engaging in sophisticated cyberwarfare, directed against U.S. "soft" commercial and civilian targets or against U.S. Central Command (CENTCOM) or other U.S. Department of Defense networks. Ilan Berman, in testimony before the U.S. House of Representatives Homeland Security Committee, noted that the Iranian regime is mobilizing to fight a cyberwar, moving from defense to offense and increasing in depth and complexity.[13]

These challenges need to be addressed both by the United States and within NATO if we are serious about adapting and updating defense and deterrence planning. However, in recent years there has been growing U.S. skepticism about the Atlantic alliance. Operations in Afghanistan have soured many in the U.S. military and elsewhere on NATO. Drastic reductions in defense budgets on both sides of the Atlantic, but especially in Europe, do not augur well for the ability of alliance members to conduct out-of-area operations, let alone engage in the cyberwarfare arena, despite a growing commercial and military imperative to do so. The military intervention in Libya in 2011 revealed the existence of many shortages of equipment and munitions, together with the need for NATO-European participants to rely on U.S. capabilities such as precision weapons and cruise missiles, aerial refueling, and surveillance and electronic-warfare assets. Several NATO members refused to participate, thus reducing the operation to a coalition of the willing. Although the United States chose to "lead from behind," the Libya experience indicates limitations on the NATO-European ability to contribute to future out-of-area operations, limitations that are likely to increase as defense cuts take effect.[14] This prospect gives rise to the basic question: how will NATO's decline affect the U.S. capacity to operate overseas?

It is not within the purview of this book to assess the general strengths and weaknesses of NATO as a basis for collective military operations. Even with planned reductions, European members would retain niche capabilities that could be contributed on a selective basis. For example, SOF as well as air and naval units of individual European countries could augment U.S. forces. However, the formal, even if limited, participation of NATO-European and other coalition partners confers international legitimacy that can contribute to domestic support for military action. Publics can be assured that the United States is not acting unilaterally, although the dark side of this proposition is the possibility that allies can place onerous restrictions (rules of engagement) on how their forces operate. The result is to leave the United States with the brunt of the operation, a fact that may not be lost on the U.S. public. If NATO did not exist, the United Sates could still assemble "coalitions of the willing" on a case-by-case basis. However, the value of NATO has included the legitimacy that the alliance has conferred on multilateral operations, together with the ability of the United States and its allies to make use of NATO infrastructure to organize, train, and prepare military forces for a range of contingencies extending from the war against Islamic extremism and other terrorism to humanitarian assistance, peacekeeping, and antipiracy missions, to mention only the most obvious.[15]

REASSURING ALLIES/COALITION PARTNERS IN THE FACE OF IRANIAN PROLIFERATION

Over the last decade, U.S. thinking about deterrence has evolved as a result of al-Qaeda's aspirations to acquire weapons of mass destruction and because of the need to address nuclear challenges from smaller nations while maintaining a capacity to deter legacy threats and emerging peer competitors (e.g., China). Nonstate actors and rogue states pose particularly daunting problems for U.S. and allied planners for two primary reasons. The first is the greater likelihood of these actors using nuclear weapons because they reject Western aversion to the use of such forces. The second has to do with ideologies that may prompt nuclear weapons use. Deterring an adversary from attacking the United States or its forward-deployed forces and allies has focused on the threat of retaliating with overwhelming force against a state-centric enemy, together with increasing emphasis on the deployment of missile defenses to upset enemy attack calculations and to reassure allies and partners of the credibility of U.S. extended-deterrence guarantees. Deterring nonstate actors or rogue states requires tailored strategies based on a keen appreciation of the group's values, interests, culture, leadership, and ideological/religious factors. Both state-centric deterrence and deterring nonstate

armed groups must take into account the need to protect vital U.S. interests at home and overseas, as well as providing a deterrence umbrella
over U.S. allies and regional partners that have refrained from developing nuclear weapons. In the past, this so-called extended-deterrence concept played a key role in reinforcing U.S. alliance partnerships. In today's
world, the specter of a nuclear Iran creates the potential for extended
deterrence to play an even greater role in U.S. counterproliferation strategy by providing credible security guarantees to friends and allies as an
alternative to such countries developing their own nuclear weapons.

The United States has committed itself through formal security treaties to defending the interests of crucial U.S. allies in NATO-Europe and
with Japan and South Korea.[16] In contrast, however, implementing an
extended-deterrence strategy, absent a formal alliance security guarantee, as exists with NATO in Europe, may not be easy in other areas within
Iran's reach, especially with limitations on U.S. forward-based forces and
constraints upon U.S. access to overseas facilities. In the Persian Gulf
area, the Gulf Cooperation Council (GCC) exists as a loose framework
for discussion among the six Arab Gulf states, but it has no formal relationship with the United States, except in the realm of a "strategic dialogue" that was begun by the George W. Bush administration. In recent
years, the U.S.-GCC Strategic Dialogue has had an operational focus
and has emphasized practical collaboration in the areas of intelligence
sharing, warning, and missile defenses. In the missile-defense area, the
United States has provided assistance to GCC members,[17] whose air and
missile defense assets are electronically linked, on a national-bilateral
basis, to an information and operations center run by the United States.
There is no multilateral collaboration, although U.S. military officials
would like to see this cooperation evolve into a more robust, regionwide interconnected air and missile defense system. Thus far, however, it
has been difficult to get the GCC nations interested in multilateral collaboration, especially in relation to Iran. The GCC states have different
interests in confronting Iran, much less a nuclear Iran. One or two of
them may hope to coexist with a nuclear Iran, especially if it becomes a
more assertive power in the region. For Saudi Arabia, Bahrain, and UAE,
the perceived threat from Iran is very real. While each state is working
with the United States on missile defense, counterterrorism, and other
security planning, Saudi Arabia has made new overtures to its neighbors

concerning an enhancement of their security collaboration.[18] In part, this initiative is the result of uncertainty among U.S. Gulf allies over the credibility of American security guarantees in the face of rising Iranian power. Just how it may affect U.S. and GCC security planning and collaboration remains to be seen. Nevertheless, the intensification of ties between Saudi Arabia and Bahrain could be a harbinger of a tighter GCC security architecture that could cooperate with or operate independently of the United States, especially if the Saudi leadership were to consider its own nuclear option to balance Iran's emergence as a nuclear power.

In each of our models, extended deterrence remains central not only to U.S. reassurance strategies but also to nonproliferation efforts, as noted earlier, and to escalation control in a crisis or conflict. Extended deterrence usually includes a defense guarantee within an alliance or other security relationship. Such a formal arrangement underscores the commitment to use force, if necessary, both to the vulnerable party and to the state against which such deterrence is directed. Of course, any extended-deterrence relationship must be perceived by an adversary as sufficiently credible in the threat to bring the full force of the protector's military power against an aggressor. However, this is only one aspect of extended deterrence. The other, arguably equally important, at least from a nonproliferation perspective, is the requirement for reassurance. As explained by French strategist Bruno Tertrais, "Whereas the credibility of the 'deterrence' part is to be appreciated by the potential adversaries, the credibility of its assurance part is to be appreciated by the protected country."[19] The erosion of a security guarantee, as perceived by both a potential aggressor and in the protected country, undermines extended deterrence. In short, at the core of extended deterrence is the need to deter the opponent and reassure the ally.

In the Arab Gulf region, no such treaty commitment or alliance framework exists, although several states have in recent decades obtained "major non-NATO status," which implies a U.S. willingness to come to their defense. In recent years, this status was reinforced by Desert Storm and in the context of updating the U.S.-Gulf Security Dialogue. Early in the Cold War, Great Britain played a leading role in the creation in 1955 of the Central Treaty Organization (CENTO), which was dissolved in 1979.[20] In 1958, the Iraq monarchy was overthrown, bringing to power a government no longer allied with the West. This opened the way for increasing Soviet penetration into the Middle East. However, it was Turkey's invasion of Cyprus in 1974 and the Iranian revolution in 1979 that spelled the demise of the organization. Since that time, the United States has emerged as the major protector for the Arab Gulf states, as well as for Jordan and Egypt, since the Camp David Accords and the beginning of the Arab-Israeli "peace process."[21] The Arab Gulf states preferred a looser defense arrangement with the United States, including a small U.S. "footprint" with respect to the forward basing of its military forces. A nuclear Iran is not likely to change Arab Gulf state policy in that regard. Increasingly, however, several of the GCC states appear to view U.S. forces in the region as their "trip-wire" in the event of an Iranian attack. From this perspective, U.S. forward-based forces are essential to deterring Iran's regional ambitions. Others, notably Saudi Arabia and the UAE, may be seeking a firmer and more explicit U.S. commitment to their security. Absent an explicit statement of intent from the United States, these Gulf nations would consider other options to counter a nuclear Iran.

From this perspective, a nuclear Iran could then become a catalyst for wider proliferation. It may not matter what form an Iranian nuclear capability would take or whether Iran's leadership justifies its action on the basis of defensive considerations, as posited in Model I. Nations such as Turkey and Saudi Arabia may conclude that the best way of countering a nuclear-armed Iran is to develop or acquire their own nuclear-deterrent capability, probably missile-based. Elements of the A. Q. Khan illicit weapons network continue to operate, and through them or via state-brokered weapons or component sales, states may calculate that their security depends on nuclear technologies and, in some cases, actual weapons deployment. Obviously, this is counter to what the Iranians have in mind, as reflected in Ahmadinejad's 2007 speech in Dubai where he essentially told his Arab neighbors that once the Americans had left Iraq, the UAE could rely on Iran to provide a defense umbrella for protection against external threats.[22] If anything, Ahmadinejad's remarks indicate a worldview that sees Iran's influence in the Gulf area growing. This view obscures tensions between Iran and its Gulf neighbors, allowing Tehran to promote the idea that it is the United States and not Iran that is regarded as the imperial power in the region. Numerous factors reinforce Iranian self-confidence on this score: the overwhelming unpopularity on the "Arab street" of America's interventions in Iraq and Afghanistan; the global demand for energy products and Iran's vast oil and gas reserves; Hezbollah's ascendance in Lebanon; legacy issues between Russia and the United States, whose collaboration on sanctions against Iran continues to be problematic, despite the widely heralded "reset" in U.S.-Russian relations;[23] and, finally, the persistence of anti-American trends throughout the region and the world.[24]

Even without a nuclear weapon, Iran has attempted to assert its dominance in the Gulf. The U.S.-Gulf Security Dialogue remains the focus of American operational planning against Iran. This initiative is based on the assumption that the Gulf allies can bridge their historic differences and work together in a multilateral framework—something that may prove to be difficult and time-consuming, if not impossible, given the enmity that exists among the GCC countries. Of the Arab Gulf states, Saudi Arabia is most likely to react to a nuclear Iran by seeking to acquire its own nuclear capability if it no longer feels confident about U.S. willingness to strengthen its security relationship. For example, the former Saudi ambassador to the United States was dispatched to Washington in the fall of 2007 to gauge the potential for getting a formal treaty commitment (like NATO's article 5) from the United States.[25] Such a proposal could strengthen U.S. counterproliferation efforts by reassuring Gulf allies to put off considering nuclear weapons. However, it would be difficult to gain support for this type of commitment for countries whose human rights records are suspect. The effort would attract great political controversy, especially in light of the political turmoil and dramatic change sweeping across the Middle East from Tunisia to Yemen. Balancing these concerns against the need to prevent a cascade of countries from following Iran's nuclear example will be a complex and difficult calculus, the outcome of which will depend on the shape and nature of the Iranian breakout and how Iran chooses to deal with the consequences of its actions.

At the strategic level, it will probably be necessary to update the Nixon and Carter Doctrines with a new declaratory policy aimed at containing Iran and assuring allies in order to blunt the psychological edge of Iran's nuclear programs and aspirations. Under the Nixon Doctrine, also known as the Guam Doctrine, first set forth on July 25, 1969, the United States was prepared to honor its treaty commitments and to provide a deterrence shield over nations allied with the United States or considered to be important to U.S. vital interests. At the same time, however, the United States expected its friends and allies to assume the primary responsibility for their own defense. We would provide material and training support. In arguing for "the pursuit of peace through partnership," the Nixon Doctrine helped set the stage for the Carter Doctrine, which was announced on January 23, 1980, as part of President Carter's State of the Union address. While the Nixon Doctrine was applied during the Nixon administration to the Gulf region, with military aid going to the shah's Iran and to Saudi Arabia, the Carter Doctrine, coming after the Soviet invasion of Afghanistan in 1979, stated that the United States would use military force if necessary to protect its interests in what was widely referred to as the Persian Gulf region.[26] Subsequently, in October 1981, President Reagan explicitly proclaimed that the United States was prepared to intervene to protect Saudi Arabia in the event that Saudi interests were threatened.[27] In the intervening years, before the events of September 11, 2001, U.S.-Saudi relations were characterized by growing defense and security cooperation. After the terrorist attacks on the World Trade Center and the Pentagon, however, the U.S.-Saudi relationship experienced a decline in mutual trust. This has created a crisis of confidence in what had been a strong partnership and, in turn, has pushed the Saudis to consider other options, including their own nuclear development, an extended-deterrence guarantee from Pakistan, and even reconciliation with the regime in Tehran.[28] Toward that end, the Saudis did not object publicly to Iranian president Ahmadinejad's participation in the 2007 GCC summit in Doha, and they were willing hosts of his pilgrimage to Mecca in December 2007. From the Saudi perspective, the United States has been weakened by its military interventions in Iraq and Afghanistan while Iran's power and influence are growing in the volatile Arabian Gulf region. However, whatever hope the Saudis may have had about the possibility of closer relations with Iran was shattered by its rather clumsy assassination attempt against the Saudi ambassador in Washington, D.C., in October 2011.

Thus, for the Saudi leadership, pursuit of a nuclear option, either through the acquisition of weapons technologies (starting with the acquisition of new civilian reactor facilities, to be situated in Riyadh) or reliance on a Pakistani extended-deterrence guarantee paid for by Saudi money appears to offer an attractive approach to dealing with a nuclear Iran. In essence, this would constitute a nuclear guarantee on the part of Pakistan, perhaps based on the deployment of Pakistani weapons in Saudi Arabia, with Pakistani troops to operate and guard them. Such an arrangement would necessarily be premised on a tight Saudi-Pakistan relationship, supplemented by an increased commitment from Saudi Arabia to support Pakistan with aid and development funds. Such a deal would, however, raise questions about Saudi Arabia's ongoing support for antiterrorism activities in Afghanistan and in Pakistan's Waziristan province.[29] However, Saudi officials may have concluded that a nuclear Iran is a more serious challenge to Saudi interests and that actions to counter Iran's growing power and influence must be a top priority. The Saudi government would have determined that a nuclear deterrent would augment its national security against a nuclear Iran, especially if the rift between U.S. and Saudi security perspectives deepens. Unless the United States can restore deterrence credibility or give sufficient substance to the U.S.-Gulf Security Dialogue, the Saudis can be expected to seek other options for their defense.

In an effort to calm Arab fears and to reassure allies, the United States has accelerated the deployment of new military systems to the Gulf states, including missile defenses, and has even reformulated an offer to provide deterrence protection over its GCC coalition partners (and Jordan), with Secretary of State Clinton stopping just short in 2008 of extending a defense umbrella over the Gulf states.[30] Nevertheless, the United States has sought to underscore its commitment to come to the defense of a GCC state if it is attacked, although we have not specified precisely the roles of U.S. nuclear or conventional forces. In other words, there is ambiguity about the nature and extent of the American defense commitment to the Arab Gulf states. As far as can be determined, U.S. policy toward the Arab Gulf states includes (1) a non-treaty-based security commitment; (2) a statement that acquisition of nuclear weapons by a hostile power is dangerous; (3) the understanding that the United States is prepared to offer a missile shield to protect friends and coalition partners; and (4) no mention of nuclear retaliation against an Iranian nuclear attack. Lacking a treaty-based commitment to the Gulf states, the United States has nevertheless implemented security guarantees on a bilateral basis to Bahrain and Kuwait, which have been granted the status of "major non-NATO allies"; in essence to Qatar, which hosts U.S. Central Command's (CENTCOM) forward headquarters; and to the UAE, which has been a major U.S. partner in Afghanistan. However, this may not be sufficient for the Saudis. This may be one factor pushing Saudi Arabia to reconsider its defense-planning options, especially since 2003, when most U.S. forces were withdrawn from the Arabian Peninsula.

The problem for U.S. deterrence planning for the Gulf region is that the need to be explicit about U.S. interests and intentions, with clearly delineated red lines for Iran, conflicts with the self-imposed U.S. practice of strategic ambiguity when dealing with allies and partners in the region. Failure to reconcile the two competing aspects of U.S. deterrence planning for the Gulf region might encourage the very proliferation that U.S. policy hopes to contain while opening a door to GCC accommodation of Iran, notwithstanding the apparent contempt that the current regime in Tehran has displayed toward its Arab neighbors. This is why U.S. deterrence planning for the Gulf region needs to be highly tailored to reassure partners that Iran can be dissuaded and deterred.

ASSURING AND DISSUADING ISRAEL IN THE
FACE OF AN IRANIAN NUCLEAR BREAKOUT

Assuring allies and coalition partners of America's interest in their security remains a cornerstone of U.S. nonproliferation policy and of U.S. efforts to deter an Iranian nuclear strike. Central to such efforts is the strengthening of the U.S.-Gulf Security Dialogue and security cooperation to build missile-defense and consequence-management capabilities, as well as intelligence sharing. Just as important, however, is the need to maintain a tight defense relationship with Israel not only because we face a common threat and Israel could decide to undertake unilateral action against Iran (into which the United States would inevitably be drawn) but also because Israel is a democracy whose survival is regarded as a major U.S. interest. Without question, Israel has proven to be a difficult partner at times, and there is no doubt that on some issues U.S. and Israeli interests are not symmetrical. Nevertheless, Israel is an unacknowledged nuclear power in the Middle East, a democracy, and a state that, despite its troubled history and contested establishment, cannot be allowed to be "wiped off the face of the earth," as Iran's president so crudely suggested.

Israel is assessing its options in the face of the new deterrence dynamic created by Iran's nuclear development. Despite an official policy of ambiguity surrounding its nuclear programs,[31] Israel is embarking on a strategic modernization effort to augment and improve its second-strike capability and to diversify its nuclear retaliatory options. In concrete terms, this means an ability to punish Iran and to deny the regime access to specific military options. Notable in this regard are Israel's efforts to modernize its submarine fleet, which currently consists of three German-produced Dolphin diesel-electric attack submarines, with two additional Dolphins on order.[32] There are also indications that Israel is working on electromagnetic weapons and on updating the Begin Doctrine, which provided the strategic context for Israel's preemptive action against Iraq's Osirak nuclear facility in June 1981. A survivable Israeli second-strike force together with missile defenses, as discussed below, might be sufficient to deter a direct Iranian attack against Israel, especially in our Defensive Iran model.[33] However, an Aggressive Iran that is emboldened by possession of nuclear weapons might not be easily contained and deterred from launching a strike against Israel.

For this reason, Israel is also focusing on covert and clandestine measures to undercut or stop Iran's nuclear progress. Numerous Israeli covert options are possible in this regard, including targeting key Iranian scientists, cyberwarfare against Iran's nuclear facilities and energy infrastructure, and other efforts that would undermine Iranian confidence in its nuclear weapons programs. The implementation of the Stuxnet and Flame viruses illustrates a new domain of warfare that is being practiced almost on a daily basis by state and nonstate actors. Iran's nuclear programs are alleged to be highly susceptible to sabotage, although whether such activities would stop Iran from crossing the nuclear threshold remains to be seen. Ever mindful of Israel's 1981 preemptive strike against the Osirak reactor, Iranian authorities have deliberately dispersed Iran's nuclear programs and have taken additional precautions by pursuing both uranium enrichment and plutonium reprocessing, creating redundant capabilities and using duplicative infrastructure that also contains other legitimate technology and manufacturing processes. Iran is probably leveraging dual-use technologies, capabilities, and development processes to deceive and cover up its illegal nuclear activities. That is why Israel also appears to be implementing sanctioned assassinations of key Iranian military personnel and scientists associated with Iran's nuclear-power programs. Israel has provided individual names of targeted-sanctions lists and is participating in global activities designed to counter Iran's illicit trafficking in nuclear-relevant technologies, materials, and capabilities.

Israel's third focus is on missile defenses. Through U.S.-Israeli cooperation, Israel has developed and deployed a layered missile defense architecture that includes the Arrow and Patriot ballistic-missile systems. Israel has also pursued development of an indigenous capability, called the Iron Dome, for use against missiles of up to 70 kilometers range, such as those that were fired against the country by Hezbollah in the 2006 conflict. On March 12, 2012, Iron Dome intercepted twenty-three of thirty-one rockets fired by Gaza militants following an Israeli air strike against a Palestinian guerrilla leader. Subsequently, Iron Dome had a nearly 85 percent success rate against rockets launched into Israel in November 2012 from Gaza. Such rocket strikes are a harbinger of what could be launched, by both Hamas and Hezbollah, in the event that Israel were to attack Iran's nuclear facilities. Israel's Iron Dome system will be augmented by a medium-range intercept capability called David's Sling, which is designed to defeat short-to-medium range ballistic missiles and fill the capability gap that exists between the Iron Dome system and the Arrow system (developed to intercept longer-range missiles such as the Iranian Shahab). For early-warning detection and tracking of missile threats, Israel would rely on a U.S. supplied high-power X-band radar, capable of detecting missile launches up to 1,500 miles away. These capabilities, when netted together in a comprehensive missile-defense architecture, and perhaps supplemented by U.S. Aegis technologies based offshore in the Mediterranean or even onshore in Israel, have the potential to provide a robust layered missile-defense network.

As part of its layered missile-defense system, Israel will deploy the upgraded Arrow III by 2015 and seek to expand its missile defense cooperation with NATO Mediterranean Dialogue countries and to participate in the U.S. Navy's Aegis architecture. This is one reason the Israeli navy has been interested in purchasing the littoral combat ship (LCS). However, the LCS configuration was not viable for the Israeli navy, and the costs for modification to meet Israeli requirements were considered too great. As a result, Israel is developing its own LCS variant, based on a German corvette design. At a minimum, Israel's leadership is seeking to link its defense capabilities to the emerging U.S. ground-based missile-defense architecture in Europe under the Obama administration's Phased Adaptive Approach (PAA).[34] Although Israel and Turkey had at one time discussed cooperative defense architectures, relations between the two countries began to deteriorate following the collapse of the Middle East peace process and the Israeli military operation in Gaza during the winter of 2008–2009. Subsequently, Israeli-Turkish relations broke down completely in the aftermath of the *Mavi Marmara* incident on May 31, 2010, in which the Israel navy intercepted and boarded a Turkish flotilla carrying aid to Gaza, resulting in the death of nine Turkish citizens. Since the incident, tourism, business ties, and military cooperation between the two countries have come to a near halt. However, as one Turkish expert noted, "the emerging dynamics in the Middle East hold out the possibility of bringing Turkey and Israel back together. Turkey's recent calls for the Assad regime to go have angered Iran's leadership. That, together with a decision to comply more fully with the UN sanctions regime by cutting oil imports from Iran, have created new tensions in the relationship, which the Istanbul talks failed to paper over. These things may be enough to bring Turkey and Israel closer to each other under the guise of emerging *realpolitik* factors."[35] The fact that Turkey is participating in the U.S. Phased Adaptive Approach by allowing the establishment of a U.S. X-Band radar installation—similar to the one deployed in Israel in 2008 for early-warning missile detection—is another factor to be considered. Once it is in place, sensor netting of the two missile-defense architectures (Israel's and NATO's) could create a powerful incentive for enhanced collaboration, especially in light of Iran's growing ballistic-missile threat.

MISSILE DEFENSES AND CONSEQUENCE-MANAGEMENT CONSIDERATIONS

During and since the Cold War, U.S. strategic analysts widely assumed that nuclear threats could be deterred by strategic nuclear forces. The worst-case Cold War threat of massive nuclear attack from the Soviet

Union provided the baseline for planning for other contingencies, including China or a smaller nuclear state such as North Korea.[36] The strategic force structure developed to deter the Soviet Union and to reassure U.S. allies was generally seen as having an intrinsic capacity to deter China's greatly inferior strategic forces. However, when considering a smaller adversary force oriented to support a deliberately aggressive foreign policy or a radical (religious) cause, the threat of a massive U.S. retaliatory strike might not be credible against a determined adversary that believes it has little to lose and much to gain from either striking first with nuclear weapons or escalating to nuclear use in the course of a conventional attack that was not succeeding. While far from certain, it is conceivable that a "use them or lose them" mindset might influence Iranian calculations at some point, especially if the threat or actual use of nuclear weapons was deemed to be necessary in order to assure regime survival. However, there might also be doubts that the United States would use its Cold War nuclear weapons against a smaller state.

Against a nuclear Iran, U.S. defense and deterrence planning must include missile defenses. In place of mutual assured destruction, greater emphasis should be placed on detection, prevention, dissuasion, crisis management, and damage limitation. Missile defenses—anti-cruise- and anti-ballistic-missile capabilities—and passive techniques, including consequence management, "render-safe" technologies, and chemical-biological incident response force units, have major deterrence roles to play in reducing the level of confidence that a nuclear-armed adversary may have in its ability to attain desired outcomes from either threatening or actually using nuclear weapons.

For Israel, the GCC, NATO, and the United States, missile defense constitutes an increasingly important element of deterrence against a nuclear Iran in each of our three models. In addition to declaratory policy and strategic communications, missile defenses provide a means of influencing and countering the Iranian nuclear program by deterring or degrading the effectiveness of missile attacks. A robust, layered missile defense may discourage or even deter a nuclear attack by increasing dramatically the uncertainty of success, especially for a country or nonstate actor deploying a small number of nuclear weapons, as would be the case in Models I and III and possibly in Model II, though that depends on the robustness of an Aggressive Iran's missile-development programs. Politically, missile defenses can contribute to crisis manage-ment and enhance the potential for escalation control. Psychologically, missile defenses may influence enemy thinking about offensive opera-tions and the endgame of nuclear escalation. Missile defenses may also have positive psychological effects on otherwise vulnerable civilian pop-ulations, which was apparently the case with Iron Dome in November 2012. The deployment of missile defenses, either on board U.S. Navy Aegis ships in Persian Gulf or Mediterranean waters, or more advanced capabilities deployed on land, at sea, or even in space, has the poten-tial to profoundly change to the U.S. advantage the deterrence dynamics between the United States and Iran.

In the face-off between a nuclear Iran and the United States, espe-cially in Models II and III, the United States will have to set priorities and synchronize policies in a way that has not been done since the Cold War, when containment of the Soviet Union provided the strategic framework for policy. If it can do so while also setting in place stronger deterrence and defensive options within the Persian Gulf region, it will significantly enhance the prospects for denying Iran the opportunity to achieve regional dominance via its acquisition of nuclear weapons. If it cannot, then the more worrisome scenarios involving a nuclear Iran out-lined in this book are more likely to materialize, bringing with them the requirement for an even more robust and diverse set of diplomatic and military initiatives on the part of the United States and its regional allies and partners.

However the United States ultimately chooses to deal with Iran as a nuclear weapons state, regional U.S. policy choices will have broader implications beyond Iran. The reverse has undoubtedly also been the case, and it is likely that Tehran has paid close attention to U.S. words and deeds related to North Korea's development of nuclear weapons. The United States placed its credibility on the line in dealing with North Korea's nuclear program by setting red lines, only to have Pyongyang repeatedly cross them. Then the United States retreated to new red lines, only to retreat again once these new lines were crossed, in effect reward-ing bad behavior.[37] North Korea's breakout from the NPT may eventu-ally be seen as a far less significant development in comparison to the regional and global consequences of Iran as a nuclear weapons state because of Iran's greater overall power. Undoubtedly, the ability of North

Korea to build a nuclear weapon despite the opposition of the international community has not been lost on Iran, which far outstrips North Korea in national capabilities, measured, for example, in energy production and population and geographic size, as well as in its overall regional status. As noted already, there is a danger of nuclear cascading in the Middle East and the Asia-Pacific area. In this sense, regional actions have potentially transregional consequences. While Iran may be viewed as largely a bilateral or at most a regional problem in the United States, this is no longer sufficient. For its part, Iran considers its actions in a broader context. They are part of a comprehensive strategy to promote Iranian power and influence on the global stage. With this in mind, as it updates its strategic vision for the Middle East within a broader global strategic context, the United States must anticipate and begin to deter a nuclear Iran, and this includes the requirement to anticipate Iran's use of irregular warfare and asymmetric threats to meet its strategic objectives.

7
Dealing with a Nuclear Iran and Asymmetric Challenges

Nuclear weapons will greatly enhance Iran's ability to conduct hybrid warfare with a broad range of instruments through a combination of techniques from asymmetric and irregular warfare. These include the use of nonstate armed groups (Hezbollah and Hamas), together with high-end military technologies such as cyberwarfare capabilities, missiles, and, potentially, nuclear weapons. Hybrid warfare can be conducted against the military forces and civilian populations of other states, and against nonstate armed groups. When military operations are necessary to achieve specific strategic objectives, nonlinear, innovative tactics are favored to defeat a stronger adversary, such as the United States. However, direct action is only one avenue for waging irregular warfare. As with counterinsurgency operations, hybrid warfare can include efforts to build support among local populations as a means of shaping perceptions and the strategic choices of friends and foes alike. Indirect action supports the conduct of irregular warfare and contributes to what the military calls "phase-zero" operations in which peacetime and precrisis activities can be leveraged to build confidence and reassure allies and partners.

Hybrid warfare has an important psychological dimension in that it seeks to break the will of an enemy and in doing so to shape perceptions and policy. It also may be protracted and may use all elements of power, including the ballot box, as Hamas with the Palestinian Authority and Hezbollah in Lebanon have done to achieve political power. A nuclear Iran, especially in Model II: An Aggressive Iran and Model III: An Unstable Iran, can be expected to engage in hybrid warfare, using sophisticated cyberattacks and lower-end military capabilities. Iran is already using asymmetric operations, including proxies, to strike at soft targets as well as covert financial and political campaigns to enhance its influence and undermine that of the United States in and beyond the Middle East. As noted by one U.S. pundit, Iran "is adept at intermingling aggressive operations and diplomacy."[1] As a strategy designed to maximize Iran's opportunities and reduce its risks, covert activities (to allow for plausible deniability), the use of proxies, and, if necessary, intimidation via nuclear threats would be the preferred means of dealing with the United States in Model II or III.

HEZBOLLAH AND ASYMMETRIC OPERATIONS

Iran has already made use of Hezbollah to conduct a range of asymmetric operations against Israel, U.S. coalition partners in the Arab world, and American forward-based forces. Hezbollah has a presence in the United States and an even larger one in South America, particularly in the triborder region where Brazil, Uruguay, and Argentina converge. Although much of Hezbollah's activity in this region has been focused on fund raising, money laundering, and drug and human trafficking, U.S. Southern Command (SOUTHCOM) officials point to indications that the organization is building an operational presence in the area, including terrorist training camps.[2] In 1994, Hezbollah was identified as having been behind the bombing of a Jewish community center in Argentina, and there are fears that Hezbollah or other terrorist groups could infiltrate the southern border of the United States or enter the country in other ways from South America, Hezbollah operations in the triborder region are facilitated by the sizable community of Lebanese (and, to a lesser extent, Syrian) immigrants who have settled there, many through forced migration after the 1948 Arab-Israeli war and after 1985 and the Lebanese civil war. A younger generation of disaffected and radicalized Arab immigrants is being actively recruited by Hezbollah in South America to undertake missions against the United States. (Colombia's Revolutionary Armed Forces, or FARC, and Peru's Shining Path terrorist group, as well as drug smugglers, also operate in this region. According to some experts this is the reason that Hezbollah, Hamas, and al-Qaeda may have located here.)[3] Hezbollah also maintains support and infrastructure in the United States, and, depending on the perceived stakes, Iran could leverage those Hezbollah assets to strike within the United States, complicating deterrence and placing the onus for retaliation in a crisis or conflict on the United States.

Deterring an Unstable Iran will be much more difficult than dealing with a state-centric Iran, as postulated in the Defensive and Aggressive Iran models, simply because we have at least some knowledge about the Iranian leadership and government structures, and these will probably be lacking in a disintegrating Unstable Iran in which the leadership would have undergone rapid change, perhaps bringing to power new and unfamiliar figures. Nevertheless, what deters U.S. action may not deter the leadership of an Unstable Iran. This contrasts sharply with the Defensive Iran of Model I, in which we could assume that Iran's leaders would not recklessly risk the destruction of their country. A crisis might spiral out of control if Iran had already descended into chaos, as posited in Model III. Another concern, as noted previously, is that especially in the Aggressive Iran model, Iranian leaders are likely to fail to understand U.S. red lines and therefore may be prone to miscalculation about U.S. interests and our resolve to protect them. At some point in the future, depending on the Iranian regime, threat-reduction initiatives similar to those that were established between the United States and Russia after the Cold War could be useful and important to pursue.[4] In the meantime, the problem of deterring a nuclear Iran depends on the ability to convey to the Iranian leadership the capacity and willingness of the United States to protect its vital interests in a crisis and to use military force, if necessary, to secure those interests. With this in mind, and against a rogue state or a nonstate actor, human-terrain mapping and building an understanding of what an adversary values emerge as critical elements of deterrence planning against an Unstable Iran.

In the case of Model III: An Unstable Iran, the potential for nuclear use would be heightened if the leadership concluded that it was in a "use them or lose them" situation. An Unstable Iran would also be more likely to proliferate weapons systems or components to a third party than would a Defensive Iran (Model I), especially if competing regime elements believed that they stood to gain from doing so, assuming, of course, that these elements had access to some or all of Iran's nuclear weapons. It is also consistent with Model III that control of nuclear weapons would no longer remain in the hands of the central government. Otherwise, operational control of Iran's nuclear weapons would almost certainly reside with the Supreme Leader and the IRGC. Experts contend that Ayatollah Khamenei has nurtured the IRGC and used it to engineer the first election of Ahmadinejad as president in 2005. Before Khamenei assumed the mantle of leadership in Iran, the IRGC was actively discouraged from participating in Iran's political discourse by no less than the first revolutionary leader, Ayatollah Ruhollah Khomeini, according to one dissident IRGC member.[5] This all changed in 1997, however, with the election of Mohammad Khatami, a popular president whose power threatened to eclipse that of the Supreme Leader. By empowering the IRGC, Khamenei may have hoped to strengthen his own position while establishing a basis for a political challenge to the Khatami presidency. In so doing, he probably sought to avoid creating what one Iranian analyst has referred to as the "Gorbachev effect," or a situation in which Khatami's reform initiatives developed a momentum of their own and threatened to destabilize the regime.[6] In 2009, with the election results in dispute, Ayatollah Khamenei faced this nightmare, and as a result he further empowered the IRGC with the support of the president, who named an unprecedented number of military men to serve in the government. In recent years, the Ayatollah has sought to use the IRGC against Ahmadinejad, who is not a cleric, by appealing to their religious credentials. Many of the current members of the IRGC have been educated at the Revolutionary Guards Theological Seminary or have otherwise received political indoctrination courses in Qom at the Martyr Mahallati University, making them clerics as well as IRGC members and leaders. Ahmadinejad's successor, Hassan Rouhani, was allowed to run for office by the Guardian Council. Even though he has been associated with Rafsanjani and Khatami, he aligned himself with the Supreme Leader, who kept him on the National Security Council after Ahmadinejad dumped him.

NUCLEAR WEAPONS AND ASYMMETRIC OPERATIONS

Outside Iran, the IRGC is also flexing its muscles. Its Qods Force has been instrumental in training Hezbollah terrorists, and it has facilitated the Shia insurgencies in Iraq and Bahrain. Even as the Arab-Persian enmity continues to influence Iran's regional relationships, Qods Force elements are known to be working with Hamas. Furthermore, despite conventional wisdom to the effect that Iranian Shi'ites would never collaborate with Sunni groups, this in fact has been the case with Iran and Hamas, raising the prospect that in a contingency in which rival factions were vying for power in Iran, IRGC elements could seek to move weapons out of Iran or, in the event of a regional war, detonate a nuclear device either to escalate a conflict deliberately or to provoke a reaction from the United States or Israel. In the latter scenario, radical Islamists may hope to goad Israel or the United States into attacking Iran as a means of unifying domestic opinion in support of their cause or certain leadership elements. This is a variant on the catalytic war concept discussed in chapter 5.

However unlikely, this contingency represents one possibility if we accept Noah Feldman's thesis that orthodox Shia ideology might support the idea of nuclear war to achieve its goals.[7] The idea that defensive jihad requires extreme measures was also suggested by Mohsen Garavian, a cleric and disciple of Ayatollah Mesbah-Yazdi, who, as noted earlier, remains closely associated with the Supreme Leader and may be seeking to succeed him.[8] Nuclear weapons are the ultimate means for asymmetric warfare, and their threatened (or actual) use on behalf of proxy groups—Hezbollah or perhaps even Hamas or al-Qaeda— remains a troubling prospect that cannot be rejected out of hand as a part of "fourth-generation" warfare.[9] Terrorists would not need actually to use nuclear weapons to alter the balance of power and to incite terror in indigenous populations. The very possibility of their use would be expected to induce greater caution on the part of Iran's enemies. By the same token, the possession of nuclear weapons, perceived or actual, might give Iranian leaders a bolder sense of foreign policy. An Iran with primitive delivery systems would be seen as capable of using other delivery means such as shipping containers, or even improvised nuclear devices (INDs). A nuclear Iran and the increasing availability of nuclear materials could bring terrorist groups closer to actually acquiring such weapons. Psychologically, the possibility of such access could instill additional constraints in the behavior of their likely or intended targets. For example, a terrorist group claiming to have a nuclear weapon could assert its demands with greater credence. In a world with multiple nuclear actors, this prospect increases in likelihood if rudimentary nuclear forces or nuclear materials are vulnerable to theft or if a regime in possession of nuclear weapons consciously decides to sell nuclear technologies to the highest bidder. By exploiting the vulnerabilities of modern-day societies, nonstate actors or state-sponsored elements with perceived access to nuclear weapons could impose tremendous costs with relatively little effort. It is logical to assume that these same considerations might be at play if Iranian regime elements seek to attract support for their cause by demonstrating their prowess outside Iran. They might also consider threatening to use nuclear weapons to force a political solution to the problem of Lebanon's division or in support of Hamas efforts against Israel. In essence, regime elements in an Unstable Iran or even an Aggressive Iran can be expected to give much greater consideration to regional initiatives as a means of influencing both external audiences and domestic opinion.

DETERRING ROGUE ELEMENTS OR NONSTATE ARMED GROUPS

Despite the complexities associated with deterring rogue elements or nonstate armed groups, it may be possible to deter such actors if deterrence by punishment and deterrence by denial are combined. Specifically, in the case of deterrence by punishment this means that, whenever possible, terrorists and their supporting infrastructure, including training bases, leadership, and enablers, should be targeted and destroyed by preventive and preemptive action. The United States is already using the Joint Special Operations Command (JSOC), which is spearheading a number of innovative kinetic operations techniques.[10] In Iraq the JSOC was instrumental in degrading al-Qaeda's network and capabilities, and it was responsible for the capture or attrition of key terrorist targets. It also developed a comprehensive psychological warfare strategy that contributed to the "Anbar Awakening."[11] In Afghanistan, special operations forces (SOF) have identified the Taliban's finance networks and interdicted key terrorist leaders. Their activities in Iraq and Afghanistan illustrate the effectiveness of punitive operations. However, retaliation by armed groups means that deterrence based on the threat of punishment has failed. The question then becomes whether future threats will be deterred as a result of past successes.

Denial is a feasible basis for deterrence, especially if it drastically lowers the adversary's likelihood of mission success or if it imposes substantial costs on the terrorists, their networks, or their state sponsors. In the case of Iran's support for Hezbollah, or even in the unlikely event of Iran's disintegration, deterrence could come from tailored approaches to combining punitive and denial threats, for example, targeting the supporting network of those associated with a particular activity. There is also the potential to embolden opposition forces within Iran, consistent with classic counterinsurgency strategies. Thus far, Western nations have been less successful in cultivating popular opposition to the regime, and, indeed, as noted earlier, many of the leaders of the Green Movement have been imprisoned, making it virtually impossible to build a coherent political opposition among Iran's elites. There is, however, a prospect of doing so among dissident minorities, which have suffered at the hands of the Persian nationalists. In this regard, Azeri nationalism and Baluch opposition are growing in Iran, despite the best efforts of the regime to keep these tribal minorities under control. Such unrest may provide another opening for U.S. SOF to leverage differences and to support opposition to the ruling regime. However, as noted already, Iran's "nuclear clock" is advancing faster than Iran's "democratic clock," and any effort to leverage and help build a resistance movement inside the country in the hope that it might help stall Iran's nuclear drive must be regarded as a long-shot at best.

Before launching Operation Desert Storm after the Iraqi occupation of Kuwait in 1990, U.S. and allied analysts engaged in intensive debate about the relevance of nuclear deterrence to nonnuclear WMD use, namely against Iraqi chemical weapons. For example, the French government issued specific guidance that became the basis for French declaratory policy—that any WMD use against vital French interests would be met by a nuclear response. The United States preferred a strategy based on ambiguity regarding the nature of its likely response, believing that such an approach provided a stronger, more convincing deterrent.[12] While the strategic policies of France and the United States have evolved since Desert Storm, the appropriate deterrent to use of nonnuclear WMD continues to be debated. To deter rogue regimes or nonstate actors, we must be able to put at risk those things that are most valued by those groups. Understandably, the application of this concept to suicide terrorists becomes problematic. However, even in this case, it may be possible to find valued objects to hold at risk. For example, Hezbollah may attach greater importance to its leadership and support networks. U.S. strategies that employ human-terrain mapping and nodal analysis may have an especially important role to play. Deterring a nuclear Iran will require extensive knowledge of key leaders and institutions and the relationships among them, as well as an intimate understanding of Iranian values, interests, and generational issues, together with the capacity to act if deterrence fails in a situation where, for example, U.S. forward-deployed assets are attacked. It will also require much more creative thought and tailored strategies to deter the variety of threats that a nuclear Iran might pose.

One area that requires innovative thought is that of cyberwarfare and its potential to contribute to deterrence strategies, including deterring nonstate actors and rogue regime elements. As previously discussed, in 2010 the Iranian government claimed that a malware known as Stuxnet had infected as many as 30,000 computers essential to operating the nuclear centrifuges at Iran's uranium enrichment facility at Natanz. (Nuclear centrifuges are needed for enriching uranium to fuel reactors or to produce nuclear weapons.) Stuxnet reportedly encompassed two key elements, one intended to make Iran's nuclear centrifuges malfunction and one to dupe Iran's plant operators into thinking that the centrifuges were functioning normally. According to experts, Stuxnet accelerated the rotational speed of rotors in the nuclear centrifuges, which caused them to spin out of control. As a result, Iran encountered substantial problems with its centrifuge operations, setting back its enrichment programs.[13]

Even though many experts believe that Stuxnet was a product of Israeli and U.S. collaboration, the difficulty of establishing unambiguous attribution for such attacks makes them an attractive form of warfare against Iran's nuclear complex. However, the United States and other advanced countries are also highly vulnerable to this form of attack, which could become part of an Iranian strategy in each of the models set forth in this study.[14]

We are also highly vulnerable to EMP attack. According to the 2004 report of the Commission to Assess the Threat to the United States from Electromagnetic Pulse Attack, an EMP even from a single nuclear warhead could have catastrophic consequences.[15] An EMP is generated by a nuclear weapon burst at any altitude above a few dozen kilometers, with the height of burst significant in determining the area exposed to EMP. The EMP threat arises from the ability, whether by terrorists or states, to launch relatively unsophisticated missiles with nuclear warheads to detonate at altitudes from 40 to 400 kilometers above the earth's surface. These short-range ballistic missiles could be launched from vessels such as freighters, tankers, or container ships off U.S. shores. The rationale for such action would be the high political-military payoff in the form of devastating consequences. An EMP attack would constitute a highly successful asymmetric strategy against a society as heavily dependent as the United States is on electronics, energy, telecommunications networks, transportation systems, the movement of inventories in its manufacturing sector, and food-processing and distribution capabilities. No national strategy either addresses the EMP threat or underwrites a serious program to counter the delivery of EMP by a ballistic missile launched from a vessel off our coasts. Commissions, studies, and hearings have produced no action beyond the byproducts of efforts to defend the United States against ICBMs that might be launched by a country such as Iran or North Korea, or to defend our overseas troops, friends, and allies against shorter-range ballistic missiles.[16]

While in no way discounting the need for effective missile defenses against an ICBM threat, it is also imperative that the United States address the more immediate threat posed by the possible attack by shorter-range missiles and EMP in particular. Although some enemies of the United States are developing long-range missiles, they and others already have short- and medium-range missiles that could be launched from ships near our coasts. Several years ago, Iran tested a short-range ballistic missile in a way that indicated an interest in developing an EMP capability—so this threat is not hypothetical. It also must be remembered that terrorists might purchase such missiles—even possibly armed with nuclear weapons.

A would-be EMP attacker might be deterred by an integrated missile-defense system with an ability (1) to detect a ship carrying one or more ballistic missiles and initiate interdiction activities (e.g., via the Proliferation Security Initiative and the Global Initiative to Combat Nuclear Terrorism)[17] before that ship could reach striking distance of the United

States and, failing detection and interdiction (2) to intercept the attacking missile, following tactical warning of its launch, before detonation of its nuclear EMP-producing warhead. Beyond deterrence and active defenses, our goal should be to reduce casualties and provide infrastructure reconstitution.

DETERRENCE PLANNING FOR THE TWENTY-FIRST CENTURY

The models set forth in this study underscore the continuing importance of critical infrastructure protection as an essential aspect of twenty-first-century deterrence planning. They also suggest an important role for missile defenses for crisis management, conflict mitigation and consequence management, and strategic-deterrence protection. This includes defenses against homeland attacks, potentially including EMP as well as dirty bombs or INDs. Deterrence in the twenty-first century is more complex and multifaceted than ever before because it also must address illicit trafficking and networks that may try to smuggle WMD or dirty-bomb elements into the country as well as attacks that might be mounted by Hezbollah or by home-grown terrorists acting in sympathy with, or directly on behalf of, Iran. Because of the potentially devastating effects of such attacks, it is important to strengthen consequence-management capabilities and to leverage military forces such as National Guard units for "event mitigation" and "render-safe" missions—keeping in mind, of course, the limitations on the use of military forces in the U.S. domestic setting based on Posse Comitatus and other considerations.[18]

Although nonnuclear strategic capabilities are critically important, nuclear weapons remain unique in their deterrence role. Therefore, the United States needs a nuclear force tailored to twenty-first-century threats, together with the supporting development and manufacturing infrastructure. The United States is the only nuclear power that is not modernizing its nuclear arsenal even as it makes major post–Cold War reductions.[19] As the United States puts into place a credible tailored-deterrence strategy to address emerging nuclear threats and challenges as may be posed by a nuclear Iran, the development of modern warhead technologies is essential to maintain a credible basis for future planning and force-structure development.

In a world with multiple nuclear actors, nuclear forensics and attribution constitute crucial aspects of deterrence, and the need for such capabilities will be reinforced by the emergence of a nuclear Iran. The United States must not only deter a nuclear Iran as a state actor but also be prepared to prevent the transfer of nuclear know-how and hardware to proxies. This makes essential the ability to trace such transfers to their origins. This is particularly important in our Model III: An Unstable Iran model, where attribution for nuclear weapons use or a dirty-bomb detonation might be difficult. Iran prefers strategic deniability; the most recent example is Iran's collusion with al-Qaeda in the 1996 Khobar Towers bombing in Riyadh, Saudi Arabia.[20] Attribution of origin, therefore, facilitated by the maturation of appropriate technologies, is an indispensable tool to help prevent nuclear-technology transfers. While promising developments on this front are on the horizon, programs applicable to this task should be given high priority to reduce or remove gaps in U.S. intelligence.[21] Nuclear forensics and attribution provide new tools for deterrence by increasing the likelihood of tracing fissile material or nuclear hardware to its point of origin. A paper based on the proceedings of the April 2010 Washington Nuclear Security Summit states that even though the science is being developed to identify the fingerprints of the nuclear weapon or material from which it was constructed, the "required systems of policies and processes have not been fully analyzed." The author concludes that both the scientific procedures and coordination of policies for attribution should be afforded high priority as an essential element of a deterrent posture aimed at holding state sponsors of terrorism accountable.[22] The 2012 Nuclear Security Summit was held in Seoul, South Korea; the Joint Declaration, echoing much of what was said at the earlier Washington Nuclear Summit, stated: "We encourage States to work with one another, as well as with the IAEA, to develop and enhance nuclear forensics capabilities . . . [in order to] combine the skills of both traditional and nuclear forensics through the development of a common set of definitions and standards, undertake research and share information and best practices, as appropriate. We also underscore the importance of international cooperation both in technology and human resource development to advance nuclear forensics."[23]

Reassuring allies constitutes another requirement of twenty-first-century deterrence planning, especially in the face of technology diffusion, which may contribute to proliferation. Security assurances can take many forms, and facing a nuclear Iran, the United States would have to intensify efforts to build niche capacities for its partners in the Persian Gulf region and in Europe, where NATO allies generally have been reluctant to contribute the resources necessary to redress critical shortfalls in military capabilities. U.S. extended deterrence continues to be important to deterring a nuclear Iran and to achieving key nonproliferation goals. Nuclear weapons remain essential to U.S. and alliance security and to efforts to reduce incentives for nuclear cascading. However, a nuclear Iran will weaken the Non-Proliferation Treaty. To the extent that U.S. security assurances are perceived as credible and reliable, they remain essential to mitigating the effects of a nuclear Iran.

Although the NPT is only one of the tools to help achieve U.S. non- and counter-proliferation objectives, its demise or weakening would portend further proliferation. Much more dangerous, however, might be the weakening of controls over material transfers and weapons trafficking. As pointed out in an Institute for Foreign Policy Analysis report on this topic, "the control and regulation of nuclear and radiological materials are being complicated by the broader dissemination of commercial nuclear technology. Growing energy demands continue to increase interest in nuclear power plants, particularly in view of ongoing concerns with regard to future fossil fuel resource scarcity. As a result, nuclear and radiological materials and related technology are being more widely dispersed, increasing as a result the opportunities for WMD-related trafficking and expanding the danger of nuclear weapons proliferation."[24] Therefore, ensuring that nuclear weapons or fissile materials do not end up in terrorist hands is an important aspect of deterrence, especially in Model II: An Aggressive Iran and Model III: An Unstable Iran. Efforts such as the Proliferation Security Initiative and the Global Initiative to Combat Terrorism to interdict the movement and transfer of fissile materials, weapons components, and delivery systems are critically important, together with intelligence to identify nodes in the trafficking networks and their sources of funding.[25] In this respect, deterrence should be based on efforts to address asymmetric challenges, a broader foundation that includes, for example, credible means for network interdiction and the disruption of the flow of resources for WMD-related development and activities.

8
U.S. Deterrence Planning and Iran

Deterring a nuclear Iran will be challenging and difficult. Success will depend on how Iran emerges as a nuclear weapons state and the purpose of its nuclear deployments. A Defensive Iran (Model I) may be more easily deterred. However, this may not be the model that we will face. Much will depend on the evolution of Iran's leadership. Iran may be not only determined to cross the nuclear threshold but also prepared at least to threaten to use nuclear weapons to expand its power and influence in and beyond the Middle East, as postulated in Model II: An Aggressive Iran. Even without nuclear weapons Iran's international behavior is proving problematic. Because its leadership may not understand Western deterrence concepts, our ability to communicate in a crisis will be limited, and escalation may be inevitable. Each side must comprehend the other's red lines, and this must be accompanied by clear and concise messaging about U.S. and allied interests and our willingness to use force to protect such interests. This, in turn, will require creative thinking about defense and deterrence, together with innovative ideas about reassurance to allies, crisis management, and conflict escalation and termination.

Although it is necessary to rethink deterrence and force structure to meet the challenges posed by a nuclear Iran, public opinion in the United States is cool to the nuclear enterprise. In an era of decreasing defense budgets, many of the programs necessary to modernize the U.S. deterrence posture have not been funded. In addition, there are calls for further strategic force reductions beyond those contained in the New START Treaty. The implications of such cuts for deterrence in a world with multiple nuclear actors are troubling, especially if the United

States were to face two or more states in possession of nuclear weapons, for example, a nuclear Iran aligned with Russia or China against the United States. As the size of the U.S. nuclear capability declines to levels perhaps comparable to other nuclear forces, the ability of the United States to manage the escalation process in a crisis could be reduced or even eliminated.

Additional possessors of nuclear weapons will make twenty-first-century deterrence more complex. According to Kenneth Waltz's thesis, discussed in chapter 1, such proliferation could be a stabilizing phenomenon as nuclear weapons lead possessors to more cautious strategies because of their unique destructive characteristics. If Iran evolves according to Model I: A Defensive Iran, it might hold that the goal of nuclear weapons is to deter an attack against Iran. However, a nuclear Iran in any of our models could produce a nuclear cascade by lowering the nuclear threshold if regional adversaries believe that nuclear weapons compensate for deficiencies in conventional forces. A nuclear Iran, especially in keeping with Model II, raises the possibility of catalytic war, as discussed in chapter 5. For example, Israel, perceiving an existential threat, could take military action against Iran. Iran, in turn, might retaliate against Israel and broaden the conflict to attack U.S. interests in the region or even to strike against the United States itself. This suggests, moreover, that escalation dominance can no longer be presumed to reside with the United States, as regional actors look to nuclear weapons to provide an asymmetric capability against superior U.S. forces. Understanding third-party options in a crisis will become a more important aspect of U.S. deterrence, extended deterrence, and strategic communications.

There is a need for innovative thinking about the implications of an Iran capable of conflict escalation by using nuclear weapons first in a conventional war, widening the scope of violence to target U.S. coalition partners in the region, or relying on proxy forces engaging in hybrid or irregular warfare or asymmetric strategies and tactics. We face a comparable situation in the case of a nuclear North Korea, which might decide to use nuclear weapons first. In both instances, however, deterring an adversary from attacking the United States directly may have a better chance of success than efforts to deter it from using nuclear weapons or other WMD against regional allies. Thus, while deterring an enemy attack against the United States must remain a central focus of U.S.

deterrence planning, other considerations, including the need to dissuade other states from taking proliferation decisions and to reassure anxious allies and coalition partners, are also important elements in U.S. deterrence planning. In the past, the extended-deterrence concept has played a key role in reinforcing U.S. alliance partnerships. In today's world, extended deterrence should continue to play a great part in U.S. non- and counter-proliferation strategy. Extended deterrence should remain at the center of U.S. reassurance strategies and escalation control in contingencies involving Iran.

EXTENDED DETERRENCE IN THE "SECOND NUCLEAR AGE"

U.S. efforts to reassure allies and coalition partners in a world with multiple nuclear actors will call for a broader array of tools and a whole-of-government approach. As with deterrence itself, extended deterrence in the "second nuclear age," as characterized by both Paul Bracken and Keith Payne, will demand unique formulas for key regional theaters and states. U.S. deterrence in the Middle East will affect Asia-Pacific allies, and vice versa. However, the security commitment that the United States provides to NATO and on a bilateral basis to its allies in Japan, Taiwan, and South Korea will probably not be replicated elsewhere, except in relation to Israel.

In NATO, the U.S. extended-deterrence commitment was embodied in the collective-defense concept set forth in article 5 and manifested in the forward deployment of American forces in Europe. It also was given substance by basing U.S. tactical nuclear weapons in Europe and sharing this mission with European NATO allies. NATO's nuclear-capable or dual-capable aircraft, as they have been called, remain an integral aspect of the alliance's concept of "shared risks" and "burden sharing." No such formula was put into place in the Asia-Pacific area, which lacked a multilateral framework comparable to that of NATO. Nevertheless, for Japan and South Korea, the extended-deterrence guarantee was reinforced by the forward deployment of U.S. forces, which, as in NATO, were regarded by their host governments as "trip-wire forces" necessary to ensure the steadfast nature of the U.S. commitment to come to the defense of its allies in a crisis, with nuclear weapons if necessary. In South Korea, the

United States deployed sizable military forces to oversee the Korean War armistice. In Japan, the United States Navy home-ported one of its aircraft carriers at Yokosuka while the marines deployed forces on Okinawa, the army at Camp Zama, and the air force at bases near Tokyo and on Hokkaido, all to reinforce extended deterrence. Extended deterrence has always been a contentious concept. In the absence of the forward deployment of U.S. military forces, it is likely that the willingness of the United States to put itself at risk to protect allied interests would have been more widely questioned. Despite the fact that some U.S. allies (France, Israel, and, for a time, Taiwan and South Korea) chose to go down the nuclear path, most of the NATO nations and Japan were satisfied that they shared a common threat perception and trusted the United States to come to their defense if necessary.

In the first decades of the twenty-first century, divergent threat perceptions have given rise to contending approaches to dealing with would-be proliferators and legacy challenges. Nevertheless, reassuring allies remains a crucial element of twenty-first-century deterrence planning. In the absence of consensus about threats, that reassurance function has become more difficult. In the wake of the U.S. engagements in Iraq and Afghanistan and as the United States continues to reposition its forces, transform its overseas presence, undertake a "pivot" to the Asia-Pacific area, and modernize capabilities as it withdraws from combat operations in Afghanistan, extended deterrence becomes less certain. In Europe, divergent perspectives on Russia and Iran have divided alliance members over strategy and article 5 (collective defense) and article 4 (crisis intervention) missions. In the Middle East and elsewhere Iran's progress toward nuclear status is cause for concern. In some countries it is prompting debate over offensive options, including nuclear acquisition. In Israel, as we have seen, it has stimulated new thinking about nuclear strategy and the deployment of second-strike forces, with networked missile defenses to protect both the country and its deterrence posture. In the Middle East, where the United States has relied on off-shore deployments to lend substance to its security commitments to allies and partners, extended deterrence is probably more difficult to achieve than it was in NATO Europe, or even in Korea and Japan, where U.S. conventional forces have been deployed on the territory of allies.

A strategic-communications/information-operations roadmap is essential to reassure allies and convey the seriousness of U.S. intentions to prospective adversaries. In place of strategic ambiguity, this would mean a clear statement of U.S. intentions communicated to allies and adversaries alike. The United States could explore the option of providing an explicit extended-deterrence guarantee to Israel while moving forward with plans to tighten the integration of Israeli and U.S. missile-defense capabilities, early-warning systems, and intelligence sharing. At the same time, the United States might also seek to tie Israel closer to NATO, although European resistance to this idea might allow only for discussion of enhanced "partnership" options.

Taking into account its history and its regional aspirations, Iran, especially in our Defensive Model I, can probably be deterred if the threatened retaliation is sufficiently credible to leave no doubt about American interests, intentions, and red lines. While there have been times when ambiguity has served us well, such as with respect to responding to non-nuclear WMD threats, countering a nuclear Iran calls for a declaratory policy that is clear, concise, and leaves no room for misinterpretation. A declaratory policy that affirms a U.S. commitment to respond to any Iranian aggression—nuclear, other WMD, or conventional—arguably could open debate among Iranians about nuclear weapons. It might have the effect of devaluing Iranian nuclear weapons. Admittedly, we face the challenge of communicating intent to an Iranian regime that may not share our understanding of deterrence. Lack of familiarity with Iran's value structures and with the perspectives of key leaders contributes to such uncertainty. In the absence of adequate communication between Iran and the United States (or Israel) regarding the other's red lines, there is danger of miscalculation and crisis escalation.

CYBERWARFARE AND NETWORK OPERATIONS

Cyberwarfare introduces a new and potentially powerful dimension of defense and deterrence planning. Cyberoperations must be considered in each of our three models. Iran can be assumed to be prepared for cyberwar as part of a future crisis with Israel and the United States, just as Israel and the United States have allegedly engaged in cyberwar against Iran with the Stuxnet virus. Cyberoperations to disable or destroy military capabilities are likely to be a part of crises between the United States and its adversaries. Cyberwarfare attacks have already been mounted against civilian infrastructures, including electric power grids. As demonstrated by the Stuxnet virus, offensive operations against computer networks open the door to options that have implications for deterrence planning. Before it was discovered, Stuxnet had infected Iran's centrifuges and undermined the country's uranium-enrichment and -processing capacity. Long-term malware like Stuxnet had the potential to confound Iran's nuclear development plans. The introduction of new-generation centrifuges at the Natanz and Fordow complexes has delayed the timelines of Iran's nuclear programs. Cyberwarfare has the potential to attack critical military and civilian infrastructure without the overt use of military forces, and attack attribution will be difficult to establish. Indeed, although much speculation exists about the origins of Stuxnet, neither the U.S. nor Israeli government has formally claimed the credit for its creation.[1] To do so would open the door to retaliation and would legitimize this covert form of cyberwarfare as an aspect of defense and deterrence planning.

These new forms of attack invite comparison with the beginning of the nuclear age. In 1945 we entered an era in which the political-military environment was decisively shaped by nuclear weapons of mass destruction, although looking back from our twenty-first-century vantage we know that many conventional wars were waged instead. In 1946 the celebrated nuclear strategist Bernard Brodie speculated: "Thus far the chief purpose of our military establishment has been to win wars. From now on its chief purpose must be to avert them."[2] In retrospect we now know that Brodie was only partly correct but nonetheless insightful. As he foresaw, there has never been a full-scale war between nuclear-armed states, although such states have gone to war against nonnuclear states and nonnuclear entities have engaged nuclear powers. Nonstate armed groups also have engaged in wars that have not escalated to the nuclear level. Does the rise of cyberwarfare in the form of Stuxnet herald the beginning of a new era characterized by cyberweapons of *precise destruction*? If so, we stand at the threshold of a political-military setting about which we have inadequate knowledge. Unlike the nuclear weapon of mass destruction, however, a cyberweapon, because of its ability to provide precise destruction, may prove to be far more usable and therefore come to be much more widely employed. If this is the case, its effects may be even more profound and wide-ranging than the nuclear weapon was for the Cold War and even the post–Cold War political-military setting.

The United States had a near monopoly on nuclear weapons for the first decade after 1945, even though the Soviet Union conducted its first nuclear test in 1949. Thus we had time to develop our thinking about the new nuclear world. We spawned an extensive and seminal literature on the meaning of nuclear weapons for national security. This contrasts sharply with the cyberworld of today in which the pace of innovation and the spread of technologies are accelerating so rapidly that we no longer have the luxury of a decade to grasp the implications for cyber-warfare. In contrast to nuclear weapons, the price of entry into the world of cyberwar is relatively low, and the technology is far more widely available now than nuclear weapons ever have been. Furthermore, cyber-weapons will become increasingly available to states and nonstate armed groups alike in the years ahead. Because they have already been used against and by Iran, cyberoperations are likely to be part of the future crisis landscape between Iran and its principal adversaries.

The introduction of novel technologies leads almost inevitably to speculation about their implications for future warfare. There are numer-ous analyses, such as the recent literature on the revolution in military affairs and writings on air power in the generation between the World Wars, that examine the transformative effect of technology on strategies and tactics for the conduct of warfare. Only with the passage of time do we begin to grasp the meaning of such innovation, and even then trans-formation is more a journey than a destination. Nevertheless, given the nature of the cyberwarfare domain, we face a rapidly evolving, dynamic technological environment in which capabilities will continue to prolif-erate at an accelerating speed, often with quite volatile and unpredictable consequences. To the extent, therefore, that cyberwar has been "legiti-mized" by Stuxnet, it is essential to begin to develop a fuller understand-ing of its strategic implications for U.S. deterrence and security planning.

The deterrence of cyberoperations adds an important new dimension to the security relationship among states in a world with multiple nuclear actors. In our discussion of twenty-first-century nuclear deterrence we have emphasized offensive and defensive elements—punishment based on retaliation as well as denial based on defense, prominently including missile defense. Key to punishment-based deterrence (retaliation) is the need to establish attribution—to know who perpetrated the act as a basis for retaliation. This is a widely cited problem in discussions of cyberdeterrence unless cyberoperations are a part of a conflict that includes conventional or nuclear weapons launched from another state. The greater the ambiguity about the origins of the attack and the greater the difficulty in establishing attribution in a timely fashion, the more difficult it will be to credibly threaten retaliation. In light of the multiplicity of actors and points from which cyberoperations can be launched, the problems of attribution enhance the need for denial-based cyberdeterrence in each of the three models set forth in previous chapters.

In conclusion, the United States must consider the following as it prepares for a nuclear Iran:

- Revitalize deterrence planning and concepts, especially in the aftermath of Iran's acquisition of nuclear weapons, and tailor them to meet the requirements of specific contingencies
- Develop options to dissuade Iran's leadership or leadership elements from transferring nuclear weapons, materials, or systems components to other states and armed nonstate actors
- Modernize U.S. deterrence force posture to incorporate innovative offensive technologies, robust missile defenses, and cyberwarfare planning
- Counter the potential of a nuclear Iran for pursuing asymmetrical strategies such as an EMP attack that would disable or destroy our electronic systems
- Address the implications of a nuclear Iran for homeland security and specifically nuclear use within the United States by a terrorist proxy such as Hezbollah
- Give greater priority in defense and deterrence planning to attack attribution and forensics
- Update thinking about extended deterrence and tailor force-structure decisions to meet the unique circumstances of specific contingencies and regional settings

- Enhance intelligence efforts in Iran and in collaboration with key partners to gain a better understanding of actors, networks, and their relationships across borders and with proxy groups

Each model set forth in this study presents unique challenges, for example, the greater likelihood of proliferation inherent in Models II and III. But in any scenario a nuclear Iran would confront the United States with the need to plan for a range of contingencies. For example, a Defensive Iran (Model I) might transform into an Aggressive Iran (Model II) or an Unstable Iran (Model III) as a result of domestic forces as Tehran expands its nuclear arsenal or broadens its foreign policy ambitions. Although a nuclear Iran might evolve toward greater caution, the reverse situation should not be discounted. As a nuclear Iran acquires more advanced nuclear capabilities and supporting technologies, it might become more willing to support an aggressive foreign policy, as described in Model II: An Aggressive Iran. A nuclear Iran, especially Model II, might be prone to miscalculate the resolve of the United States in a crisis, concluding that nuclear weapons confer greater latitude to pursue expansionist aims against its weaker Gulf neighbors only to find that the United States was not prepared to acquiesce to such behavior. An unstable Iran with nuclear weapons would be more dangerous than a disintegrating Iran without nuclear weapons. Preparing for a nuclear Iran is the basis for deterring such a crisis or at least limiting its escalation. Deterring a nuclear Iran is the fundamental basis for a strategy that first contains and then hopefully helps transform Iran.

NOTES

1. INTRODUCTION: SETTING THE SCENE FOR IRAN'S EMERGENCE AS A NUCLEAR POWER

1. The Non-Proliferation Treaty (NPT) was designed to limit the spread of nuclear weapons. It was opened for signature on July 1, 1968, and entered into force in 1969. Only five states (France, the former Soviet Union and now Russia, China, the United Kingdom, and the United States) were recognized as nuclear weapons states. These five states, in signing the NPT, have committed, in article 1, not to transfer nuclear weapons or their components to non–nuclear weapons states and not to use their nuclear weapons against non–nuclear weapons states except in response to a nuclear attack or a conventional attack by a state allied with a nuclear weapons state.

2. On March 19, 2011, a multistate coalition began a military intervention to implement UNSC Resolution 1973, which called for a naval blockade and no-fly zone over Libya and to protect civilians under threat of attack. What was initially supposed to be a neutral intervention quickly morphed into an operation in support of the rebel movement that was trying to topple the Qaddafi regime. NATO took control of the arms embargo operation on March 23, 2011, under the name of Unified Protector. One day later, NATO agreed to take control of the no-fly zone enforcement effort, with targeting on the ground remaining under the control of national coalition forces. Qaddafi's death in October 2011 effectively ended the fighting in Libya, and a new government, formed out of the rebels' Transitional National Council (TNC), was established.

3. Nuclear weaponization is defined here as the mating of an operational warhead to a delivery system that can then be employed against an adversary target.

4. Nuclear latency is a situation in which a state possesses the personnel, technologies, and infrastructure necessary to test, build, and deploy nuclear weapons. A nuclear weapons capability (weaponization) could be deployed in a relatively short time if the state with nuclear latency chose to do so. Nuclear latency is sometimes referred to as the "Japanese option" because it is commonly accepted that Japan possesses the technological capability, infrastructure, and required supply of plutonium to produce nuclear weapons. However, because of historical, ideological, and

political reasons, together with its defense alliance with the United States, Japan has decided not to cross the nuclear weapon threshold.

5. Farideh Farhi, "'Atomic Energy Is Our Assured Right': Nuclear Policy and the Shaping of Iranian Opinion," in *Nuclear Politics in Iran*, ed. Judith Yaphe, an Institute for National Security Studies (INSS) Paper, Center for Strategic Research, Middle East Strategic Perspectives Series, No. 1 (May 2010). Most significant in this regard, she argues, was the decision in 2005, just before Khatami left office, to resume conversion of uranium yellowcake to UF-6 at Iran's Isfahan plant. She also suggests that it was during the Khatami presidency that the foundations for a nationalist justification for Iran's nuclear programs were laid and that "framing the Iranian nuclear program in terms of the country's scientific and technological progress made it much more difficult to challenge" (9).

6. The Green Movement refers to a popular protest movement in Iran that emerged during the 2009 presidential election campaign. It reflected the re-emergence of a "reformist" faction in Iranian politics, which had come to light during the presidency of Mohammad Khatami (1997–2005). During his term in office, Khatami supported a "Dialogue of Civilizations" and sought liberal reforms in Iran's society. In 2009, disillusioned by the "conservatives" in power, Khatami decided to run for president of Iran again, but his candidacy was short-lived. In February 2009, he withdrew from the race, throwing his support to his friend and cofounder of the Green Movement, Mir Hossein Mousavi. There has been much speculation about the results of the 2009 election, with many in Iran claiming the results were fraudulent. Mousavi, who served as prime minister of Iran in the 1980s, remains the leader of the opposition, but the activities of his Green Movement are severely restricted by the Iranian authorities. Mousavi and another key opposition leader, Mehdi Karoubi, have both been under house arrest since early 2011. In March 2011, members of the Green Movement could not get their names placed on the ballot, and the election results, while representing a slap in the face for the incumbent president, Ahmadinejad, nevertheless were a victory for the conservative faction of the Supreme Leader.

7. The Qods Force is an elite, special operations–like element of the IRGC. It is responsible for operations outside of Iran, including the training of Hezbollah and other proxy forces.

8. The United Nations has enacted four sets of sanctions against Iran: Security Council resolutions 1737, 1747, 1803, and 1929, as depicted on table 1.1. Their goal is to make it more difficult for Iran to acquire equipment, technology, and finance to support its nuclear activities. The sanctions ban the sale to Iran of material and technology related to nuclear enrichment, heavy-water activities, and ballistic-missile development; restrict dealings with certain Iranian banks and individuals; stop the sale of major arms systems to Iran; and allow some inspections of air and sea cargoes. They do not, however, stop the trade in oil and gas, the main source of income for Tehran. However, on November 22, 2011, the United States, in coordination with Britain and Canada, enacted sanctions aimed at Iran's central bank and commercial banks. The United States also imposed sanctions on companies involved in Iran's nuclear

industry, as well as on its petrochemical and oil industries, adding to existing measures with the goal of weakening the Iranian government by denying its ability to refine gasoline or invest in its petroleum industry. In addition, the European Union, in January 2012, imposed sanctions on Iranian oil imports, which went into effect in July 2012. These new punitive sanctions, which include an embargo on Iranian natural gas imports to EU countries, also include measures that will adversely affect Iran's trade and banking exchanges with EU countries. According to a report by the U.S. Congressional Research Service (CRS), "Together, these sanctions have reduced Iranian oil exports to about 1 million barrels per day as of October 2012, a dramatic decline from the 2.5 million barrels per day Iran exported during 2011. . . . The loss of hard currency revenues from oil—coupled with the cutoff of Iran from the international banking system and the reported depletion of Iran's foreign exchange reserves—caused a collapse in the value of Iran's currency, the rial, in early October (2012). . . . In response, Iran has tried to impose currency controls and arrested some illegal currency traders, although these steps are unlikely to restore public confidence in the regime's economic management" (see Kenneth Katzman, *Iran Sanctions*, Congressional Research Service, a Report for the U.S. Congress, October 15, 2012, executive summary).

9. Anoushiravan Ehteshami, "Iran's Tenth Presidential Election: Implications for Iran and the Region," in *Nuclear Politics in Iran*, ed. Judith Yaphe, an Institute for National Security Studies (INSS) Paper, Center for Strategic Research, Middle East Strategic Perspectives Series, No. 1 (May 2010), 38.

10. Bahman Baktiari, "Seeking International Legitimacy: Understanding the Dynamics of Nuclear Nationalism in Iran," in *Nuclear Politics in Iran*, ed. Judith Yaphe, an Institute for National Security Studies (INSS) Paper, Center for Strategic Research, Middle East Strategic Perspectives Series, No. 1 (May 2010), 20–22. Baktiari notes that the Persian word for dignity, "*sherafat*," has deep roots in Persian culture, and it is often associated with respect, or "*ehteram*." A violation of dignity causes humiliation. For many Iranians, "the core of what is identified as their national dignity largely coincides with the Iranian state's material interest in security."

11. Iranians typically point to the 1828 Treaty of Turkmenchai, by which Iran lost Central Asian territory to Russia, as one of the most humiliating events in its history. Iran's nationalization, in the 1950s, of oil brought it into conflict with Great Britain, and the close U.S. relationship with the shah's regime ensured that America would become a prime target for Iran's Islamic Revolution, which culminated with the taking of American hostages in 1979. On this latter topic, see Mark Bowden, *Guests of the Ayatollah: The First Battle in America's War with Militant Islam* (New York: Atlantic Monthly Press, 2006).

12. The non–nuclear weapons states (NNWS) that are signatories to the NPT have committed not to receive, acquire, or develop nuclear weapons (article 2), and, in article 3, to accept the safeguards and verification regimes implemented by the International Atomic Energy Agency. Article 6 of the NPT stipulates the responsibility of the nuclear weapons states toward disarmament and article 4, which is

controversial, implies a "right" of access by NNWS to civilian nuclear technologies, but only if these states comply with the safeguards and transparency stipulated in article 2. Article 10 of the NPT allows for a signatory's withdrawal from the treaty, after a three-month notification period has passed, and only if an extreme national emergency dictates withdrawal. Originally, the NPT was slated to be in force for twenty-five years. On May 11, 1995, at the 1995 Review and Extension Conference of the Parties to the Treaty on the Non-Proliferation of Nuclear Weapons, however, the treaty was extended indefinitely.

13. Article 4 of the NPT refers to the "inalienable right" of all treaty signatories to "develop research, production, and use of nuclear energy for peaceful purposes." Moreover, as a nonnuclear signatory of the NPT, Iran signed the Additional Protocol, a program that was initiated in 1993 to strengthen and extend the NPT safeguards system; by the end of 2010, 139 countries had signed the Additional Protocol. However, the Iranian parliament (Majlis) has not ratified the Additional Protocol. Nevertheless, Iran is still subject to IAEA inspections, and until 2003 it had more or less complied with IAEA requests and allowed for on-site inspections at some facilities. The problem has been that Iran has failed to declare all of its nuclear-related infrastructure, and some sites, such as that at Isfahan, were only discovered using defector information. The four sites declared by Iran and which are now under IAEA safeguards and monitoring include Natanz, Isfahan, Fordow, and Arak. Of these, Natanz has both a pilot centrifuge facility and a larger commercial facility, buried underground, which is capable of holding more than 47,000 centrifuges to produce uranium enriched up to 5 percent. The pilot facility is being used to enrich uranium up to 20 percent and to test more advanced centrifuges. According to a 2012 Congressional Research Service report, by February, Iran had installed approximately 9,100 centrifuges in the commercial facility at Natanz and is "feeding uranium hexafluoride into as many as 8,808 of those centrifuges." At Fordow, a site that is built into the side of a mountain, the facility contains about 3,000 centrifuges, which—according to Tehran—will be configured to produce uranium enriched to both 5 and to 20 percent. Isfahan is an above-ground facility used to convert uranium oxide into uranium hexafluoride that can be enriched to produce nuclear weapons. Arak is the site of an operational water reactor. Bushehr is the site of a light-water reactor but is of less concern than the Arak facility. To date, Iran has refused to allow IAEA unimpeded access to "sites of interest." Moreover, there are fears that much of Iran's nuclear program remains hidden from view in military installations or other concealed facilities.

14. These contentions are reinforced by analysts in a collection of essays, written by Iranians, for publication by the National Defense University. See Judith S. Yaphe, ed., *Nuclear Politics in Iran*, an Institute for National Security Studies (INSS) Paper, Center for Strategic Research, Middle East Strategic Perspectives Series, No. 1 (May 2010); see, in particular, Farhi, "'Atomic Energy Is Our Assured Right,'" 9.

15. Baktiari, "Seeking International Legitimacy," 25.

16. The NIE on Iran was released in 2007 and generated much debate. For many, the key judgments in the NIE were overstated and reflected, perhaps, a reaction to

previous intelligence-community judgments that overestimated Iraq's WMD capabilities. Moreover, the decision to define Iran's nuclear weapons program in terms of its weapons design and weaponization work and covert uranium-enrichment-related work necessarily bounded the assessment in ways that in hindsight are not realistic and, as a result, skew understanding of the scope of Iran's nuclear development programs. Thus, for example, the key judgment that Iran terminated its nuclear weapons program in 2003 failed to consider the full implications of Iran's resumption of its declared uranium-enrichment program at Natanz for Iran's weaponization or the implications of revelations about the Fordow facility, which were made public in the fall of 2009. Nor did the NIE address Iran's ongoing ballistic-missile-development efforts or the plutonium-enrichment path on which Iran is also embarked. Most of all, it failed to address the extent to which Iran may have put into place a parallel and covert military program, as well as the extent to which Iran may have benefited from the A. Q. Khan network—a factor that raises the possibility that Iran has had access to weapons blueprints and advanced miniaturization designs.

17. The NIE of 2007 was, however, confusing in this regard, even if the impression it left was that Iran indeed had stepped back from its nuclear "work." What the 2007 NIE actually contended was that the "intelligence community had moderate confidence" that Iran's "nuclear weapons work" had halted in 2003. However, in a footnote, the NIE stated that "weapons development work" was defined as warhead design and not the enrichment of uranium, which continued unabated in Iran, with the expansion of related facilities and centrifuges for uranium enrichment, which is necessary to produce weapons-grade fissile material. In September 2009, Iran was forced to admit that it was constructing a secret uranium-enrichment facility near Qom. Analysts for the IAEA contend that at least two other suspect sites for uranium enrichment probably exist. Beyond this, intelligence sources contend that there is evidence that Iran is actively working on building and testing nuclear "trigger" technology, based on a four-year plan to test a neutron initiator, the component of a bomb that triggers the explosion. Technical documents that have been translated from Farsi describe the use of a neutron source, uranium deuteride, which experts contend was used in Pakistan's bomb, from which Iran obtained its nuclear blueprints. Moreover, uranium enrichment is not the only nuclear path that Iran appears to be pursuing. In October 2009, IAEA inspectors in Iran to inspect the newly revealed Qom facility discovered at Khonab, a small nuclear facility near Isfahan, 600 barrels of "heavy water," which is used in making weapons-grade plutonium. When asked about the origin of the heavy water, Iranian officials reported that it had been manufactured in Iran. The 2011 NIE on Iran's nuclear program, which reportedly said that Iran is keeping the nuclear weapons option open, was not made public.

18. In May 2012, the Associated Press released a drawing of an explosives-containment chamber of the type needed for nuclear tests that it said was based on information received from an official of a country tracking Iran's nuclear program. According to the AP press release, this drawing "proves the structure (at Parchin)

exists, despite Tehran's refusal to acknowledge it" (see George Jahn, "Drawing Shows Iran Has Nuclear-Arms Test Chamber," *San Francisco Chronicle*, May 14, 2012).

19. Cited in "Iran's Nuclear Timetable," Iran Watch: Tracking Iran's Mass Destruction Capabilities, http://www.iranwatch.org/ourpubs/articles/iranucleartimetable .html, updated February 25, 2013. Figures were estimated by IAEA experts, based on those cited in Director-General of the International Atomic Energy Agency, "Implementation of the NPT Safeguards Agreement and Relevant Provisions of Security Council Resolutions in the Islamic Republic of Iran," IAEA Board of Governors, http://iranwatch.org/international/IAEA/iaea-iranreport-022113.pdf, August 30, 2012, updated February 21, 2013. Reportedly, Iran has also produced 5,974 kilograms as of February 2013 of 20% enriched uranium and purified about 6 tons of 5% or below. Uranium is considered "weapons-grade" at about 90% enrichment.

20. "The Defense Secretary: An Interview with Leon Panetta," *60 Minutes*, January 29, 2012, http://www.cbsnews.com/8301-18560_162-57367997/the-defense -secretary-an-interview-with-leon-panetta/. The United Kingdom holds to a similar assessment about the timelines for an Iranian nuclear breakout, assuming a strategic decision has been made to do so. In July 2012, the head of MI-6, Sir John Sawers, stated that Iran will probably have a nuclear weapon by 2014 (quoted in Christopher Hope, "MI-6 Chief Sir John Sawers: 'We Foiled Iranian Nuclear Weapon Bid,'" *Telegraph*, July 12, 2012, http://www.telegraph.co.uk/news/uknews/terrorism-in-the -uk/9396360/mi6-chief-sir-john-sawers-we-foiled-iranian-nuclear-weapons-bid .html). The release of the August 2012 IAEA report, cited in note 19, was used as the basis for analysis by the widely respected Institute for Science and International Security (ISIS) in Washington, D.C. According to the analysis of Dr. David Albright, a former UN nuclear inspector, Iran "could produce enough highly enriched uranium for one atomic bomb, about 25 kilograms, in two to four months, using its largest uranium-enrichment facility near the city of Natanz." The ISIS report concluded that Iran's growing stockpile of highly enriched uranium, together with expanding numbers of centrifuges for spinning the uranium, provided the basis for estimating a faster timeline than that offered by Prime Minister Netanyahu of Israel during his speech before the UN General Assembly on September 27, 2012. According to ISIS, Tehran could "combine its stockpiles of low-enriched and higher-enriched uranium to make a dash for weapons-grade fuel, which is around 90% purity. The Iranians could do that by synchronizing the enrichment of these two grades of uranium and cutting out some intermediary steps that slow the process. 'Growth in the stock of near 20% (purity) reduces the time to breakout.' Iran has a stockpile of 280 kilograms of uranium enriched to 20% purity, according to the IAEA. An additional 25 kilograms of the material is committed for conversion into fuel rods for Tehran's research reactor. ISIS said its faster estimates for Iran acquiring the highly enriched uranium would require Tehran to use its total stockpile of 20% enriched uranium" (quoted in Jay Solomon, "Iran Seen as Closer To Bomb-Grade Fuel," *Wall Street Journal*, October 10, 2012).

21. Rick Gladstone and David E. Sanger, "Nod to Obama by Netanyahu on Iran Bomb," *New York Times*, September 28, 2012. Equating a nuclear-armed Iran to a nuclear-armed al-Qaeda, Netanyahu analyzed the implications for Middle Eastern stability and went on to suggest that in the spring or summer of 2013, Iran would have enough fissile material to make a bomb. Netanyahu based his calculations on IAEA estimates (Director-General of the IAEA, "Implementation of the NPT Safeguards Agreement") and suggested that in contrast to assertions by the U.S. administration, the intelligence indicators of an Iranian decision to cross the nuclear threshold would be readily apparent, starting with the expulsion of the IAEA inspectors, Iran could assemble a bomb clandestinely anywhere in the country, out of sight of inspectors and intelligence efforts. Recalling previous intelligence failures surrounding al-Qaeda and Iraq, Netanyahu asked the rhetorical question of whether we "want to risk the security of the world on the assumption that we would find in time a small workshop in a country half the size of Europe?"

22. The Stuxnet virus was a form of cyberwarfare that was unleashed on Iran's first generation of centrifuges, which had been manufactured in Germany. The computer virus was designed to disrupt the functioning of the centrifuges and set back Iran's efforts to enrich uranium for weapons use. Officially, no country has come forward to claim credit for the effort, but suspicions abound that the Stuxnet virus was developed by a team of U.S., European, and Israeli scientists. In April 2012, Iran appears to have suffered another serious cyberattack, this one aimed at Iran's oil industry. Reportedly, Iran had to disconnect several of its main oil terminals from the Internet on April 23, 2012, to combat a serious computer virus called Wiper. According to public reports, the virus was first noticed in March 2012, but its effects were only felt when the Kharg Island terminal went down. Typically, Kharg Island accounts for about 80 percent of Iran's crude oil exports, amounting to perhaps 2.2 million barrels per day. See Thomas Erdbrink, "Facing Cyber Attack, Iranian Officials Disconnect Some Oil Terminals from Internet," *New York Times*, April 24, 2012. A more in-depth analysis of Stuxnet and the Olympic Games, as they were called by policy makers, is found in David E. Sanger, *Confront and Conceal: Obama's Secret Wars and Surprising Use of American Power* (New York: Crown, 2012), esp. prologue, chap. 8, and 262–65.

23. In October 2009, the IAEA presented a proposal to Iran that called for its agreement to ship most of its low-grade enriched uranium out of the country for reprocessing in Russia. Russia, in turn, was to send the reprocessed uranium to France, where it would have been converted into fuel rods for use in a medical reactor in Iran. From the Western perspective, the advantage of this proposal was that it would have moved most of Iran's stockpile of nuclear fuel (at that time) out of the country, leaving Iran without enough fissile material to convert into a nuclear weapon. Iran, for its part, rejected the proposal, arguing that if it were to send uranium out of the country, Iran would have to be compensated with the right to buy additional nuclear fuel from external sources.

24. In April 2012, the P-5+1 (the five permanent members of the United Nations Security Council plus Germany) and Iran held negotiations in Istanbul. Following the Istanbul meeting, a framework was tabled at the next round of talks between Iran and the P-5+1 (held in Baghdad on May 23, 2012). It was based on an idea of George Perkovich and Ariel Levite of the Carnegie Endowment for International Peace. According to one report, the Carnegie experts proposed a "nuclear traffic light" system in which "green" represents the approved category (i.e., civilian power plants, medical reactors, and academic research); the "red" represents forbidden activities (i.e., warhead design, procurement of bomb-making technologies, and warhead testing); while the "yellow" represents dual-use activities, around which firewalls would have to be carefully constructed. In the "yellow" category, some uranium enrichment (i.e., 5 percent or below) would be permitted, if verified. However, neutron triggers would be banned, except for those configured for oil exploration, but those would have to be imported, not developed in Iran. Moreover, this proposal depends on a great deal of transparency, which the Iranian government has yet to accommodate, and its implementation would require concessions from both sides, including a halt of work at Fordow, the site that has been identified as being used to enrich uranium above the 5 percent level.

25. More recently, however, China appears to be more sensitive to Western concerns about Iran's nuclear efforts. In the spring of 2012, China began to cut back its purchases of oil from Iran. While China experts doubt that this is a reflection of a new embrace by the government in Beijing of sanctions as an effective policy tool, there is disagreement on other possible Chinese motives. One school of thought suggests that China might have been trying to extract a better price for its crude-oil imports. With Japan and South Korea cutting Iranian oil purchases to avoid being affected by the new U.S. sanctions, which went into effect in July 2012, Iran is stockpiling oil in tankers in the Persian Gulf region. Another assessment, however, contends that China was trying to position itself in a positive light to get the Obama administration to waive its compliance with the provisions of the July 2012 sanctions regime. This new round of sanctions imposes penalties on countries that continue to import Iranian energy products. As China is Iran's largest market for energy products, it must either gain a waiver from the United States (which it did) or demonstrate a "significant reduction" in imports from Iran to avoid the U.S. sanctions. See Mark Landler and Steven Lee Myers, "U.S. Is Seeing Positive Signs from Chinese," *New York Times*, April 27, 2012.

In May 2012, it was reported that Iran was accepting Chinese renminbi and Indian rupees for its oil exports to those two nations. Tehran, in turn, is using the currencies on goods and services imported from China and India. During her 2012 trip to Beijing and New Delhi, Secretary of State Hillary Clinton urged both countries to further reduce their trade with Iran. Since the tightening of the sanctions against Iran, China and India have had to find alternative ways to finance their purchases. Initially, the nonbarter portions of China's transactions with Iran were settled through renminbi accounts at the Bank of China. Now, much of the money that is to be transferred to Iran from China is processed through Russian banks, which apparently take large commissions on the transactions. See Henny Sender, "U.S. Sanctions Force Iran to Accept Renminbi in Oil Trades with China," *Financial Times*, May 8, 2012.

26. A. Q. Khan is considered the father of Pakistan's nuclear weapons program. During the 1990s, intelligence emerged that Khan was discussing the sale of nuclear technology to other countries, such as North Korea. By early 2000, it became clear that Khan was at the center of an international nuclear-proliferation network. At the urging of the United States, the Pakistani government began investigating Khan. In early February 2004, Pakistan reported that Khan confessed that he had supplied Iran, Libya, and North Korea with designs and centrifuge technology to assist in nuclear weapons programs. Pakistani officials added that the government had not been complicit in his proliferation activities. Fearing a negative domestic reaction if the highly popular Khan remained under arrest, former Pakistan president Musharraf pardoned him on February 5, 2004.

27. Joby Warrick, "Smugglers Had Design for Advanced Warhead," *Washington Post*, June 15, 2008.

28. Founded in the early 1960s, MeK began as an urban guerrilla group opposed to the monarchy of Shah Mohammad Reza Pahlavi. While it participated in the 1979 revolution, MeK broke with Ayatollah Khomeini over ideology and in 1981 went underground. Currently based in Iraq and Europe, MeK seeks the overthrow of the theocratic government in Tehran, and for that reason, Iraq is seeking its expulsion. Since 1997, the U.S. State Department has designated MeK as a terrorist organization, although in September 2012 Secretary Clinton took MeK off the terrorist list. MeK was used by Saddam Hussein to attack the Iranian government during the Iran-Iraq war in the 1980s. Before the U.S. invasion of Iraq in 2003, MeK carried out many of its operations from Camp Ashaf, a U.S.-protected refugee compound along Iraq's eastern border with Iran where the majority of MeK members reside. In late 2011, the United Nations and the Iraqi government agreed to relocate the Ashraf Camp to a new facility in Iraq. However, because of conditions at Camp Liberty, many MeK members have been sent to Albania as political refugees. MeK's affiliated political organization, the National Council of Resistance in Iran (NCRI), has supplied vital intelligence on Iran's clandestine nuclear programs and other projects. It was the MeK that provided the West with information regarding the Natanz and Qom nuclear sites.

29. See Yaakov Katz, "Tehran Is Accelerating Nuclear Weapons Program, Says Iranian Opposition Report," *Jerusalem Post*, May 13, 2012.

30. In 2010, Turkey and Brazil proposed a new initiative designed to ease the crisis between Iran and the West over Iran's nuclear development programs. Spearheaded by Luiz Inacio Lula, Brazil's (then) president, and Turkey's prime minister, Recep Tayyip Erdogan, this agreement called for Iran to send abroad some of its low-enriched uranium stocks for reprocessing up to 20 percent for medical isotope use, in exchange for higher enriched uranium rods imported into Iran for use in medical research. This initiative was very similar to an earlier IAEA proposal to which Iran

had agreed and then reneged. This time, however, Iran was facing a new (fourth) round of sanctions, and many suspect that Iran agreed to the Brazilian-Turkish initiative as a way to forestall the imposition of the sanctions regime. However, the deal ultimately fell through because of Iran's intransigence about talks aimed at more than the stocks needed for the medical reactor.

31. The Russian plan included full supervision by the IAEA over Iran's nuclear activities, based on adherence to the NPT's Additional Protocol and Subsidiary Arrangement, which includes agreement to limit uranium enrichment activities inside of Iran to LEU up to 5 percent, a halt to the production and installation of new-generation centrifuges capable of enriching uranium to 20 percent or more, limiting enrichment sites to one disclosed location, and being more transparent about past technical ambiguities and questions concerning specific military sites.

32. See Hossein Mousavian, "There Is an Alternative to the Impasse Between Iran and the West," *Financial Times*, May 23, 2012. In the run-up to the 2013 presidential election in Iran, an escalating battle of wits has broken out between "conservative" clerics and their "pragmatic/technocrat" peers. Iran's then-president, Mahmoud Ahmadinejad was ineligible to run for reelection, so he tried to influence its outcome by bolstering a "conservative" candidate of his choosing. Rafsanjani, a cofounder of the Green Movement and a former president of Iran, worked against Ahmadinejad. He is joined in this endeavor by a "band" of influential Iranian clerics who supported Hassan Rouhani, who won the 2013 presidential election without a run-off vote.

33. The Islamic word "fatwa" means opinion. In a religious or legal context, a fatwa is a ruling on a point of Islamic law/religion given by a recognized authority on the matter. The authority needs to supply evidence from Islamic sources to support the opinions. In February 2010, Iran's Supreme Leader issued a religious edict against nuclear weapons and said that his country would never produce them. This is in sharp contrast to his earlier views, however, and according to an internal UN document, Ayatollah Sayyed Ali Khamenei embraced the idea of an Iranian nuclear weapon nearly two decades ago, in 1984, saying, essentially, that they were needed to protect Iran's revolutionary government. This document was obtained by the Washington, D.C.–based Institute for Science and International Security and is published on their website.

34. In 2012, differences were apparent among prominent Israeli politicians and military leaders over the efficacy of a strike against Iran's nuclear infrastructure. While some prominent politicians, the prime minister included, have contended that a military strike might be necessary to end Iran's nuclear progress, others, such as the former chief of Israeli intelligence and a former Mossad leader, believe that a preemptive Israeli strike against Iranian nuclear sites would probably accelerate, not end, Iran's nuclear ambitions. See Jodi Rudoren, "Defense Minister Adds to Israel's Recent Mix of Messages on Iran," *New York Times*, April 27, 2010.

35. The Arab Spring refers to the "revolutionary" events that sparked political changes in countries from Tunisia to Egypt and beyond in the Arab world. While the hope was that political reform and democratic elections would usher in a new

era of stability and prosperity in the Arab world, the reality is less clear, and further instability seems likely, including in one or two of the autocratic Arab Gulf states. Moreover, in Egypt, where elections have taken place, "Salafist" parties, which have a conservative agenda, have attracted support among the electorate.

36. Irregular warfare is defined by the Department of Defense as "a violent struggle among state and non-state actors for legitimacy and influence over the relevant populations. Irregular warfare favors indirect and asymmetric approaches, though it may employ the full range of military and other capabilities, in order to erode an adversary's power, influence, and will" (U.S. Department of Defense, *Irregular Warfare Joint Operating Concept*, version 1 [July 2007], 4).

37. Department of State, Office of the Coordinator for Counter-Terrorism, *Strategic Assessment: Country Reports for 2011*, July 31, 2012, http://www.state.gov/j/ct/rls/crt/2011/195540.htm. Also see Siobhan Gorman, "U.S. Sees Shift in Threat from Iran and al-Qaeda," *Wall Street Journal*, August 1, 2012.

38. The Taliban practice a form of Islam that descends from Deobandism, a reform movement originating in India, with the aim of rejuvenating Islamic society in a colonial state. Deobandism remained prevalent in Pakistan after its partition from India and has emerged as a principal influence on the Taliban movement, which implements Islamic law through a combination of Saudi Wahhabism (as a result of the proliferation of Saudi-financed "schools" in Afghanistan and Pakistan) and tribal custom. According to reports, Iran has allowed the Taliban to open an office in eastern Iran and has discussed the possibility of providing them with surface-to-air missiles. One analyst suggests that this is part of a broader Iranian effort to enhance the country's options for retaliation should it face an attack on its nuclear facilities. Another suggests that Iran and the Taliban have a common view of the United States as their main threat and on that basis, "Iran is willing to put aside ideology and . . . deeply held religious values . . . for their [*sic*] ultimate goal: accelerating the departure of U.S. forces from Afghanistan" (quoted in Maria Abi Habib, "Tehran Builds on Outreach to Taliban," *Wall Street Journal*, August 1, 2012).

39. Ibid.

40. An EMP is a burst of electromagnetic radiation that could disable critical infrastructure through the production of damaging current and voltage surges as a result of a nuclear detonation or other high-energy explosions or sudden fluctuations in the earth's magnetic field. EMP effects have long been recognized by nuclear weapons countries as a means of disabling and crippling an adversary's civilian and military systems and networks, and work is underway in many countries today to harness EMP technologies for defense and deterrence planning.

41. Scott D. Sagan and Kenneth N. Waltz, *The Spread of Nuclear Weapons: A Debate* (New York: Norton, 2002). See especially chapter 1, by Waltz ("More May Be Better"). See also Kenneth N. Waltz, "Why Iran Should Get the Bomb," *Foreign Affairs* (July–August 2012): 2–5; and Colin H. Kahl and Kenneth N. Waltz, "Iran and the Bomb," *Foreign Affairs* (September–October 2012): 157–62.

2. THE DETERRENCE DYNAMICS OF AN IRAN WITH NUCLEAR WEAPONS

1. Sectarianism in Kuwait has not been an issue thus far. The Shia in Kuwait are integral to the country's society, its leadership, and its merchant class. Constituting about 30 percent of the population, Shia Muslims have existed side by side with Sunni Muslims for years. As events in Bahrain have demonstrated, the politicization of Shia sectarianism could eventually affect Kuwait, where some neighborhoods are becoming more homogenously Shi'ite. Ironically, however, the fact is that many Kuwaitis of Arab origin are historically Shia while those of Persian origin are Sunni, the reverse of what is expected and of what is fomenting new concerns about Iran's perceived, growing influence in Kuwait. Kuwait's Shia population tends to follow Ayatollah Ali al-Sistani of Iraq and not Ayatollah Khamenei of Iran, which is a legacy partly of the Iran-Iraq War and Iran's animosity toward all Arabs and partly of the Gulf War, when all Kuwaitis suffered at the hands of Saddam Hussein. Fueling the potential for sectarian division in contemporary Kuwait is the Shia opposition to the prime minister, who is widely regarded as corrupt. If the Shia are made to feel separate and isolated in Kuwait, then the prospects for political activism will increase. Against this prospect, the Kuwaiti government has adopted a practical line, which is also reflected in Kuwait's regional security strategy, which condemned what it termed the Saudi invasion of Bahrain, and its "softer" line on Iran's nuclear policies. As a small country wedged between two powerful neighbors, Kuwait has a vested interest in keeping the peace and moderating polemical rhetoric.

2. Iran contests the UAE's claim to ownership of the Greater and Lesser Tunbs and Abu Musa, located near the Strait of Hormuz. Recently, tensions over the islands have escalated, and Iranian commanders threatened military action to assert Iran's control. In November 2012, reports emerged that Iran had set up a naval base near Bandar-e Lengeh. Together with Bandar-e Lengeh, the three contested islands are strategically vital to Iran's control of the Strait of Hormuz. Iran's sovereignty claims go back to 1971, when the United Kingdom ended its protectorate role in the Persian Gulf region. At that time, Iran under the shah agreed to administer the islets jointly with Sharjah (now a member of the UAE). Since then, however, Iran has sought to militarize all three islets and has encouraged Iranian migration to Abu Musa, the only islet that is inhabited, as a means of changing its demographic composition. Iran has built a military base and installed an airport on Abu Musa. The UAE has repeatedly called for international arbitration of the status of the islets but Iran continues to refuse.

3. The term "Finlandization" refers to a Cold War phenomenon. The strength of the Soviet Union relative to that of its neighbors in Europe and the Baltic states encouraged some smaller nations, particularly those who were not members of the NATO alliance, to ameliorate their foreign and security policies to support, or at least not to oppose, the interests of the Soviet Union.

4. Extended deterrence refers to one nation's willingness to use its nuclear forces on behalf of nonnuclear allies or coalition partners. It originated in the commitment

contained in article 5 of the North Atlantic Treaty and was extended to include Japan and South Korea as part of U.S. security treaty commitments to those two countries. In part, the rationale for extending deterrence coverage over allies was related to U.S. efforts to dissuade allies and other key security partners from crossing the nuclear threshold. Conceived as such, the extended deterrence concept was implemented to deter both nuclear and conventional attacks against allies, but its credibility was called into question when the United States itself became vulnerable to Soviet and, years later, Chinese nuclear attack.

5. Partly as a result of the anticipated withdrawal of U.S. forces from Afghanistan and in light of public opinion in the United States, which has grown weary of U.S. involvement in the wider Middle East, U.S. defense guidance has "pivoted" toward Asia. This also reflects growing concerns about China's military modernization efforts and worries about stability on the Korean Peninsula after Kim Jong-il's demise.

6. Iran's candidate is Ayatollah Mahmoud Hashemi Shahroudi, an Iraqi-born cleric who led Iran's judiciary for a decade. He is said to be sympathetic with militant Islam and at odds with the traditions of Najif, Iraq's Shi'ite spiritual center, which advocates keeping a "measured distance from politics." Intervention in political affairs is sanctioned only when it is deemed important. See Tim Arrango, "Iran Presses for Official to be Next Leader of Shi'ites," *New York Times*, May 12, 2012.

7. Amitai Etzioni, "Can a Nuclear-Armed Iran Be Deterred?" *Military Review* (May–June 2010): 120. In this article, Etzioni refers to a third category of decision-making behavior (in addition to "rational" and "irrational" behaviors), called "non-rational" behavior. The notion of "non-rational behavior" has been championed by the sociologist Talcott Parsons, and it contends that as people have been willing to kill and even die for their beliefs, a religious fanatic may believe that God commands him toward some specific action.

8. The Nuclear Posture Review was released by the Obama administration in April 2010. It describes the purposes of nuclear weapons as more or less limited to deterring nuclear weapons threats, moving away from previous policy that suggested nuclear weapons could be used to deter or respond to other threats from weapons of mass destruction, notably, the use of biological weapons. The Obama NPR also forswears the use of nuclear weapons against nonnuclear states in compliance with their nonproliferation obligations under international treaties. The Obama NPR can be found on the Department of Defense website at http://www.defense.gov/npr/.

9. The U.S. analyst Edward Luttwak is credited with coining the phrase "post-nuclear age," which he used to describe the shift in attention to advanced conventional weapons and a new emphasis on the concept of "conventional deterrence." Subsequently, the phrase was employed by former Soviet president Mikhail Gorbachev in 1989 to promote nuclear disarmament.

10. Keith B. Payne, *The Great American Gamble: Deterrence Theory and Practice from the Cold War to the Twenty-First Century*, (Fairfax, Va.: National Institute Press, 2008), 348.

11. Etzioni, "Can a Nuclear-Armed Iran Be Deterred?" 120.

12. This branch of Islam contends that Ali, Muhammad's cousin and brother-in-law, is the most important figure in Islam after the Prophet. Shia Muslims believe that Ali was the anointed successor to Muhammad but his rule was contested and after his murder his main rival claimed the caliphate. Ali's son, Hussein, was martyred in battle against the "illegitimate" caliph. Shia Muslims hold that the Twelfth Iman, Muhammad al-Mahdi, is still alive but disappeared and will return when the time is right. This belief is called "occultation."

13. Payne goes on to note that "such motivations and values are perplexing to Western observers. . . . Iranian President Ahmadinejad claims special knowledge underlying his confidence that the United States 'would not dare' to strike Iran, in part because, 'I believe in what God says,' to wit, 'God says that those who walk in the path of righteousness will be victorious. What reason can you have for believing that God will not keep this promise?'" (cited in Payne, *The Great American Gamble*, 349–50).

14. Emanuele Ottolenghi, executive director of the Transatlantic Institute in Brussels, quoted in Etzioni, "Can a Nuclear-Armed Iran Be Deterred?" 123.

15. Global Zero refers to a movement founded in December 2008 to abolish nuclear weapons across the globe. The initiative picked up steam in 2009, after President Barack Obama embraced its goals in a speech in Prague, Czech Republic. While many Global Zero proponents recognize that nuclear weapons will not be abolished any time soon, they maintain that over time, as nations commit to dramatic reductions in their nuclear stockpiles, the value of nuclear weapons to national security planning will diminish. The problem is that most nuclear weapons nations hold the opposite view and all, with the exception of the United States, are modernizing and upgrading their national nuclear inventories. For arguments justifying the embrace of Global Zero, see George P. Shultz, William J. Perry, Henry A. Kissinger, and Sam Nunn, "A World Free of Nuclear Weapons," *Wall Street Journal*, January 4, 2007; and the Campaign for a Nuclear Free World, http://nuclearweaponsfree.org/aboutus/. For President Obama's 2009 Prague speech on the goal of eliminating nuclear weapons, see http://www.whitehouse.gov/the_press_office/Remarks-By-President-Barack-Obama-In-Prague-As-Delivered.

16. Andrew F. Krepinevich and Robert C. Martinage, *Dissuasion Strategy* (Center for Strategy and Budgetary Assessments, 2008), http://www.csbaonline.org/publications/2008/05/dissuasion-strategy/, xi: "What might appear 'irrational' from the perspective of American observers could be entirely logical when the target's culture, religious beliefs, political concerns, personal jealousies, life experiences, and other psychological factors (e.g., the degree of stress to which the target is exposed) are taken into consideration."

17. A 2012 Congressional Research Service report concluded: "Department of Defense and other assessments indicate that sanctions have not stopped Iran from building up its conventional military and missile capabilities, in large part with indigenous skills. However, sanctions may be slowing Iran's nuclear program somewhat by preventing Iran from attaining needed technology from foreign sources. . . .

Despite the imposition of what many now consider 'crippling' sanctions, some in Congress believe that economic pressure on Iran needs to increase further and faster" to stop Iran's nuclear programs. However, both Russia and China object to the imposition of harsher sanctions, and, despite their support for previous UNSC sanctions, they are unlikely to support additional action in this regard. China is worried about its future access to Iranian energy products, and Russia appears to be more concerned about retaining Iran as an arms market and enhancing its influence with the country at the expense of the West. See Kenneth Katzman, *Iran Sanctions*, Congressional Research Service, a Report for the U.S. Congress, October 15, 2012, executive summary. Also, as reported by the *Washington Post*, Turkey is proving crucial to keeping Iran's economy afloat. "Turkey relies heavily on Iranian oil and was granted an exemption to new U.S. sanctions in return for voluntary efforts to reduce its imports from Iran" (James Ball, "Sanctions Hurting Iran's Oil Exports, New Data Show," *Washington Post*, October 17, 2012). However, few analysts believe that Turkey will cut off all imports from Iran, and it is proving willing to aid Iran's economy in other ways. "Iran is increasingly sourcing its imports through Turkey as other trading partners become unwilling to deal." Iran also imports goods and food from Turkey. As a result, according to one U.S. economist, "the broad picture is that sanctions against Iran are proving effective, but not decisive. . . . The government has some maneuverability to shift the pain around and make sure that the people who are more likely to support it suffer less, while people who have both the means to withstand the sanctions and are less supportive of the government will bear a greater portion of the pain." According to Djavad Salehi-Isfahani of Virginia Tech, "This is not the equivalent of the one good example of sanctions having an effect, which was South Africa, where the majority of the population, even if they suffered, identified with the cause" (quoted in Ball, "Sanctions Hurting Iran's Oil Exports").

18. Ball, "Sanctions Hurting Iran's Oil Exports." For example, in March 2010, Pakistan and Iran signed an agreement for construction of a gas pipeline valued at $7.4 billion. Despite continued opposition by the United States, Pakistan says it will move forward with the Iranian pipeline, which is expected to export 8.7 billion cubic meters of Iranian natural gas per year to Pakistan beginning in 2014 or 2015.

19. Jo Becker, "Web of Shell Companies Veils Trade by Iran's Ships," *New York Times*, June 8, 2010. The Proliferation Security Initiative was launched by the George W. Bush administration on May 31, 2003. Its purpose was to stop shipments of weapons of mass destruction, their delivery systems, and related materials. Stemming from the 2002 National Strategy to Combat Weapons of Mass Destruction, the PSI was also created to support and help implement United Nations Security Council Resolution 1540, which calls on all states to prevent WMD trafficking.

20. Geoffrey Kemp, "Iran's Nuclear Options," in *Iran's Nuclear Options: Issues and Analysis* (The Nixon Center, 2001), http://www.iranwatch.org/privateviews/NIXON/perspex-nixon-irannuclearweaponsoptions-0101.pdf.

21. The full text of Ahmadinejad's statement can be found at http://www.globalsecurity.org/wmd/library/news/iran/2005/iran-050919-irano2.htm. Access to

civilian nuclear technologies is explicitly contingent upon NPT member-state compliance with the IAEA safeguards and verification regimes. As an NPT member, North Korea developed nuclear weapons and then abrogated its treaty responsibilities when it crossed the nuclear threshold. However, most NPT members have foregone nuclear weapon programs as a precondition for gaining access to peaceful nuclear energy technologies under international safeguards and inspections.

22. India seeks to deter a nuclear-armed China while Pakistan, which cannot match India in conventional forces, views nuclear weapons as a deterrent to invasion by India.

23. In his seminal work *A World Restored: Europe After Napoleon: The Politics of Conservatism in a Revolutionary Age* (New York: Grosset and Dunlap, 1964), Henry Kissinger explores the interactions of a "revolutionary" power (Napoleonic France) and status quo powers, notably England and Austria, while commenting on the mechanisms for pursuing peace and stability. He writes, "The foundation of a stable order is the *relative* security—and therefore the *relative* insecurity—of its members. Its stability reflects, not the absence of unsatisfied claims, but the absence of a grievance of such magnitude that redress will be sought in overturning the settlement rather than through an adjustment within its framework. An order whose structure is accepted by all major powers is 'legitimate.' An order containing a power, which considers its structure oppressive is 'revolutionary.' The security of a domestic order resides in the preponderant power of authority, that of an international order in the balance of forces and in its expression, the equilibrium. . . . The major problem of an international settlement, then, is so to relate the claims of legitimacy to the requirements of security that no power will express its dissatisfaction on a revolutionary policy, and so to arrange the balance of forces as to deter aggression produced by causes other than the conditions of the settlement" (144–47). The book is based on Dr. Kissinger's dissertation, completed at Harvard University in 1964.

24. It is important to recall that the Soviets withdrew their missiles from Cuba, though in exchange for American agreement to dismantle U.S. Jupiter missiles in Turkey. A book describing the Cuban missile crisis asserts that "Khrushchev had done his best to disguise the fact that the Soviet Union was the weaker superpower with spectacular public relations feats. He had launched the first man into space and tested the world's largest bomb. 'America recognizes only strength,' he told his associates. His son Sergei was taken aback when Khrushchev boasted that the Soviet Union was churning out intercontinental rockets 'like sausages.' A missile engineer himself, he knew this was not true. 'How can you say that when we only have two or three?' Sergei protested. 'The important thing is to make the Americans believe that,' his father replied. 'That way, we can prevent an attack.' Sergei concluded that Soviet policy was based on threatening the United States with 'weapons we didn't have'" (quoted in Michael Dobbs, *One Minute to Midnight: Kennedy, Khrushchev, and Castro on the Brink of Nuclear War* [New York: Knopf, 2008], 37).

25. "Kremlin Bans Sale of S-300 Missiles to Iran," *BBC News*, September 22, 2010, http://www.bbc.co.uk/news/world-europe-11388680.

26. "Iran: We've Produced Domestic Version of S-300 Anti-Aircraft Missiles," *Haaretz.com*, September 30, 2011, http://www.haaretz.com/news/middle-east/iran-we-ve-produced-domestic-version-of-s-300-anti-aircraft-missiles-1.387387.

27. The swarm tactic refers to the use of groups of small speedboats to ambush much larger craft such as merchant convoys or warships transiting important shipping corridors. Iran has employed swarm tactics from both coastal and off-shore staging areas. They have been used with great effect to test enemy responses, as was the case in early January 2008 against U.S. Navy platforms transiting the Strait of Hormuz. See Jonathan Marcus, "Is a US-Iran Maritime Clash Inevitable?" *BBC News*, January 10, 2012, http://www.bbc.co.uk/news/world-middle-east-16485842; Bryan Gold, "Four Reasons Why the United States Should Not Attack Iran: Part 1," February 13, 2012, http://americansecurityproject.org/blog/2012/four-reasons-why-the-united-states-should-not-attack-iran-part-1/; and Fariborz Haghshenass, "Iran's Asymmetric Naval Warfare," The Washington Institute for Near East Policy, Policy Focus Paper No. 87 (September 2008).

28. Paul Bracken has written about this problem. According to Bracken, "the dawning of a second nuclear age overturns fundamental strategic assumptions about both the techno-military balance and preserving Western dominance in other areas" (Bracken, "The Second Nuclear Age," *Foreign Affairs* 79, no. 1 [January/February 2000]: 147).

29. Bracken, "The Second Nuclear Age," 155–56.

30. Paul Bracken, *The Second Nuclear Age: Strategy, Danger, and the New Power Politics* (New York: Times Books/Holt, 2012), 8.

31. Amatzia Baram, "Deterrence Lessons from Iraq: Rationality Is Not the Only Key to Containment," *Foreign Affairs* 91, no. 4 (July/August 2012): 77.

32. Rooted in the eighteenth-century thought of Saudi religious ideologue Mohammad bin Abd-al Wahhab, Salafist, Taliban, and Deobandist ideologies all share a politico-religious philosophy that is characterized by violence and intolerance. Al Wahhab's interpretation of Islam rejects all innovation and reduces the religion to absolute monotheism, i.e., restricting worship to Allah alone. Under this interpretation, the notion of "lesser jihad" (*jihad kabeer*, or armed struggle) took precedence over "greater jihad" (*jihad akbar*, or inner spiritual struggle). Deobandism migrated to India and Pakistan thanks to the teachings of Syed Ahmed. By the late 1970s Deobandi influences had infiltrated Pakistan's military and intelligence services.

33. The Baluch are an Iranian ethnic group found in southern parts of Afghanistan, western Pakistan, the Federally Administered Tribal Areas (FATA) to the north, and southeastern Iran. Sistan or Baluchestan is the largest province in Iran and is home to Iran's Baluchi Sunni minority. In Afghanistan, Baluchistan covers a vast area in Nimroz, south of Helmand, Kandahar, and southwest of Farah province. Most likely, the Baluch are an off-shoot of the Kurds. Baluchistan is also the largest province in Pakistan and a major supplier of natural gas. It is also the site of Pakistan's space-launch center and the Sonmiani missile-test range.

34. The Pashtun people are an eastern Iranian ethno-linguistic group with tribes in Afghanistan, Pakistan, and Iran and a sizable community in India and the Persian Gulf states, where they work as migrant laborers. They are the main ethnic contingent of the Taliban, and they practice Pashtunwali, which embraces a traditional code of conduct and honor.

35. Kemp, "Iran's Nuclear Options."

36. The Kargil crisis was a conventional conflict between India and Pakistan that occurred between May and July 1999 in the Kargil district of Kashmir and elsewhere along the Line of Control (LOC) that divides Indian- and Pakistani-administered Kashmir. The conflict began when Pakistan's forces infiltrated into Indian-controlled territory in the Kargil area. Pakistan thought that its nascent nuclear capability would prevent any major move by India, especially across the international border into Pakistan. In addition, Pakistan believed that the government in India was weak and unstable and consequently would be unable to marshal a firm response. It was only after international intervention and pressure on Pakistan (particularly by the United States), together with the threat of Pakistan's international isolation, that the embattled government of Prime Minister Nawaz Sharif backed down. Sharif was later removed from power in an October 1999 coup d'état led by the army chief and, Pervez Musharraf, who later became president of Pakistan and who is believed to be largely responsible for the planning and initiation of the Kargil campaign.

37. C. Wergin and H. Strausberg, "Iran plant Baue einer Raketenstellung in Venezuela," *Die Welt* (Hamburg), November 25, 2010.

38. Quoted in Ephram Kam, *A Nuclear Iran: What Does It Mean and What Can Be Done?* Memorandum No. 88. (Tel Aviv: Institute for National Security Studies, 2007), 81.

39. The "insider problem" is discussed in Shahram Chubin, *Iran's Nuclear Ambitions* (Washington, D.C.: Carnegie Endowment for International Peace, 2006), 48–63. Iran's Revolutionary Guards Corps (IRGC) was founded in 1979 by Ayatollah Ruhollah Khomeini, the father of Iran's Islamic Revolution. Originally, the IRGC was intended to monitor the ideological commitment of the remnants of the shah's Imperial Army and to disarm non-Islamic members of the Revolution. From its operations in the War of the Cities (against Iraq, 1980–1988), the IRGC's fame and stature grew, having "established a reputation as an efficient military force, and political influence soon followed." According to one assessment, "The nature of the Islamic Republic is changing from a system governed by the Shi'ite clergy and guarded by the IRGC into a regime dominated by the military (Ali Alfoneh, "How Intertwined Are the Revolutionary Guards in Iran's Economy?" American Enterprise Institute for Public Policy, paper no. 3 [October 2007]). The involvement of the IRGC in the Iranian economy started after the Iran-Iraq war. Battered by almost ten years of war and revolution, reconstruction of the economy was Iran's main priority, and the IRGC had the manpower to engage in reconstruction activities. Over the next two decades, the IRGC became an economic force in Iran, dominating the energy, construction, telecommunications, auto-making, and banking and finance sectors. See Alireza

Nader, "The Revolutionary Guards," in *The Iran Primer* (United States Institute of Peace, 2011), http://iranprimer.usip.org/resource/revolutionary-guards; and Greg Bruno and Jayshree Bajoria, "Iran's Revolutionary Guards," Council on Foreign Relations, updated October 12, 2011, http://www.cfr.org/iran/irans-revolutionary-guards/p14324.

40. Dan Strumpf, "Iran Sanctions Are Having a Quicker Impact Than Expected," MarketBeat, *WallStreetJournal.com*, March 7, 2012, http://blogs.wsj.com/marketbeat/2012/03/07/iran-sanctions-are-having-a-quicker-impact-than-expected/.

41. Ali Larijani is one of five brothers, two of whom sit at the top of different branches of Iran's government. Ali Larijani is the speaker of the Majles, while his brother Sadegh is the chief of the Judiciary. Coming from a clerical family, Ali Larijani remains close to the Supreme Leader, but differences have emerged over Larijani's failure to condemn the Green Movement. During the 2012 parliamentary elections, Larijani challenged Ahmadinejad's candidate in Qom, Mojtaba Zonnouri, a cleric who also served for thirty years in the IRGC, and who had the backing of Ayatollah Mohammad Taqi Mesbah-Yazdi, the cleric who has suggested that Iran should develop nuclear weapons. By all accounts, Mesbah-Yazdi aspires to succeed Ayatollah Khamenei as Supreme Leader, and his views are more conservative and hardline. Even he, however, parted ways with Ahmadinejad, suggesting that he was "out of control" and not willing to work with Iran's clerical community.

42. Chubin, *Iran's Nuclear Ambitions*, 28.

43. The so-called China model refers to an alternative framework for building the Iranian economy. As such, it is said to incorporate elements of Western economic liberalism within an autocratic political context in which limited "freedoms" are accorded to individuals while the government still controls the parameters of how far and to what extent such freedoms are tolerated to ensure that they do not deviate too widely from Sharia law and customs.

44. Ali Alfoneh, "Ahmadinejad Versus the Technocrats," American Enterprise for Public Policy, Paper no. 4 (May 2008). According to Alfoneh, Ayatollah Mohammad-Reza Mahdavi Kani, the general secretary of the Society of Combatant Clergy and a member of the Assembly of Experts, harshly rebuked Ahmadinejad for his April 16, 2008, speech in Qom during which the president accused foreign hands and Iran's internal enemies of engaging in a conspiracy against the government and plotting to raise inflation to 80 percent. Ayatollah Kani also was reported to say, "We are not allowed to blame others for the ills of society . . . and (Ahmadinejad) should not expect praise from our side." Alfoneh reports that this opened the floodgates for others to criticize the government and the president. More recently, Iran's political life has been disrupted by accusations and countercharges over responsibility for the country's double-digit inflation, high unemployment rate, and the devaluation of the rial, Iran's national currency. While President Ahmadinejad has sought to blame members of the Larijani and Rafsanjani families, they have united in charging Ahmadinejad with responsibility for Iran's economic upheavals. Supporting them are many of the Shi'ite clerics and military leaders who had once endorsed

Ahmadinejad. This increasingly acerbic rivalry is playing out in public and will ultimately help determine the extent to which Ahmadinejad retains influence after he steps down from the presidency. See, for example, Tomas Erdbrink, "Iran's Political Infighting Erupts in Full View," *New York Times*, October 23, 2012.

45. On March 8, 2011, former Iranian president Akbar Hashemi Rafsanjani was replaced as head of the Assembly of Experts, the committee charged with electing the Supreme Leader, supervising his activities, and removing him from office if he is deemed incapable of fulfilling his duties. See "Iran: Rafsanjani Ouster a Defeat for Regime's Anti-Ahmadinejad Camp," *Time*, March 8, 2011, http://globalspin.blogs.time.com/2011/03/08/iran-rafsanjani-ouster-a-defeat-for-regimes-anti-ahmadinejad-camp/#ixzz1fmt1xnbD. In September 2012, Rafsanjani's daughter, Faezeh Hashemi who has been politically active, was arrested, allegedly for inciting antistate propaganda. By most accounts, however, this is a blatant attempt by "conservative" factions to undermine the Green Movement and Rafsanjani's aspirations to return to politics.

46. As it is often described, the essence of the so-called grand bargain would involve an end to sanctions, normalization of relations, and the provision of a negative security guarantee by the United States (not to attack Iran) in exchange for an end to Iran's nuclear programs and its support to terrorism. It is also important to note that Rafsanjani's influence has waned as a result of the events surrounding Iran's 2009 election and his removal in 2011 as head of the Assembly of Experts (see note 45).

47. The Proliferation Security Initiative is a set of activities, not a formal, treaty-based organization, based on partnerships established by participating nations, of which there are fifteen core countries, including the United States, Russia, Japan, France, Germany, and the United Kingdom, and seventy-one other nations that have agreed to cooperate on an ad hoc basis. See also note 19. The Global Initiative to Combat Nuclear Terrorism is a multilateral partnership that aims to strengthen the global capacity to prevent, detect, and respond to nuclear terrorism. In 2006, it was established by the United States and Russia and has now expanded to include eighty-two nations and four observing parties. To gain membership, nations must endorse its nonbinding Statement of Principles, which includes several goals: enhancing the security of civilian nuclear facilities; improving the ability to detect nuclear and other radioactive materials and substances to prevent illicit trafficking; improving partners' capabilities to regulate unlawfully held nuclear and radioactive materials; preventing the provision of safe havens to terrorists; ensuring adequate legal frameworks are implemented to hold accountable those who are illegally seeking these materials; improving response, mitigation, and investigation capabilities; and promoting the sharing of information among parties. The GICNT has completed a number of activities, including workshops, practical exercises, and information sharing, including the use of the Global Initiative Information Portal, an unclassified, secure website that enables partner nations to communicate and collaborate in one centralized location.

48. Unconventional Warfare (UW) is defined by the U.S. Special Operations Command (SOCOM) as "activities conducted to enable a resistance movement or insurgency to coerce, disrupt, or overthrow a government or occupying power by operating through or with an underground, auxiliary and guerrilla force in a denied area." UW is not only about overthrowing governments, however. It is about tribal initiatives, such as those that have been successful in Iraq and are now underway in Afghanistan. It is about counterterrorism planning and security cooperation and the training and equipping of partners. It even may involve antidrug operations and planning to interdict illicit trafficking and to counter the influence of criminal organizations. UW by its nature involves long-term planning, and intelligence-supported operations. See Dave Maxwell, "Why Does Special Forces Train and Educate for Unconventional Warfare?" *Small Wars Journal*, April 25, 2010, http://smallwarsjournal.com/jrnl/art/why-does-special-forces-train-and-educate-for-unconventional-warfare.

3. CONSIDERATIONS INFLUENCING IRAN'S NUCLEAR EMERGENCE

1. The U.S.-Indian civilian nuclear-power deal has been controversial from its inception in July 2005, both in the United States and India and among members of the broader international community. There are many who believe that this deal sets a bad precedent for global nonproliferation efforts because India still refuses to sign the Non-Proliferation Treaty unless the treaty is significantly revamped. Second, elites in India are concerned about the effect that this deal will have on Indian efforts to modernize India's strategic nuclear force. According to reports surrounding the 2008 Nuclear Suppliers Group approval of the accord, India has committed to allowing IAEA inspections of its civilian programs to show the world that it is not using civilian nuclear technologies for its nuclear weapons-modernization program. Third, concerns about another round of nuclear testing also are providing a basis for opposing this deal. Some proliferation-security analysts fear that India may be emboldened to undertake new nuclear tests once this deal has provided India with the uranium stores it needs to supply its existing reactors and to fuel new sources of energy supply (i.e., new-generation civil nuclear reactors). Against that prospect, analysts worry that other countries, especially Pakistan but also China, will follow suit. This could, it is hypothesized, affect a nuclear-threshold country such as Iran and send the message that if you are important to the global economy, as India and Iran now see themselves, then the world will acquiesce in nuclear activities that pave the way to weapons status. For an overview of this agreement, see Jayshree Bajoria, "The U.S.-India Nuclear Deal," Council on Foreign Relations, November 5, 2011, http://www.cfr.org/india/us-india-nuclear-deal/p9663.

2. This idea was argued in Noah Feldman, "Islam, Terror, and the Second Nuclear Age," *New York Times*, October 29, 2006, http://www.newyorktimes.com/2006/10/29/magazine/29islam.html. However, there are those who disagree with this thesis and point out that prominent Islamic scholars have issued fatwas against the use of nuclear weapons in the name of Islam. In a *New Yorker* article, Lawrence Wright,

author of *The Looming Tower: Al-Qaeda and the Road to 9/11* (New York: Knopf, 2006), reports on the rebellion within radical Islamist circles over the use of terrorist tactics to promote jihad against the West. According to Wright, the chief architect of this controversy is none other than Dr. Fadl (also known as Sayyid Imam al-Sharif), who was founder of the Egyptian terrorist group Al Jihad, a mentor to both Osama bin Laden and Ayman Al-Zawahiri, and a source of inspiration for al-Qaeda's sophistry. The murder of civilians is at the root of much of the controversy, and this extends to Sunni-on-Shia violence as well. WMD use, from the perspective of the reformers, could only be seen as "indiscriminate murder" and therefore illegal under Islamic law, which, in any case, Fadl argues, restricts the possibility of holy war to extremely rare circumstances. See Lawrence Wright, "The Rebellion Within: An al-Qaeda Mastermind Questions Terrorism," *The New Yorker*, June 2, 2008, 37–53.

3. Colin Freeman and Philip Sherwell, "Iranian Fatwa Approves Use of Nuclear Weapons," *Telegraph*, February 18, 2006, http://www.telegraph.co.uk/news/world news/middleeast/iran/1510900/Iranian-fatwa-approves-use-of-nuclear-weapons .html. The fatwa issued by Mohsen Gharavian contradicts the fatwa issued in September 2004 by Supreme Leader Ayatollah Khamenei at Friday prayers, which stated that the production, stockpiling, and use of nuclear weapons are forbidden under Islam and that the Islamic Republic of Iran shall never acquire these weapons. In June 2008 Ayatollah Khamenei asserted that "no wise nation" would pursue nuclear weapons but also stated that Iran would continue to develop a nuclear program for peaceful purposes. However, it should be noted that fatwas are issued in response to particular circumstances and can be adjusted to changing situations. For example, the Supreme Leader has in the past altered his stance on several issues, including taxes, women's right to vote, and military conscription. Consequently, Ayatollah Khamenei could modify his fatwa on nuclear weapons should conditions dictate a change.

4. Proposed by President Dwight D. Eisenhower in a speech to the United Nations General Assembly on December 8, 1953, Atoms for Peace was established with the objective of using nuclear science to support medicine, energy development, and other peaceful applications. In this address, Eisenhower proposed that peaceful nuclear technology would be made available to all nations under appropriate international controls. The speech had two major focal points: constraining the proliferation of nuclear weapons and using nuclear research to benefit all people. Atoms for Peace led directly to the creation of the International Atomic Energy Agency in 1957, numerous multilateral nonproliferation agreements, the creation of the civilian nuclear-power industry, and a flowering of scientific innovation that included advances in nuclear medicine and fundamentally new perspectives about the nature of matter and energy that have led to dozens of Nobel Prizes. On the occasion of the fiftieth anniversary of President Eisenhower's Atoms for Peace address, the Institute for Foreign Policy Analysis organized a conference for the U.S. Department of Energy. The conference report, *Atoms for Peace Plus 50*, contains extensive information not only about the Atoms for Peace address but also its impact on

subsequent nuclear science and technology. It can be downloaded at http://www
.ifpa.org/pdf/DOEFlet.pdf.

5. See chap. 1, notes 16–17.

6. Iran has the largest and most diverse ballistic-missile arsenal in the Middle
East. Most were acquired from foreign sources (North Korea, China, and Russia),
although Iran also has an indigenous capability, based on technologies acquired
from abroad. The U.S. Department of Defense (DOD) states that the Shahab-3 or
Meteor-3 medium-range liquid-fueled ballistic missile (estimated range of 800–1200
miles and 760–1100 kg payload) is based on North Korea's No Dong missile, but has
also benefited from Russian technologies. With this capability, Iran is able to target
Israel, Turkey, and Saudi Arabia. DOD reports that a Shahab-3 variant with a longer range capability (1,200–1,500 miles) may also have been deployed, and there is
much speculation about Iran's development of an even longer-range ballistic missile,
which is projected to have intercontinental capability. U.S. officials think that Iran
may field such a longer-range ICBM sometime between 2015 and 2020. In addition
to the ICBM, Iran is working on a solid-fueled medium-range missile, called the
Sajjil, and a space-launch vehicle program using Safir rockets. A follow-on vehicle,
called the Simorgh, was unveiled in 2010, and with the Safir rockets, Iran has demonstrated sophistication in multistate propulsion and separation technologies. See
Alexander Wilner and Anthony H. Cordesman, *Iran and the Gulf Military Balance*
(Center for Strategic and International Studies, 2011), http://csis.org/files/publication
/111128_Iran_Gulf_Military_Bal.pdf, 74–75,. A newer system, referred to as the Sha-
hab-4, is subject of much speculation. Media and intelligence reports on the Sha-
hab-4 have frequently been contradictory and do not furnish definitive details about
this missile, leading some to speculate that it does not actually exist. Others, however,
speculate that it is a derivative of North Korea's No Dong and Taepodong missiles,
with three stages and therefore a longer range (up to 1660 miles) and using Russian
SS-4 rocket propulsion. See "Shahab-4," *MissileThreat.com*, the Claremont Institute,
2011, http://missilethreat.com/missiles/shahab-4/.

7. Quoted in Ephram Kam, *A Nuclear Iran: What Does It Mean and What Can
Be Done?* Memorandum No. 88. (Tel Aviv: Institute for National Security Studies,
2007), 79.

8. Over the past decade, Iran has hidden a large part of its nuclear development
underground and has developed a complex network of tunnels to facilitate access to
specific facilities. In doing so, Iran not only has been able to obscure the extent and
nature of its nuclear infrastructure but also is creating a means of protecting these
facilities from a conventional and perhaps even a nuclear attack (depending on warhead size, accuracy, altitude of burst, and the physical conditions of the tunnels and
their locations.) See William J. Broad, "Iran Shielding Its Nuclear Efforts in Maze of
Tunnels," *New York Times*, January 6, 2010.

9. See Emile Hokayem, "Iran and Hezbollah: The Balance of Power Shifts in Lebanon," in *The Iran Primer* (United States Institute of Peace, 2011), http://iranprimer.usip
.org/blog/2011/jan/27/iran-and-hezbollah-balance-power-shifts-lebanon; and Nimrod

Raphaeli, "The Iranian Roots of Hezbollah," Middle East Media Research Institute report no. 448 (June 17, 2008), http://www.memri.org/report/en/0/0/0/0/0/88/2712.htm.

10. Greg Bruno and Jayshree Bajoria, "Iran's Revolutionary Guards," Council on Foreign Relations, October 12, 2011, http://www.cfr.org/iran/irans-revolutionary-guards/p14324.

11. Jay Davis, former director of the Defense Threat Reduction Agency (DTRA) has observed, "As a technologist and an operator, I keep a standing mental list of the five hardest technical problems of which I am aware. Nuclear forensics and biological forensics each make that list. There is no assurance that we can work backward from the effects of these horrific events to uniquely determine a perpetrator. . . . What I suggest is a process that can lead us to knowledge of what is possible, and a way to structure our work so that we will have the largest possible credibility in attempting this daunting task" (Jay Davis, "The Attribution of WMD Events," ANSER Institute for Homeland Security, April 2003). A 2010 study by the Committee on Nuclear Forensics, under the auspices of the National Research Council, stated that the United States has demonstrated a nuclear forensics capability in both actual incidents as well as in simulations/exercises of required actions after a nuclear detonation. However, it identified several concerns that if not rectified will result in a deterioration of such capabilities. Recommended actions include streamlining the organizational structure of the Department of Homeland Security, which is responsible for coordinating U.S. nuclear forensics activities; developing and issuing a coordinated and integrated implementation plan for sustaining and improving the program's capabilities; implementing a plan to develop/maintain the needed nuclear forensics workforce; and adapting nuclear forensics to the challenges of real-life situations, for example, by conducting more realistic exercises. See Committee on Nuclear Forensics, *Nuclear Forensics: A Capability at Risk*, (Washington, D.C., National Research Council, 2010).

12. Claude Salhani, "Iran Nearing Nuclear Weapons Capability," *Middle East Times*, June 3, 2008, http://www.ncr-iran.org/en/news/nuclear/4842-iran-nearing-nuclear-weapons-capability; and Bret Stephens, "The NIE Fantasy," *Wall Street Journal*, December 11, 2007: http://www.online.wsj.com/article/SB119734115058520384.html. Speculation about personalities and their roles in Iran's nuclear programs has become a cottage industry in Israel and the United States. The Israelis contend that they have been able to identify key officials connected to Iran's nuclear programs. Information about Iranian scientists and officials involved in the country's nuclear programs has also been made available to the West by the Mujahedin-e Khalq of Iran, or MeK, a group that was taken off the U.S. State Department's Terrorist Watch List in 2012. Rumors also abound that MeK members, trained and financed by Israel, have been involved in the assassination of Iranian nuclear scientists and engineers. It was clear from interviews in Israel that the Israelis have registered success in this area and that they might be responsible for punitive actions against key individuals. One such person was identified as Moshen Fakrizadeh, the military official in charge

of Iran's nuclear efforts. A senior officer in the IRGC, who for a time was sidelined but is back at work on the development of a nuclear trigger, among other things, Fakrizadeh has been compared to Robert Oppenheimer, who had chief scientific responsibility for the Manhattan Project, the nuclear program that produced the first atomic weapon. A colleague, Fereydoun Abbasi-Davani, heads Iran's Atomic Energy Organization, and, like Fakrizadeh, he appears to be instrumental in forwarding Iran's nuclear development.

13. Thomas Schelling, quoted in Thomas Barnett, "Nuclear Ringtone: The Lasting Peace Provided by Nuclear Weapons," *Scripps News*, September 7, 2007, http://www.scrippsnews.com/node/26648.

14. Ibid.

15. Kenneth N. Waltz, "Why Iran Should Get the Bomb," *Foreign Affairs* 91, no. 4 (July/August 2012): 2–5.

16. Bret Stephens, "Iran Cannot Be Contained," *Commentary* (July/August 2010): 3, http://www.commentarymagazine.com/article/iran-cannot-be-contained/.

17. Stephens, "Iran Cannot Be Contained," 4.

18. To borrow from the lexicon of suicide terrorism, this would be more or less akin to what is termed the "lone-wolf" phenomenon.

19. John Agresto, former president of St. John's College in New Mexico, who went on to observe: "We don't understand either killing for God or dying for God. But others do" (quoted in Keith B. Payne, *The Great American Gamble: Deterrence Theory and Practice from the Cold War to the Twenty-First Century* [Fairfax, Va.: National Institute Press, 2008], 351). Agresto served in Iraq in 2003 and 2004 as the senior advisor for the Coalition's Provisional Authority to the Iraqi minister of education.

20. Of course, as suggested by the Carnegie expert Karim Sadjadpour, Ahmadinejad's ties to the IRGC, while important, are not nearly as significant as those of the Supreme Leader. Indeed, according to Sadjadpour, while Khamenei's clerical credentials have always been suspect, his ties to the military are strong, and that is his power base, along with his relationship to Iran's other power institutions, including the judiciary and the Guardian Council. See Karim Sadjadpour, *Reading Khamenei: The World View of Iran's Most Powerful Leader* (Washington D.C.: Carnegie Endowment for International Peace, 2009), v.

4. NUCLEAR WEAPONS OPERATIONALIZATION: WHAT TYPE OF NUCLEAR FORCE?

1. The Strait of Hormuz, through which approximately 17 percent of the world's oil passes, separates the Persian Gulf from the Gulf of Oman and the Indian Ocean. At its narrowest point, it is twenty-one miles (i.e., thirty-four kilometers) wide. Following a takeover of three small (UAE) islands in the Gulf in 1971, Iran positioned itself to control the traffic in and out of the Gulf, and since 2006 Iranian leaders have overtly referenced Iran's capacity to close the strait to commercial traffic. In that same year, Iran conducted military maneuvers in the strait to highlight its ability to do just that. Later, on the seventeenth anniversary of Ayatollah Khomeini's death, his successor,

Ayatollah Khamenei, proclaimed, "If the Americans make a wrong move toward Iran, the shipment of energy will definitely face danger, and the Americans would not be able to protect energy supplies in the region" (quoted in Simon Henderson, "Facing Iran's Challenge: Safeguarding Oil Exports from the Persian Gulf," Washington Institute for Near East Studies, July 6, 2007, http://www.washingtoninstitute .org/policy-analysis/view/facing-irans-challenge-safeguarding-oil-exports-from-the-persian-gulf. More recently, in December 2011 and January 2012, Iran threatened to close the Strait of Hormuz in response to sanctions imposed on Tehran by the United States and the European Union, respectively (see chap. 1, note 8). To coincide with this threat, Iran conducted military exercises in international waters near the Strait of Hormuz. Even though many analysts think Iran would suffer economically if it sealed off the Strait of Hormuz, military experts say Tehran could attempt to do so by mining the Strait, and by using air strikes, sabotage, and swarming tactics. Both Defense Department and the U.S. Navy officials have stated that American warships and other U.S. assets would be used to prevent an Iranian blockade of the strait if necessary.

2. Richard L. Garwin, "When Could Iran Deliver a Nuclear Weapon," *Bulletin of the Atomic Scientists,* January 17, 2008, http://www.thebulletin.org/web-edition/ features/when-could-iran-deliver-a-nuclear-weapon. "Counterforce refers to the targeting of military forces, bases, and their infrastructure by an opposing force. Ideally, a counterforce strike would diminish so-called collateral damage and civilian casualties. In contrast, a countervalue strike would be optimized to target civilian casualties and in some instances to destroy specific socioeconomic entities, such as industrial sectors and cultural sites. During the Cold War, counterforce targeting was often equated with efforts to develop a first-strike capability, where nuclear weapons would be used to wipe out an enemy's ability to retaliate. This concept was also associated with that of limited nuclear war and the notion of escalation management.

3. Department of Defense Report to Congress, "Military Power of Iran," April 2010, http://www.armscontrolwonk.com/file_download/226/2010_04_19_Unclass_ Report_on_Iran_Military.pdf.

4. In March 2005, Peter Vincent Pry, a senior staffer with the Commission to Assess the Threat to the United States from Electromagnetic Pulse Attack, testified about Iran's efforts to develop an EMP weapon for use against the United States. According to Dr. Pry, "An Iranian political-military journal, in an article entitled, 'Electronics to Determine the Fate of Future Wars,' suggests that the key to defeating the United States is an EMP attack. According to the article's authors, 'Advanced information technology equipment exists which has a very high degree of efficiency in warfare.' . . . Iranian flight-tests of their *Shahab-3* medium-range missile, that can reach Israel and U.S. forces in the Persian Gulf, have in recent years involved several explosions at high altitudes, reportedly triggered by a self-destruct mechanism on the missile. The Western press has described these flight tests as failures, because the missiles did not complete their ballistic trajectories. Iran has officially described all of these same tests as successful. The flight-tests would be successful if Iran were

practicing the execution of an EMP attack. . . . Iran has also successfully test-fired a missile from a vessel in the Caspian Sea. A nuclear missile concealed in the hold of a freighter would give Iran, or terrorists, the capability to perform an EMP attack against the United States homeland, without developing an ICBM, and with some prospect of remaining anonymous. Iran's *Shahab-3* medium-range missile . . . is a mobile missile, and small enough to be transported in the hold of a freighter" (statement of Peter Vincent Pry, EMP Commission Staff, before the United States Senate Subcommittee on Terrorism, Technology, and Homeland Security, March 8, 2005).

5. See the Independent Working Group 2009 report entitled *Missile Defense, the Space Relationship, and the Twenty-first Century* (Cambridge, Mass.: Institute for Foreign Policy Analysis, 2009), http://www.ifpa.org/pdf/IWG2009.pdf, 11–13. For a fictional depiction of the potential consequences of an EMP attack, see William Forstchen, *One Second After* (New York: Forge/Tom Doherty, 2009).

6. Iran's Air Force operates an aging and deteriorating inventory of approximately 300 aircraft, the bulk of which were acquired before the 1979 revolution or obtained after the defection of Iraqi pilots to Iran in 1991 at the onset of Operation Desert Storm. Iran's fleet includes U.S.-manufactured F-14s, F-4Ds, F-5s, and F-4Es; French Mirage F-1Es; Chinese F-7s; and Soviet Su-24s, Su-25s, and MiG-29s. However, because of poor maintenance, a scarcity of spare parts, and the cannibalization of aircraft to keep others flying, it is believed that only 50 percent of Iran's aircraft are operational at any given time. Tehran is attempting to counter these shortcomings by the acquisition of modern air-to-air missiles from Russia, the conversion of U.S. HAWK ground-to-air missiles to long-range air-to-air systems, and the purchase of Chinese and Russian aircraft. These purchases, however, have been stymied by UN sanctions. See International Institute for Strategic Studies, *The Military Balance, 2012* (London: Routledge Taylor and Francis Group for IISS, 2012), 323–36.

7. Countervalue targeting aims to instill terror and to uphold the tenets of assured destruction, which was established in the Cold War when nuclear weapons technologies were less accurate and produced considerable collateral damage. Over time, as nuclear weapons technologies matured, weapons became more precise and the potential for collateral damage was reduced significantly, leading to the development of targeting strategies focused on interdicting an adversary's military forces or industrial infrastructure.

8. Barry Posen, *A Nuclear-Armed Iran: A Difficult but Not Impossible Policy Problem* (New York: New Century Foundation, 2006), 17, suggests that "fearing preemption by a neighbor, Iran could adopt a 'hair-trigger' alert posture, or due to poor command and control, a fearful Iran might in a crisis inadvertently launch a nuclear weapon."

9. David S. McDonough, *Nuclear Superiority, The 'New Triad' and the Evolution of Nuclear Strategy*, Adelphi Paper 383 (London: International Institute for Strategic Studies, 2006), 74. According to McDonough, "At the very least, a rogue state would begin to rely on ever-more destabilizing employment strategies for its own deterrent, especially if the goal is to provide a degree of positive control during the more

complicated situation of intra-war deterrence. A good example is Saddam Hussein's reported pre-launch delegation authority over Iraq's [chemical and biological] weapons to local commanders during the Gulf War. The temptation to 'launch-under-attack' in order to assure retaliation in the event of intra-war deterrence failure or to launch-on-warning against an impending first-strike would be especially dangerous given their uncertain early-warning and C3 capabilities" (75).

10. Even today, NATO consideration of missile defense is controversial when it comes to identification of potential threats. The lack of consensus among NATO members about Iran's emerging threat or challenge to European security has resulted in a situation in which Supreme Headquarters Allied Powers Europe (SHAPE) planners cannot undertake "prudent planning" vis-à-vis Iran. Instead, planners rely on mythical scenarios and fabrications to consider concrete options and alliance taskings. At their Chicago Summit in 2012, alliance leaders reaffirmed their support for the missile defense concept that was articulated in 2010 at the Lisbon Summit and declared that an "interim" capability was in place and operational. "This interim capability will provide the Alliance with a limited but operationally meaningful and immediately available capability against a ballistic missile threat. It is a first step, but a real step, toward providing full coverage for all NATO populations, territory and forces in Europe" (Anders Fogh Rasmussen, "NATO's First Steps on Missile Defense," *Wall Street Journal*, May 14, 2012).

11. As much as anything, concerns about nuclear sharing and the credibility of the American extended-deterrence guarantee motivated the French and British leaderships to develop independent national nuclear capabilities. Under the charismatic president Charles de Gaulle, the French undertook their first nuclear test on February 13, 1960. France's first squadron of nuclear-capable Mirage-IV bombers became operational in 1964. While the United Kingdom had participated in the U.S. Manhattan Project during World War II, the decision to develop an independent nuclear weapon capability was taken by the Churchill government, with the UK's first atomic device detonated on October 3, 1952. A global strategy paper published in the same year established nuclear deterrence as the only possible counter to the threat of a nuclear attack. See Jacquelyn K. Davis, *Reluctant Allies and Competitive Partners: U.S.-French Relations at the Breaking Point?* (Dulles, Va.: Brassey's/Institute for Foreign Policy Analysis, 2003); and Jeremy Stocker, *The United Kingdom and Nuclear Deterrence*, Adelphi Paper no. 386 (London: The Institute for Strategic Studies, 2007).

12. It is far more likely, however, that the leadership of the Emirates would opt to acquire a nuclear capability either in the form of whole-up systems purchased from, say, Pakistan or China, or, more realistically, that it would, in essence, buy an extended deterrence guarantee, as Saudi Arabia may in fact have already done, from Pakistan, which is a nuclear weapons state and deploys nuclear-tipped missiles.

13. Carrier vulnerability is an increasingly important issue for the U.S. Navy, particularly given China's development of the DF-21D antiship ballistic-missile system whose range was reported by the Pentagon in 2011 as exceeding 1,500 km (comments

by Chinese military officials in *China Daily* put its range at 2,700 km). See Hu Yinan, Li Xiaokun, and Cui Haipei, "Official Confirms China Building Aircraft Carrier," *China Daily*, July 12, 2011, www.chinadaily.com.cn/china/2011-07/12/content_12881089.htm. Senior U.S. Navy officials have stated that the Chinese have begun to deploy the DF-21D. This system, when fully operational, could significantly impact U.S. expeditionary operations. See Office of the Secretary of Defense, *Annual Report to Congress: Military and Security Developments Involving the People's Republic of China, 2011,* www.defense.gov/pubs/pdfs/2011_cmpr_final.pdf.

14. For recognized nuclear powers, such as Russia and China, and states deemed not to be in compliance with the NPT and other nonproliferation obligations, such as Iran, North Korea, and perhaps Syria, the 2010 NPR makes clear that the United States will reserve the right to use nuclear weapons first or in response to an attack even if that attack does not include nuclear weapons. The NPR notes, however, that the United States would only consider the use of nuclear weapons in "extreme circumstances to defend the vital interests of the United States or its allies and partners." As Secretary of Defense Robert Gates stated in his April 6, 2010, remarks on the NPR's release, nuclear weapons are "obviously a weapon of last resort." However, for these states, the NPR foresees "a narrow range of contingencies" in which the United States might still use nuclear weapons to deter an attack with conventional, chemical, or biological weapons. In contrast, the 2001 NPR reportedly said that nuclear weapons "provide credible military options to deter a wide range of threats, including WMD [weapons of mass destruction] and large-scale conventional military force." Although the Obama NPR states that the "fundamental role" of U.S. nuclear weapons is to "deter nuclear attack on the United States, our allies, and partners," other roles remain. This falls short of the policy declaration that some experts were advocating, that the "sole purpose" of U.S. nuclear weapons is to deter nuclear attack. The NPR notes that the United States will continue to strengthen its conventional capabilities "with the objective of making deterrence of nuclear attack on the United States or its allies and partners the sole purpose of U.S. nuclear weapons."

15. Robert E. Harkavy, "Triangular or Indirect Deterrence/Compellence: Something New in Deterrence Theory," *Comparative Strategy* 17, no. 1 (January–March 1998): 64.

16. The Global Strike concept was developed by U.S. Strategic Command in coordination with the air force and navy after 9/11, basically to provide prompt global strike and nonnuclear options to the president, as discussed in greater detail in chapter 6 of this book.

17. One of the direct consequences of the sanctions against Iran has been the enhancement of IRGC business interests. The IRGC is using its business and engineering companies to replace European firms that have abandoned Iran because of the sanctions. Typically, the IRGC contracts the most complex work to Chinese companies. This is possible because, although China voted in June 2010 for United Nations Security Council sanctions against Iran for failure to suspend its

uranium-enrichment program, China adheres only to the letter of the UNSC sanctions, which contain no explicit limitations on energy investment or trade.

18. Sheikh Nasser bin Hamed, a well-known Saudi cleric associated with al-Qaeda, wrote *A Treatise on the Ruling Regarding the Use of Weapons of Mass Destruction Against the Infidels*. The treatise came in response to a question raised following media reports regarding al-Qaeda's intention to use WMD against the United States. The question was aimed at clarifying Islamic law's view of the permissibility of using WMD in the framework of jihad, and specifically whether such permissibility would be inclusive or limited only to the hour of need. In one chapter of Sheikh Hamed's lengthy response, "Proof that the Use of Weapons of Mass Destruction Is Permissible," Sheikh Hamed stated that it was permissible to use WMD against ten million Americans specifically, and against infidels in general, and that support for their use could be found in Islamic religious sources. According to Sheikh Hamed, it is allowable to strike America with WMD in order to repay it in kind. After citing Koranic verses, Sheikh Hamed wrote, "Anyone who looks at America's acts of aggression against the Muslims and their lands over the recent decades will permit this based only on the section of Islamic law called 'Repayment in Kind,' without any need to indicate the other evidence." For further information see "Contemporary Islamist Ideology Authorizing Genocidal Murder," MEMRI Special Report no. 25 (January 27, 2004), http://www.memri.org/report/en/0/0/0/0/0/0/1049.htm.

19. Department of Defense, "Military Power of Iran." An explosively formed penetrator is a special type of shaped charge designed to penetrate armor at standoff distances.

5. IMPLICATIONS FOR U.S. STRATEGIC AND OPERATIONAL PLANNING

1. Michael Eisenstadt and Mehdi Khalaji outline three broad approaches of radical Shi'ite theology: the *quietist*, which calls upon believers to pray and undertake acts of piety as they patiently await the return of the Mahdi; the *activist*, which summons the faithful to engage in revolutionary action to bring about a revolutionary Islamic government committed to purging corruption and injustice; and the *apocalyptic*, based on violence that would include the use of nuclear weapons. See Michael Eisenstadt and Mehdi Khalaji, "Nuclear Fatwa: Religion and Politics in Iran's Proliferation Strategy," Washington Institute for Near East Policy, Policy Focus no. 115 (September 2011): xi.

2. Michael Eisenstadt, "Deter and Contain: Dealing with a Nuclear Iran," in *Getting Ready for A Nuclear-Ready Iran*, ed. Henry Sokolski and Patrick Clawson (Carlisle, Pa.: Strategic Studies Institute, 2011), 225–55.

3. The phrase "catalytic warfare" was first used in 1960 by Herman Kahn. From Kahn's perspective, the greater the number of countries that possessed nuclear weapons, the greater the potential for catalytic warfare. He also suggested that it might be possible for one country to attack another country with the intention of having the attack attributed to a third country. The result would be that the country

actually initiating the attack would not be the party against which retaliation was mounted. The goal of the country initiating the attack would be to have the country that it had attacked engage in a destructive nuclear exchange with its presumed attacker. The result would be a situation in which the country initiating the attack would emerge unscathed while the other two countries would have devastated or destroyed each other. If the United States during the Cold War had been attacked with nuclear weapons, in all likelihood we would have assumed that the attack came from the Soviet Union. We would have retaliated against the Soviet Union, with the Soviet Union and the United States possibly engaging in repeated nuclear exchanges. If China had initiated the attack, it would be the presumed beneficiary in a world without the United States or the Soviet Union. In a variant of catalytic warfare, an exchange between two smaller states could bring into play a larger conflict between major powers having an alliance or other treaty-based security commitment to one of the lesser states. For example, the crisis that led to World War I began with a confrontation between the Austro-Hungarian Empire and Serbia. Russia backed Serbia and Germany supported Austria based on their respective security commitments. The crisis escalated to war between Germany and Russia and led ultimately to the destruction of their ruling regimes.

Today there is considerable discussion of catalytic war in relation to the Middle East. If, for example, Israel struck Iran's nuclear infrastructure, Iran might retaliate against Israel and the United States. The United States might be drawn into the Iran-Israel conflict in order to prevent Israel's destruction. In each of these examples, the escalatory process would not be easily controlled. The current Middle East example is not based on any Israeli desire to see the United States and Iran destroy each other. However, the effect of an Israeli strike against Iran's nuclear complex would be to draw the United States into the conflict. See Herman Kahn, *On Thermonuclear War* (Princeton, N.J.: Princeton University Press, 1960), 231–32; Donald H. Kobe, "A Theory of Catalytic War," *Journal of Conflict Resolution* 6, no. 2 (June 1962): 125–42.

4. The United States is in the midst of a concerted effort to strengthen alliance relations and build partner capacities in the face of Iran's nuclear efforts and prospective "breakout." Secretary of State Hillary Clinton even raised the prospect of creating a commitment like that set forth in NATO's article 5 for the Arab Gulf states, although this idea may be a bridge too far when it comes to congressional approval or even administration support. Short of that kind of commitment, however, the Obama administration, like the Bush administration before it, is providing missile-defense assets to countries at risk from Iran's military modernization, and it is endeavoring to develop specific and focused responses to a range of Iranian contingencies.

5. Notable examples in this regard include the 1994 attack on a Jewish community center in Buenos Aires and the 1996 bombing of the Khobar Towers in Saudi Arabia. In both instances, local Hezbollah affiliates carried out the attacks, and Iran denied any culpability even after evidence was found in the Khobar Towers case linking Iran to Hezbollah in Saudi Arabia.

6. For example, on February 2, 2012, during Friday prayers, Supreme Leader Ayatollah Ali Khamenei promised to retaliate against recent oil sanctions on Iran as well Western threats of military action. He warned that any attack "would be 10 times worse for the interests of the United States" than it would be for Iran. This was followed several days later by Iranian ambassador to Russia Seyed Mahmoud-Reza Sajjadi's statement that the United States is "well aware of our people's unity. . . . And that's why Iran is fully able to deliver retaliatory strikes on the United States anywhere in the world" if there is a U.S. attack on Iran (Vladimir Soldatkin, "Iran Says It Can Hit U.S. Interests Worldwide If Attacked," *Reuters*, February 8, 2012, http://www.reuters.com/article/2012/02/08/us-iran-russia-usa-idUSTRE8170TM20120208). Such remarks are representative of the type of blustering assertions Iranian civilian and military leaders have been making for several years. For example, in October 2007 Brigadier General Mahmoud Chaharbaghi, commander of IRGC artillery and missile forces, said: "In the first minute of an invasion by the enemy, eleven thousand rockets and cannons would be fired at enemy bases . . . This volume and speed of firing would continue. . . . If a war breaks out in the future, it will not last long because we will rub their noses in the dirt. . . . Now the enemy should ask themselves how many of their people they are ready to have sacrificed for their stupidity in attacking Iran. . . . We have identified our targets and with a close surveillance of targets, we can respond to the enemy's stupidity immediately" (Agence France Presse, "Iran to Fire '11,000 Rockets in Minute' If Attacked," October 20, 2007).

7. Patrick Clawson and Michael Eisenstadt, "Deterring the Ayatollahs: Complications in Applying Cold War Strategy to Iran," Washington Institute for Near East Policy, Policy Focus no. 72 (July 2007): 5–6.

8. In June 2011, the British foreign secretary stated that Iran had recently conducted secret tests of medium-range ballistic missiles capable of delivering nuclear payloads and hitting targets in Israel and parts of Europe. See UK Foreign Ministry, "Foreign Secretary William Hague Statement on North Africa and the Middle East," June 29, 2011.

9. Clawson and Eisenstadt, "Deterring the Ayatollahs," 5–6.

10. See Caitlin Talmadge, "Closing Time: Assessing the Iranian Threat to the Strait of Hormuz," *International Security* 33, no. 1 (Summer 2008): 82–117. Iran threatened to close the Strait of Hormuz in December 2011 and January 2012 following sanctions enacted by the United States and the European Union.

11. In "nuclear cascading," one state becomes a nuclear weapons possessor, leading other states to develop a nuclear capability of their own. While the precise rationales differ from state to state or for a nonstate actor, in the current strategic environment any number of events could spark the proliferation. A new entrant to the nuclear club could provoke similar responses by others in the region. See Graham Allison, "Nuclear Disorder: Surveying Atomic Threats," *Foreign Affairs* 89, no. 1 (January/February 2010): 74–86; and Mitchell Reiss, "The Nuclear Tipping Point: Prospects for a World of Many States," in *The Nuclear Tipping Point: Why States Reconsider*

Their Nuclear Choices, ed. Kurt Campbell, Robert Einhorn, and Mitchell Reiss (Washington, D.C.: Brookings Institution Press, 2004), 3–4.

12. Shahram Chubin, *Iran's Nuclear Ambitions* (Washington, D.C.: Carnegie Endowment for International Peace, 2006), 54, 55. Chubin also notes, "The Iranian political system even after twenty-seven years still functions more like a conspiracy than a government" (48). Moreover, decision making for national security—as was noted at an IFPA Workshop on Iran held in Washington, D.C., on September 24, 2007—has been concentrated in a few hands. This is a cause for concern, especially in the nuclear area, because these decision makers are relatively unfamiliar with deterrence theory and the lessons from the Cold War in this regard.

13. This scenario was credibly drawn by Jason Zaborski, "Deterring a Nuclear Iran," *Washington Quarterly* 28, no. 3 (Summer 2005): 153–67. However, if the August 2008 confrontation between Russia and Georgia is any indication, the willingness of the United States and NATO to become involved in what could become an escalatory confrontation with Russia was limited by the lack of substantive options. The fact that Georgia was not at the time a NATO member or on its way to becoming a NATO member—recall that the April 2008 Bucharest NATO Summit rejected, for the time being, Georgia's application to begin the Membership Accession Process— may have encouraged Russia to take a calculated risk to reassert sovereignty over South Ossetia. This is an arguable point, but depending on how one assesses the implications of Russia's actions for U.S. efforts to promote democracy in Central Asia and the Black and Caspian Sea regions, NATO membership and U.S. extended-deterrence guarantees may be perceived as less valuable to states facing stronger potential adversaries.

14. Game theory in international relations refers to a decision-making approach that assumes rational behavior in which each actor tries to maximize gains or minimize losses, even under conditions of uncertainty and incomplete information. In a two-actor zero-sum game, one side benefits at the other's expense. This, apparently, is how many Iranians appear to view the U.S.-Iranian relationship.

15. The New START Treaty was signed and ratified by the United States Senate, based on an administration commitment to budget and implement certain nuclear-modernization initiatives. To date, the administration has not followed through on its commitments in this regard, and with Senator Jon Kyl's departure from the Senate, there appears to be no Senate champion to ensure that this modernization will in fact be funded. Congressman Robert Turner of Ohio has stepped up to the plate on this issue in the House. However, interest in the Senate on nuclear modernization appears to be low, and proponents of modernization will have to educate a new generation of members and staffers about deterrence-related issues.

16. Kahn, *On Thermonuclear War*, 231, 217. Also see Herman Kahn, *Thinking About the Unthinkable* (New York: Horizon Press, 1962), 57; and this chapter, note 3.

17. In June 2008, Israel conducted an exercise that appeared to observers to be practice for an attack on Iran. The exercise involved more than one hundred Israeli

F-15 and F-16 aircraft, refueling planes, and search and rescue helicopters. "The Israeli aircraft flew more than 900 miles, roughly the distance between Israel and Natanz, Iran's main nuclear enrichment facility" (Jay Solomon and Yochi J. Dreazen, "Israeli Maneuvers Demonstrate Unease Over Iran," *Wall Street Journal*, June 21, 2008). More recently, Israel has been preparing for potential retaliation following a possible attack on Iran's nuclear facilities by bolstering its civil defense capabilities and implementing active defense measures. Iran is also said to have deployed indigenously developed air defenses around important military sites and research centers. See Ronen Bergman, "Will Israel Attack Iran?" *New York Times Magazine*, January 25, 2012.

18. Walter Pincus "At the Pentagon and in Israel, Plans Show the Difficulties of an Iran Strike," *Washington Post*, February 9, 2012; Abdullah Toukan and Anthony H. Cordesman, *Study on a Possible Israeli Strike on Iran's Nuclear Development Facilities* (Washington, D.C.: Center for Strategic and International Studies, 2009), http://csis .org/files/media/csis/pubs/090316_israelistrikeiran.pdf.

19. See Director-General of the International Atomic Energy Agency, "Implementation of the NPT Safeguards Agreement and Relevant Provisions of Security Council Resolutions in the Islamic Republic of Iran," IAEA Board of Governors, November 8, 2011, http://www.isis-online.org/uploads/isis-reports/documents/Iran_ safeguards_report_November_2012.pdf; Alexander Wilner and Anthony H. Cordesman, *Iran and the Gulf Military Balance*, (Washington D.C.: Center for Strategic and International Studies, 2011), http://csis.org/files/publication/111128_Iran_Gulf_ Military_Bal.pdf.

20. See Bergman, "Will Israel Attack Iran?"; Ken Dilanian, "U.S. Sees Limited Military Options on Iran," *Los Angeles Times*, February 17, 2012; and Elisabeth Bumiller, "Iran Raid Seen as a Huge Task for Israeli Jets," *New York Times*, February 20, 2012.

21. The Israeli strike of September 6, 2007, remains shrouded in mystery, as neither the U.S. nor the Israeli government has been willing to provide details. Speculation abounds that the target of the strike was a nuclear reactor, modeled after a North Korean plant, and that for this reason and so as not to derail the Six-Party process, the Bush administration chose to say nothing on this topic. Based on open source reporting, Israeli intelligence had either tracked or had information that a North Korean freighter, docked in a Syrian port, had delivered cargo to the site. According to interviews with Israeli officials and with Gulf security analysts, the site that was struck by Israeli aircraft was under the control of the Syrian Air Force, which also has responsibility for overseeing Syrian ballistic missile and WMD programs. If it was a reactor site, this would have marked a significant shift in Syrian policy, reflecting the fact that Syria's leaders now felt emboldened to seek their own nuclear programs as a result of Iran's successful defiance and in light of its determination to continue to pursue its national nuclear programs. Earlier, it should be recalled, Bashar al-Assad had publicly stated that nuclear weapons were not "useable," and he supported calls for a Middle East nuclear-free zone. The evidence of a change in Syrian policy may also be explained, according to one analyst, as providing a "front" for Iran's nuclear development. In any case, even in Israel, discussion of

the strike is muted, and there is a feeling that the Israelis prefer to bide their time and focus on the more important threat—namely, that of Iran's nuclear development. For details on the Israeli attack on the Syrian nuclear site, see Daveed Gartenstein-Ross and Joshua D. Goodman, "The Attack on Syria's al-Kibar Nuclear Facility," *Focus Quarterly* 3, no. 1 (Spring 2009): http://www.jewishpolicycenter.org/826/the-attack-on-syrias-al-kibar-nuclear-facility.

More recently, David Makovsky, writing in *The New Yorker*, contends that the Israelis indeed struck a reactor facility in Syria, in support of the so-called Begin Doctrine, named after former Israeli prime minister Menachem Begin, who was responsible for agreeing to the 1981 attack against the Osirak reactor in Iraq. According to the Begin Doctrine, which holds that no Israeli adversary in the Middle East should be allowed to acquire or produce a nuclear weapon, Israel was empowered to act when Mossad found evidence of the reactor's development after a raid on the home of Ibrahim Othman, head of the Syrian Atomic Energy Commission. Subsequently, after the raid, an IAEA inspection team concluded in 2009, that the site very likely had been that of a nuclear reactor based on soil sampling and evidence of man-made uranium and graphite. See David Makovsky, "The Silent Strike: How Israel Bombed a Syrian Nuclear Installation and Kept It Secret," *The New Yorker*, September 17, 2012, 34–40.

22. Not all Israelis share these views. For example, Meir Dagan, former head of Mossad, Israel's spy service, said that an Israeli attack on Iran's nuclear facilities would create a regional war endangering Israel's existence. See "Israel Government 'Reckless and Irresponsible' Says ex-Mossad Chief," Conal Urquhart, *Guardian*, June 3, 2011, http://www.guardian.co.uk/world/2011/jun/03/israel-government-reckless-mossad-chief. Another former head of Mossad, Efraim Halevy, made the case in his memoir for engaging Iran and Syria. From his perspective, "Even if the Iranians did obtain a nuclear weapon, they are 'deterrable' because for the mullahs, survival and perpetuation of the regime is a holy obligation." On Ahmadinejad and his rhetoric, Halevy says, "I believe that behind their bombastic statements there is a desperate fear that they [Iranians] are going down a path that would have dire consequences. They don't know how to extricate themselves. We have to find creative ways to help them escape from their rhetoric" (Efrain Halevy, *Man in the Shadows: Inside the Middle East Crisis with a Director of Israel's Mossad* [New York: St. Martin's Press, 2006], 320). For an overview of the current divisions within Israel on this issue, see Benny Morris, "Israel Divided Over Attacking Iran," *The National Interest*, November 8, 2011, http://nationalinterest.org/commentary/israel-divided-over-attacking-iran-6132.

23. One example of this can be found in the statements of the head of Iran's Atomic Energy Organization, Fereydoon Abbasi. Quoted in an article on the website of *Al Hayat*, a pan-Arab newspaper published in the United Kingdom, Abbasi reportedly said that "because of espionage, his government had sometimes provided false information to protect its nuclear program, which Western powers have called a cloak to develop a nuclear weapons capability. . . . 'We presented false information sometimes in order to protect our nuclear position and our achievements, as

there is no other choice but to mislead foreign intelligence . . . sometimes we present a weakness that we do not in fact really have, and sometimes we appear to have power without having it'" (quoted in Rick Gladstone and Christine Hauser, "Iran's Top Atomic Official Says Nation Issued False Nuclear Data to Fool Spies," *New York Times*, September 21, 2012).

24. This argument is set forth in detail by Kenneth Waltz. See Scott Sagan and Kenneth N. Waltz, *The Spread of Nuclear Weapons: A Debate Renewed*, 2nd ed. (New York: Norton, 2002), chaps. 1 and 3.

25. The "Velvet Revolution" refers to Czechoslovakia's emergence as a democracy. It was a nonviolent protest movement dominated by student activism and popular demonstrations that took place between November 17 and December 29, 1989, when Czechoslovakia's communist government collapsed and the country's borders with East Germany and Austria were opened, allowing for free passage and the first democratic elections (in June 1990) since 1946. Alexander Dubcek was elected speaker of the federal parliament on December 28, 1989. On December 29, 1989, Vaclav Havel was elected president.

26. Active Endeavor is a NATO article 5 maritime counterterrorism operation focused on preventing the movement of weapons of mass destruction into and out of the Mediterranean region. In February 2003, it was broadened to include maritime operations in the Strait of Gibraltar and, subsequently, ship escort and compliant boardings to enforce international law. Naval forces from the Standing NATO Response Force Maritime Group are responsible for carrying out these operations. In September 2006, the North Atlantic Council authorized Russian participation in Operation Active Endeavor. Russia has deployed vessels twice, in 2006 and 2007. However, in August 2008, NATO voted to suspend further Russian participation in Active Endeavor following Russia's occupation of territory in Georgia. Russia has since expressed interest in resuming its involvement in Active Endeavor. Besides Russia, Ukraine, Israel, and Morocco have offered to participate in patrolling operations, and Sweden and Finland have also expressed their interest in contributing to Active Endeavor.

6. U.S. DETERRENCE PLANNING IN THE EVENT OF AN IRANIAN NUCLEAR BREAKOUT

1. Human-terrain mapping has emerged as an integral aspect of counterinsurgency planning. Essentially, it is the collection, collation, and presentation of sociopolitical information, including the identification of key players and their societal relationships, data necessary for a field unit to influence a local population. The goal is to give commanders insight into the population and how it may react in order to enhance operational effectiveness, save lives, and reduce military and civilian conflict. Understanding these connections is central to forging alliances and developing actionable intelligence. Intelligence-fusion teams in Iraq and in Afghanistan have been organized around U.S. and allied/coalition special operations forces,

intelligence professionals, forensic experts, political analysts, and mapping and computer specialists using new technologies (e.g., advanced, armed, unmanned platforms and space-related technologies). Building and training such teams is the idea behind the U.S.-inspired NATO SOF Headquarters (NSHQ) element and the notion of an Allied Effects Group (AEG) in Afghanistan. For a discussion of fusion teams in Iraq, see Jody Warrick and Robin Wright, "U.S. Teams Weaken Insurgency in Iraq," *Washington Post*, September 6, 2008.

2. Keith Payne, *The Great American Gamble: Deterrence Theory and Practice from the Cold War to the Twenty-First Century* (Fairfax, Va.: National Institute Press, 2008), 305–6.

3. Tom Scheber, quoted in Tom Scheber and Keith Payne, *Examination of U.S. Strategic Forces Policy and Capabilities* (Fairfax, Va.: National Institute for Public Policy, 2008), 4. NATO is in the process of reassessing its deterrence posture as part of a broader study on the future of Alliance Dual-Capable aircraft (DCA) deployments in Europe and arms-control considerations, including the need to capture Russian nonstrategic nuclear forces in discussions to reduce nuclear weapons in Europe. Many NATO DCA aircraft are aging, and national governments have declined to invest the resources necessary to keep this a viable mission. With aircraft being retired from national inventories, questions have emerged about their replacement and cost-effectiveness. The United States still supports development of a nuclear-capable version of the F-35, but it is of lower priority than other variants. It remains to be seen whether other European governments will actually purchase the nuclear version. At their Chicago Summit, NATO's members essentially endorsed the findings of the jumbo ministerial of 2012, in which NATO foreign and defense ministers agreed to the recommendations contained in the Deterrence and Defense Posture Review, implemented after the Lisbon Summit in 2010. Essentially, the heads of state and government agreed to endorse NATO's nuclear posture while continuing to review its implementation. They also agreed to pursue arms-control negotiations with Russia on tactical nuclear weapons deployments in Europe and to uphold the negative security pledges of each of the three NATO nuclear weapons states, which essentially imply that nuclear weapons will not be used against nonnuclear states, with certain provisos in each of the three cases. Not agreed to at Chicago and continuing to attract alliance debate was a statement to the effect that "the fundamental purpose of NATO's nuclear weapons is to deter the use of nuclear weapons against the alliance." Some newer NATO members continue to worry about a conventional attack from Russia and embrace a more comprehensive view of deterrence in and for NATO-Europe. Other members, including France, seek to include reference to nonnuclear WMD attacks. Undoubtedly, this will continue to be debated in the alliance, as will the optimal DCA posture and the issue of engaging the Russians in an arms-control discussion that includes tactical nuclear weapons.

4. Air-Sea Battle is an operational concept designed to counter the emergence of anti-access threats, including those from China and Iran. It encompasses force protection, forcible entry, cyberwarfare, and space operations. Its development coincides

with a time when overseas U.S. forward-presence deployments are changing and the need for access to key regional theaters is of increasing importance to reassure allies and partners and enable U.S. ground forces to meet their strategic objectives. For an overview of Air-Sea Battle, see "The Air-Sea Battle Concept Summary," Marine Corps website, November 10, 2011, http://www.marines.mil/unit/hqmc/Pages/TheAir-SeaBattleconceptsummary.aspx.

5. On carrier vulnerability, see chap. 4, note 13.

6. Department of Defense Directive 3000.07, December 1, 2008 defines irregular warfare (IW) as a "violent struggle among state and non-state actors for legitimacy and influence over the relevant population(s). Irregular warfare favors indirect and asymmetric approaches, though it may employ the full range of military and other capacities, in order to erode an adversary's power, influence, and will." Entities using IW flout Geneva Convention rules and use nontraditional tools, including weapons of mass destruction, improvised explosive devices, and cyberwar operations. Hybrid warfare is waged using a combination of regular and irregular warfare tools, concepts, and doctrines. Hybrid warfare appears to be the construct of choice for Iran, which maintains conventional armed forces and the IRGC, optimized for asymmetric and conventional operations. Iran also has the option of using nonstate armed groups, most notably Hezbollah, to implement irregular or regular warfare operations perhaps simultaneously.

7. Colin Gray has described the differences and relationships between preemption and prevention. According to his view, "The option of a preventive war, or of a preventive strike, must express a guess that war, or at least a major negative power shift, is probable in the future." In contrast, preemption "refers to the first use of military force when an enemy attack already is underway or, at the least, is very credibly imminent." From Gray's perspective, "To preempt is to launch an attack against an attack that one has incontrovertible evidence is either actually underway or has been ordered. . . . [It] is about self-defense." In contrast, "prevention, preventive self-defense, has at its core the proposition that the preventor, if one may coin that term, is able to detect, and to anticipate, deadly menace in the future." Preventive war, according to Gray, is consistent with former secretary of State Elihu Root's logic (propounded in 1914) in which a "state is determined to prevent 'a condition of affairs in which it will be too late to protect itself,'" raising questions about the use of force in certain circumstances. See Colin S. Gray, *The Implications of Preemptive and Preventive War Doctrine: A Reconsideration* (Carlisle, Pa.: Strategic Studies Institute, U.S. Army War College, 2007), esp. 8–14.

8. U.S. access to Diego Garcia could change in 2016 when its lease runs out. Complicating the situation is the fact that the British tenancy is under challenge from the Chagossian people, who want the island returned to Chagos, part of Mauritius. Diego Garcia was ceded to the British by France in the 1814 Treaty of Paris. When decolonization was ordered by the United Nations in the 1960s, Britain expelled the Chagossians in exchange for an agreement with the United States that involved use of the island and a deal on nuclear technologies. The Chagossians want to be

repatriated in 2016, and the United Kingdom has so shrunk its force structure that access to Diego for its purposes is no longer necessary. However, the island's strategic value to the United States (and to the UK) in the context of the troop withdrawals from Afghanistan and Iraq and against a possible Iran contingency is only likely to increase. For this reason, Britain is unlikely to arbitrate its claim to Diego Garcia, and, even if it did, the United States could conceivably build up and use a base on the Cocos Islands, use of which was recently provided by Australia.

9. Quoted in Julian Borger, "U.S. Military Chiefs Warn Israel Against Strike on Iran," *Guardian*, November 1, 2012. Reportedly, UK officials have come to this decision based on their conception that a preemptive attack against Iran would contravene international law.

10. Prompt Global Strike (PGS) is an effort to develop, as part of the Global Strike mission, a system to deliver a precision strike within an hour anywhere in the world using conventional munitions. Defense Secretary Leon Panetta announced that the U.S. Navy is seeking to develop an "undersea conventional prompt global strike option" as part of the 2013 defense budget. This system would be a ballistic missile mated with a conventional warhead launched from a submarine. In the past, critics of PGS have argued that a nonnuclear missile launch from a U.S. submarine could be misinterpreted, particularly by Russia, as a nuclear strike and generate a nuclear counterstrike. However, Defense Department officials state that advances in missile technology (e.g., the ability to alter both the missile's trajectory and its speed) would make obvious that it was not a nuclear-tipped missile.

11. In June 2006, the defense journalist Robert Kaplan spent time with a B-2 squadron in Guam. From his perspective, "As countries like North Korea and Iran put more and more of their critical facilities deep underground, in places that cruise missiles launched from such off-shore platforms as submarines lack the kinetic energy to penetrate, the B-2's ability to drop heavier (non-nuclear) bombs becomes ever more important. If the United States ever attacks Iran, expect to be reading a lot about the B-2. And if we never do, the B-2 will have been a hidden hand behind the muscular diplomacy that made an attack unnecessary." According to Colonel Robert Wheeler, USAF, then the Guam Squadron's group commander of operations, "'The deterrence effect of this airplane may be as important as its destructive capability'" (Robert D. Kaplan, "The Plane That Would Bomb Iran," *Atlantic Monthly* [September 2007], http://www.theatlantic.com/magazine/archive/2007/09/the-plane-that-would-bomb-iran/306133/.

12. To meet the operational challenge posed by buried targets, the U.S. Air Force has developed the Massive Ordnance Penetrator (MOP), a 30,000-pound bomb designed to destroy deep underground facilities. The MOP can be deployed on B-52 and B-2 bombers. See W. J. Hennigan, "Boeing Delivers First Batch of 30,000-Pound Bombs to Air Force," *Los Angeles Times*, November 16, 2011, articles.latimes.com/2011/nov/16/business/la-fi-bunker-buster-bomb-20111117.

13. By all accounts, Iran has a significant capability in the cyberwarfare arena. In testimony to the U.S. Senate Select Committee on Intelligence in January 2012,

the director of national intelligence, James R. Clapper, noted that Iran's cybercapabilities "have dramatically increased in recent years in depth and complexity." More and more, they appear to be directed against the United States (quoted in Ilan Berman, "Iran, the Next Cyber Threat: Regime Is Upgrading Its Capability for Attacking U.S. Infrastructure," *Washington Times*, May 14, 2012). In August 2012, Iran sponsored a disquieting cyberattack against the main oil company of Saudi Arabia, Aramco. Hackers, calling themselves the Sword of Justice, introduced a malicious virus code that forced Aramco to shut down operations to stop the virus from spreading. Dubbed Shamoon, this virus was designed to replace data on computer hard drives with an image of a burning American flag and to report the addresses of infected computers and information from them, forcing the company to cut off connections with the Internet to husband proprietary information. Some computer experts have suggested that this virus was created in retaliation for the Flame virus, which affected Iran's Kharg Island terminal, a conduit for 80 percent of Iran's oil exports. See Nicole Perlroth, "Cyberattack on Saudi Firm Disquiets U.S.," *New York Times*, October 24, 2012.

14. The Libyan operation has been suggested as a model for NATO as the alliance goes forward. This operation provided a framework in which NATO allies could participate in the enforcement of the embargo and no-fly zones over Libya if their member governments consented to participation, which fourteen of NATO's twenty-eight members did. It also provided a framework for collaboration with non-NATO partners, including Qatar, and it offered a template for "prudent planning" based on work that was previously done at NATO's combined joint task force headquarters. However, of the fourteen NATO member states providing military assets, only eight offered to fly ground-attack missions. In addition, the United States supplied the bulk of some essential capabilities, including ISR support, aerial refueling (necessary because most of NATO's air sorties originated from bases in Italy), electronic-warfare assets, and precision munitions. NATO stocks of precision munitions are badly depleted, and the political will to increase member defense spending to levels necessary to maintain alliance proficiencies in this and other critical areas is lacking, contributing to a situation in which NATO's transformational goals, outlined at the 2012 Chicago NATO Summit, have little chance of being realized. In Washington and some other NATO capitals this may increase skepticism about the ongoing relevance of the alliance and erode support in Congress for defense spending for NATO when other priorities are perceived to be more pressing.

15. For a concise survey of NATO from its origins to today, see Stanly R. Sloan. *Permanent Alliance? NATO and the Transatlantic Bargain from Truman to Obama* (New York: Continuum, 2010), esp. 179–80.

16. A study undertaken by the Institute for Foreign Policy Analysis explored new concepts for deterrence planning, with a particular emphasis on extended deterrence. As suggested in the IFPA assessment:

U.S. efforts to reassure allies and coalition partners of America's interest in their security remains a cornerstone both of non-proliferation policy and of U.S. efforts to mitigate the consequences of an adversary's nuclear strike. Central to American efforts in this regard is the extended deterrence guarantee that the United States provides to U.S. allies in NATO and to Japan and South Korea as part of a bilateral treaty commitment to each country. In NATO, this commitment was embodied in the Washington Treaty's collective defense concept (Article 5) and manifested in the forward deployment of American troops for the defense of Europe against a Soviet-Warsaw pact attack. In so far as nuclear strategy was concerned, this meant the possible first-use of nuclear weapons by NATO if the Soviet-Warsaw Pact attack could not be halted and reversed by conventional means alone. The U.S. extended deterrence commitment to NATO-Europe was also given substance by the peacetime basing of U.S. tactical nuclear weapons in Europe and the sharing of the nuclear mission with several NATO-European allies. NATO's nuclear-capable aircraft, or DCA, as they came to be called, remain an integral aspect of the Alliance's concepts of "shared risks" and "burden-sharing."

No such formula was put into place in Asia, which in any case lacks a multilateral framework comparable to that of NATO. Instead, for Japan and South Korea, the U.S. extended deterrence guarantee was explicitly tied to the bilateral U.S. security relationships that were developed with each country and were made manifest in the forward deployment of American forces.

These included nuclear weapons on the Korean Peninsula, until the Carter administration decided to withdraw all tactical nuclear weapons from the Korean theater. They also included the deployment in Korea and Japan of conventional U.S. forces, which were regarded as a "trip-wire" to underpin the credibility of the U.S. extended deterrent security commitment.

17. The GCC was formed in 1981 at the initiative of Saudi Arabia, which saw it as a means of countering the rise of Iranian power in the region. The six GCC member-states are Bahrain, Kuwait, Oman, Qatar, Saudi Arabia, and the United Arab Emirates. In May 2011 Morocco and Jordan submitted proposals to join the GCC.

18. In May 2012, Saudi Arabia put forth a new proposal to strengthen security ties among the GCC states. While it is likely that Bahrain and perhaps even the UAE will move forward on this initiative, Kuwait, Oman, and Qatar are not likely to want to "irritate" Iran. The Saudi proposals are directly aimed at containing Iran's power in the wider Gulf region and specifically at undermining Shia influence in Bahrain and in Saudi Arabia's eastern province.

19. Bruno Tertrais, "Security Guarantees and Extended Deterrence in the Gulf Region: A European Perspective," *Strategic Insights* 8, no. 5 (December 2009): 27.

20. CENTO membership included Iran, Iraq, Pakistan, Turkey, and the United Kingdom. The United States joined the military committee of the alliance in 1958. The organization's headquarters were initially located in Baghdad, but after the coup in 1958, it was relocated to Ankara, Turkey.

21. The Camp David Accords were signed by President Anwar El-Sadat of Egypt and Prime Minister Menachem Begin of Israel on September 17, 1978, at Camp David, Maryland. Officially called *A Framework for the Conclusion of a Peace Treaty Between Egypt and Israel,* these accords provided the basis for the 1979 treaty. They committed

the United States to providing billions of dollars in aid to the two countries, which continues today in the form of grants and foreign military sales and security assistance.

22. In May 2007, President Mahmoud Ahmadinejad made the first visit to the United Arab Emirates by an Iranian head of state since 1971. Ahmadinejad delivered a harsh speech to a rally of Iranian expatriates living in Dubai, in which he declared, "We are telling you [the United States] to leave the region." The insistence that the United States leave the Middle East was notable since Ahmadinejad's visit followed by only days a visit by Vice President Dick Cheney, who sought to strengthen ties with U.S. regional allies. Ahmadinejad countered the U.S. strategy, saying, "The nations of the region can no longer take you forcing yourself on them. The nations of the region know better how to create peace and security." The Iranian president also warned against a possible U.S. military strike against Iran, cautioning that the United States "cannot strike Iran. The Iranian people are able to retaliate. They are able to protect and defend themselves well" (Jim Krane, "Iranian President Holds Anti-U.S. Rally in Dubai," Associated Press, May 13, 2007; and Lydia Georgi, "Ahmadinejad Warns U.S. Against Military Action," Agence France Presse, May 14, 2007).

23. To attract Russian support for a fourth round of sanctions against Iran, the Obama administration made two rather significant concessions to Moscow. First, it lifted U.S. sanctions against Russia's state arms-export agency and other entities in the Russian military complex that had provided sensitive technology and weapons to Iran. Second, it agreed not to ban the sale of Russian S-300 antiaircraft batteries to Tehran, a contract that Moscow had suspended but not canceled. The United States continues to urge Russia to cancel this contract. Iran, in frustration, has announced that it is developing an indigenous system to meet the country's defensive require-ments, but this might take years to realize. The Obama administration also revived a civilian nuclear-cooperation agreement with Russia (which had been shelved after Russia's war with Georgia) in an effort to create a fresh start with what was then the new Putin presidency. Critics argue that the U.S. concessions were premature. Russia has not agreed to cancel the S-300 sale, and there is opposition to the civil-ian nuclear-power agreement as well so long as Russia continues to support Iran's Bushehr facility. See Peter Baker and David E. Sanger, "U.S. Makes Concessions to Russia for Iran Sanctions," *New York Times*, May 21, 2010, http://www.nytimes .com/2010/05/22/world/22sanctions.html.

According to former U.S. national security advisor Zbigniew Brzezinski, "Rus-sia is an increasingly revisionist state, more and more openly positioning itself to attempt at least a partial reversal of the geo-political losses it suffered in the early 1990s. In that context, an actual conflict in the Persian Gulf region may not be viewed by all Moscow strategists as a one-sided evil. The dramatic spike in oil prices would harm China and America while unleashing a further wave of anti-American hostility. . . . The stakes of a serious crisis in the Persian Gulf are thus far-reaching. They could cause a more dramatic shift in the global distribution of power than even the one that occurred after the Cold War ended" (Zbigniew Brzezinski, "A Partner for Dealing with Iran?" *Washington Post*, November 30, 2007).

24. The Arab Public Opinion Poll was conducted in October 2011 by Shibley Telhami, the Anwar Sadat Professor for Peace and Development at the University of Maryland and nonresident senior fellow at the Saban Center for Middle East Policy at the Brookings Institution. The poll surveyed 3,000 people in Egypt, Morocco, Jordan, Lebanon, and the United Arab Emirates on their attitudes toward the United States and the Obama administration, prospects for Arab-Israeli peace, the effects of the Arab awakening, the outlook for the Egyptian elections, and where the region is headed politically. A majority (59 percent) of Arabs expressed unfavorable views of the United States, but those with favorable views increased from 10 percent in 2010 to 26 percent in 2011—possibly because of the positive perception of the U.S. role in the Arab Spring. Of those polled, 52 percent remain discouraged by Obama administration policies in the Middle East, although this is down from 65 percent in 2010. See Shibley Telhami, "The 2011 Arab Public Opinion Poll" (produced in conjunction with Zogby International), November 21, 2011, http://www.brookings.edu/reports/2011/1121_arab_public_opinion_telhami.aspx.

25. This idea has been the subject of considerable discussion in U.S. and GCC analytical circles. For Saudi Arabia and possibly other GCC states, the idea would be to try to get a formal U.S extended-deterrence guarantee, using the Gulf Security Dialogue as the framework for its implementation. If, as most U.S. defense experts contend, this is not feasible given the contending threat perspectives of the GCC countries and their different levels of comfort with a closer association with the United States in the security realm, then the Saudis may decide to broach the subject with the United States, in a bilateral context, as part of the ongoing security dialogue between the two countries. However, politically, this is likely to be a hard sell, all the more so because of the challenges associated with delineating precisely what Iranian behaviors a U.S. security guarantee to Saudi Arabia, or even the GCC, would be intended to deter. See Patrick Knapp, "The Gulf States in the Shadow of Iran," *Middle East Quarterly* (Winter 2010).

26. The precise wording found in President Carter's 1980 State of the Union address is: "Let our position be absolutely clear: An attempt by any outside force to gain control of the Persian Gulf region will be regarded as an assault on the vital interests of the United States of America, and such an assault will be repelled by any means necessary, including military force."

27. In what is commonly known as the "Reagan Corollary," President Reagan proclaimed in October 1981, "We cannot permit Saudi Arabia to become another Iran."

28. Since the events of 9/11, the U.S.-Saudi relationship has suffered, especially from the fact that fifteen of the nineteen 9/11 terrorists came from Saudi Arabia. Moreover, differences over the U.S. invasion of Iraq in 2003 which resulted in a Shia government coming to power in Baghdad; Saudi attempts to preserve the status quo during democratic uprisings in the Arab world, evidenced by its intervention to stop the revolt in Bahrain, and the lack of U.S. support for Hosni Mubarak during Egypt's revolt have further complicated U.S. relations with Saudi Arabia. For a fuller treatment of the differences that continue to plague that relationship, see Anna Fifield

"Arab Spring Tests U.S.-Saudi Relationship," *Financial Times*, June 16 2011, www
.ft.com/intl/cms/s/014082dc70-984d-11e0-ae45-00144feab49a.html#axzz2B5AdfgBn;
and Joshua Teitelbaum, in Bruce Maddy-Weitzman, editor, "Has the Shi'ite Crescent
Disappeared? Saudi Arabia and the U.S. Alliance Against Iran," *Tel Aviv Notes* (The
Moshe Dayan Center), January 27, 2007, http://www.tau.ac.il/dayancenter/Has_the_
Shiite_Crescent_Disappeared.pdf.

   29. According to one report, "Private Saudi backers were the chief source of
finance for the Taliban. Members of FinTraca, the Afghan financial intelligence
unit, state that since 2006 more than £920 million from Saudi Arabia has arrived in
Afghanistan through Pakistan's tribal areas, in particular north Waziristan, which
is infamous as al-Qaeda's heartland" (Anthony Loyd, "Terror Link Alleged as Saudi
Millions Flow Into Afghanistan War Zone," *Times* (London), May 31, 2010, www
.timesonline.co.uk/tol/news/world/Afghanistan/article7140745.ece.

   30. According to Secretary of State Hillary Clinton, "We want Iran to calculate
what I think is a fair assessment, that if the United States extends a defense umbrella
to the region, if we do even more to support the military capacity of those in the
Gulf, it is unlikely that Iran will be any stronger or safer, because they won't be able to
intimidate or dominate, as they apparently believe they can, once they have a nuclear
weapons" (quoted in Mark Landler and David E. Sanger, "Clinton Speaks of Shielding Mideast from Iran," *New York Times*, July 23, 2009).

   31. This ambiguity was greatly reduced by former U.S. president Carter's revelation of Israel's nuclear holdings. In response to a question about how to deal with
Iran's nuclear threat, Carter said, "The U.S. has more than 12,000 nuclear weapons,
the Soviet Union has about the same, Great Britain and France have several hundred, and Israel has 150 or more." Reuters, "Israel Has '150 or More' Nuclear Weapons,
Carter Says," *Boston Globe*, May 27, 2008, www.boston.com/news/world/middleeast/
articles/2008/05127/israel_has_150_or_more_nuclear_weapns_carter_says.

   32. The fourth and fifth Dolphin submarines are due for delivery in 2013 and 2014,
respectively; the sixth was purchased from Germany in May 2012. Although never con-
firmed by Israel, reports have circulated since 2010 that Israel was preparing to station
one of its three German-built submarines permanently in Gulf waters. These boats
purportedly will carry nuclear-tipped cruise missiles with a range of 1,500 kilometers,
making them capable of reaching targets in Iran. Doubling the submarine fleet from
three to six will help Israel maintain a continuous naval presence in distant locations.
See Uzi Mahnaimi, "Israel Stations Nuclear Missile Subs Off Iran," *Sunday Times* (London), May 30, 2010, www.timesonline.co.uk/tol/news/world/europe/article7140282
.ece; and Edmund Sanders, "Israel's Military Looks to Sea," *Los Angeles Times*, May 11,
2012, articles.latimes.com/2012/may/11/world/la-fg-israel-navy-qa-20120511.

   33. The Israeli historian and strategist Martin Van Creveld stated (in a BBC interview, broadcast on July 8, 2008, after Iran test-fired Shahab missiles) that "Israel has
more than enough capacity to deter Iran."

   34. The Phased Adaptive Approach (PAA) refers to the Obama administration's
concept for U.S. missile-defense deployments in Europe. PAA relies on U.S. Navy

Aegis sea- and land-based capabilities, netted with a complex array of sensors and other U.S. missile-defense systems. Its stated purpose is to address Iran's short- and medium-range ballistic missile threat to Europe. It is being designed to incorporate relevant technologies quickly and cost-effectively to respond to evolving threats. See "Fact Sheet on U.S. Missile Defense Policy, A 'Phased, Adaptive Approach' for Missile Defense in Europe," The White House, September 17, 2009, http://www.whitehouse.gov/the_press_office/FACT-SHEET-US-Missile-Defense-Policy-A-Phased-Adaptive -Approach-for-Missile-Defense-in-Europe.

35. Nimrod Goren, "Israel Is Missing an Opportunity to Mend Ties with Turkey," *Haaretz.com*, March 19, 2012, http://www.haaretz.com/opinion/israel-is-missing -an-opportunity-to-mend-ties-with-turkey-1.418707.

36. For an extensive and detailed discussion of Cold War deterrence and its evolution after the fall of the Soviet Union, see Payne, *The Great American Gamble*, esp. chap. 2, for a discussion of competing approaches to deterrence represented by Herman Kahn and Thomas Schelling.

37. In February 2007, the George W. Bush administration signed, with its partners, an agreement with North Korea mandating the dismantlement of North Korea's nuclear weapons program. Even after North Korea's failure to meet the agreement's first deadline requiring a transparent declaration of its nuclear programs and holdings, the Bush administration held to the outlines of the Six-Party framework and moved forward in late 2007 to begin the process of removing North Korea from the State Department's terrorist watch list and to normalize relations. While the jury was still out on North Korean compliance and its intentions, there were worrisome indications during the summer of 2007 that the regime in Pyongyang may have tried to transfer either fissile material or missile technologies to Syria or Iran. Israel subsequently chose to strike a "facility in Syria," presumably to eliminate whatever may have been shipped from Pyongyang. In August 2008, North Korea missed its first chance to be removed from the State Department's terror watch list because of "incomplete" information about its nuclear programs and its unwillingness to allow outside verification of its nuclear declaration, which was provided in June 2008 as part of an agreement reached at the Six-Party Talks. Even as North Korea physically destroyed a cooling tower at its Yongbyon facility, in compliance with the agreement reached at the Six-Party Talks, it failed to answer specific questions about suspected nuclear activities, including how many weapons it had and the details of its involvement with Syria. North Korea has subsequently made significant advances in its nuclear program, launching a second nuclear test in May 2009 and revealing a uranium-enrichment facility to a prominent U.S. scientist in November 2010.

7. DEALING WITH A NUCLEAR IRAN AND ASYMMETRIC CHALLENGES

1. David Ignatius, "Spy Games in Iran," *Washington Post*, July 2, 2008.
2. See Roger F. Noriega and José R. Cárdenas, "The Mounting Hezbollah Threat in Latin America," The American Enterprise Institute, October 6, 2011,

http://www.aei.org/article/foreign-and-defense-policy/regional/latin-america/
the-mounting-hezbollah-threat-in-latin-america.

3. Colombia's Revolutionary Armed Forces (FARC) is a Marxist-Leninist guerrilla organization that claims to represent Colombia's rural poor in a struggle against the nation's ruling elite and affluent class. Financed primarily by kidnappings and trade in illegal drugs, the FARC has attempted to overthrow the government of Colombia, but of late it is seeking negotiations to terminate its insurgency. The United States has designated it a terrorist organization. It has frequently collaborated with Venezuelan officials who reportedly have asked FARC leaders to furnish guerrilla training to progovernment cells and to assassinate opponents of Venezuelan president Hugo Chávez. In recent years the FARC has experienced several setbacks, including the deaths of key leaders and the desertion of hundreds of members, which is why it now seeks "peace talks" with the Colombian government. See "Revolutionary Armed Forces of Colombia (FARC)," *New York Times*, http://topics.nytimes.com/top/reference /timestopics/organizations/r/revolutionary_armed_forces_of_colombia/index .html. The Shining Path, a Peruvian Maoist insurgency group, has reemerged in isolated areas of the Andes. The war against the group, which resulted in approximately 70,000 deaths, supposedly ended in 2000. However, modeling itself after FARC, the Shining Path now thrives, largely on Peru's illegal cocaine trade. While not reaching the numbers of the 1980s and 1990s, there are recent reports of growing casualties and civilians killed in the battle between the Peruvian government and Shining Path rebels. See "Shining Path," *New York Times*, http://topics.nytimes.com/top/reference /timestopics/organizations/s/shining_path/index.html.

4. The Nunn-Lugar Cooperative Threat Reduction (CTR) program began in 1991 as the result of legislation sponsored by former senators Sam Nunn of Georgia and Richard Lugar from Indiana. Initially, the legislation directing this program was centered on Russia and was designed to help Russia meet its START obligations to reduce its strategic nuclear weapons inventory. Over time, however, the emphasis of the program changed to focus on securing Russian fissile materials from potential terrorist threats and on initiatives for ensuring acceptable employment for Russian nuclear scientists, many of whom had suddenly found themselves disenfranchised and without salaries. Eventually, CTR programs were initiated in the former Soviet states of Kazakhstan, Belarus, and Ukraine, and today there is debate centered on expanding Nunn-Lugar initiatives beyond the former Soviet Union to other geographic areas, including in relation to the Six-Party Talks and North Korea's hoped-for nuclear dismantlement. In 2003, the Bush administration announced that it had extended the scope of CTR activities to include support to the global war on terrorism, and, in 2004, the Nunn-Lugar Expansion Act was passed by Congress, obligating funds to "assist the United States in resolution of critical emerging proliferation threats and to permit the United States to take advantage of opportunities to achieve long-standing proliferation goals." The expansion of Nunn-Lugar has proved to be somewhat controversial. Debate exists over CTR's globalization at a time when so much still needs to be done in Russia. That said, there is support for using some

Nunn-Lugar funding to implement projects that are limited in scope or central to achieving the denuclearization of former adversaries, such as Libya, and perhaps in the context of dealing with North Korea's nuclear dismantlement (should that come to pass). Moreover, the Russian government, under Vladimir Putin, has announced that it intends to halt its participation in Nunn-Lugar activities in 2013, when the current agreement expires.

5. Mohsen Sazegara, cofounder of the IRGC, who fell out of favor with the regime, quoted in an article published by *The Forward*, "Revolutionary Guard Meddling in Iranian Politics Began Years Ago," http://www.cnsnews.com/news/article/61599.

6. Remarks of Ali Alfoneh, a fellow at the American Enterprise Institute (AEI), noted in ibid.

7. Noah Feldman, "Islam, Terror and the Second Nuclear Age," *New York Times*, October 29, 2006, http://www.newyorktimes.com/2006/10/29/magazine/29islam.html.

8. Sherifa D. Zuhur, *Iran, Iraq, and the United States: The New Triangle's Impact on Sectarianism and the Nuclear Threat* (Carlisle, Pa.: Strategic Studies Institute, U.S. Army War College, 2006), 56.

9. Colonel Thomas X. Hammes, USMC, *The Sling and the Stone: On War in the Twenty-First Century* (St. Paul, Minn.: Zenith Press, 2006), 2, describes fourth-generation warfare as the use of "all available networks—political, economic, social, and military—to convince the enemy's political decision-makers that their strategic goals are either unachievable or too costly for the perceived benefit. It is an evolved form of insurgency. Still rooted in the fundamental precept that superior political will, when properly employed, can defeat greater economic and military power, [fourth-generation warfare] makes use of society's networks to carry on the fight. Unlike previous generations of warfare [which the author identifies as the rise of the nation-state with its massed armies and direct-fire weapons, second-generation firepower, and third-generation maneuver warfare] it does not attempt to win by defeating the enemy's military forces. Instead, via the networks, it directly attacks the minds of enemy decision-makers to destroy the enemy's will. Fourth generation wars are lengthy—measured in decades rather than months or years."

10. Joint Special Operations Command, or JSOC as it is commonly known, is a joint headquarters component of U.S. Special Operations Command, located at Pope Air Force Base and Fort Bragg, North Carolina. Its purpose is to "provide a unified command structure for conducting joint special operations and exercises." It is engaged in counterterrorism missions, strike operations, reconnaissance in denied areas, and special intelligence missions. It commands the military's Special Missions Units and is also charged with implementing counter-WMD terrorist tasks, preparation of the battlefield for special operations, and, on a case-by-case basis, support for civil authorities. The JSOC was established on December 15, 1980, after the failed hostage rescue mission in Iran.

11. The "Anbar Awakening" refers to the decision by key Sunni tribal leaders in Anbar province in Iraq to distance themselves from al-Qaeda operations in Iraq. In 2005, the Abu Mahals tribe was being forced across the Syrian border by a rival

tribe that was associated with al-Qaeda in Mesopotamia. The Abu Mahals decided to engage with the United States and broached the idea of forming an alliance to defeat al-Qaeda in this region. The United States provided arms and training. In the spring of 2006, the Anbar Awakening was initiated when Sheik Abdul Sattar al-Rishawi and his tribal allies established the Jazeera Council in Ramadi and began to work with coalition forces to pacify and stabilize Ramadi against the al-Qaeda insurgents and foreign fighters. In 2007, the movement was expanded and renamed the Iraqi Awakening, a movement to oust and defeat the foreign fighters resident in Salahadin and Diyala provinces. Sheik al-Rishawi was killed in a suicide bombing in 2007.

12. In January 1991, before the start of hostilities, Secretary of State James Baker reflected this policy line when he told the Iraqi foreign minister, Tariq Aziz, "Before we cross to the other side—that is, if the conflict starts, God forbid, and chemical or biological weapons are used against our forces—the American people would demand revenge, and we have the means to implement this" (Baghdad INA, January 9, 1991, translated and published by the Foreign Broadcast Information Service [FBIS] as "INA Reports Minutes of Baker-Aziz Meeting," January 14, 1992, FBIS-NES-92-009, 27). During this meeting, held on January 9 in Geneva, Secretary Baker also delivered a private message from President Bush to Saddam Hussein in which the same deterrence message was conveyed. According to the publication of Bush's own recollections, he wrote: "Let me state, too, that the United States will not tolerate the use of chemical or biological weapons or the destruction of Kuwait's oil fields and installations. The American people would demand the strongest possible response" (cited in George Bush and Brent Scowcroft, *A World Transformed* [New York: Knopf, 1998], 442).

13. William J. Broad, John Markoff, and David E. Sanger, "Israeli Test on Worm Called Crucial in Iran Nuclear Delay," *New York Times*, January 16, 2011. Also see David E. Sanger, *Confront and Conceal: Obama's Secret Wars and Surprising Use of American Power* (New York: Crown, 2012), esp. the prologue, chapter 8, and pp. 262–65.

14. Indeed, according to the head of Iran's Passive Defense Organization, Iran is preparing a cyberdefense strategy that includes offensive and defensive options. Supposedly, in September 2012, Iran implemented a cyberattack against two U.S. banks, although attribution of those attacks remains undocumented. In any event, we can only assume that Iran and other potential U.S. adversaries, China in particular, are engaged in cyberwarfare development, focusing their efforts on military targets but also on critical commercial and civilian infrastructure, which remains extremely vulnerable to sophisticated attacks. For this reason, incorporating the cyberwarfare dimension into U.S. defense and deterrence planning is an obvious necessity, and much more thought needs to be given to this with respect to state and nonstate actors.

15. Commission to Assess the Threat to the United States from Electromagnetic Pulse (EMP) Attack, "Critical National Infrastructures" (November 12, 2008), http://www.empcommission.org/docs/A2473-EMP_Commission-7MB.pdf. According to

the report, a single nuclear weapon exploded at high altitude above the United States will interact with the Earth's atmosphere, ionosphere, and magnetic field to produce an electromagnetic pulse radiating down to earth and also electrical currents within the earth. EMP effects are both direct and indirect. The former are caused by electromagnetic "shocking" of electronics and stressing of electrical systems, and the latter arise from the damage that "shocked"—upset, damaged, and destroyed—electronic controls then inflict on the systems in which they are embedded.

16. The February 2010 Department of Defense Ballistic Missile Defense Review Report states, "The United States seeks to dissuade such states (as Iran and North Korea) from developing an intercontinental ballistic missile, deter them from using an ICBM if they develop or acquire such a capability, and defeat an ICBM attack by such states should deterrence fail."

17. The Proliferation Security Initiative, launched by President Bush in May 2003, is a global effort that seeks to stop trafficking of WMD, their delivery systems, and related materials to and from states and nonstate actors of proliferation concern; see http://www.state.gov/t/isn/c10390.htm. The Global Initiative to Combat Nuclear Terrorism is an international partnership of eighty-one nations and four official observers to prevent, detect, and respond to nuclear terrorism by conducting multilateral activities that strengthen the plans, policies, procedures, and interoperability of partner nations; see http://www.state.gov/t/isn/c18406.htm.

18. The Posse Comitatus Act of 1878, passed after the use of the U.S. Army during Reconstruction in the states of the former Confederacy, prohibits the deployment of federal troops against civilians for the purpose of domestic law enforcement. Today it applies to all the armed forces, including the National Guard, but only when the guard has been federalized by the president (title 10) as opposed to the guard's role under the direction of a state governor.

19. For an analysis of the U.S. strategic nuclear program and deterrence requirements, see *America's Strategic Posture: The Final Report of the Congressional Commission on the Strategic Posture of the United States* (2009), http://www.usip.org/files/America's_Strategic_Posture_Auth_Ed.pdf (informally called the Perry-Schlesinger Commission Report); and *The 36th IFPA-Fletcher Conference Report on National Security and Policy—Implementing the New Triad: Nuclear and Non-Nuclear Forces in Twenty-First-Century Deterrence* (2006), http://www.ifpa.org/pdf/IFC36.pdf.

20. According to counterterrorist experts, the U.S. Federal Bureau of Investigation concluded that the Khobar bombings in 1996 were "staged by Saudi Hezbollah members" and that "the entire operation was planned, funded, and coordinated by Iran's security services, the IRGC and the MOIS (Iran's Ministry of the Interior), acting on the orders from the highest levels of the regime in Tehran" (cited in Steve Schippert, "IRGC Threat: New 'Punch' Same as the Old 'Punch,'" *ThreatsWatch*, August 20, 2007, http://threatswatch.org/commentary/2007/08/irgc-threat-new-punch-same-as/.

21. Both U-235 and Pu-239 are enriched and purified when exposed to other elements and chemicals. The exact recipe for mixing together the elements with the additives can be used to "fingerprint" the origin of the fissile material. Nuclear

forensics provides the ability to "identify a bomb's source from radioactive debris after it explodes. Building on Cold War techniques, the Pentagon has developed new methods for collecting samples from ground zero, measuring data such as isotopic ratios and the efficiency of the fuel burn in the detonation, and comparing that information to known nuclear data to determine the origin of the materials." See Arnie Heller, "Identifying the Source of Nuclear Materials," *Science and Technology Review* (January/February 2007): www.llnl.gov/str/JanFeb07/Smith.html; and Graham T. Allison, "Nuclear Accountability: How to Deter States from Giving Terrorists Nukes," *Technology Review* (July 2005): http://www.technologyreview .com/Energy/14597/.

22. Debra K. Decker, *Before the First Bomb Goes Off: Developing Nuclear Attribution Standards and Policies*, Belfer Center Discussion Paper, No. 2011-03, Harvard Kennedy School, April 2011, http://belfercenter.ksg.harvard.edu/files/Decker_ DP_2011_FINAL.pdf. On April 12–13, 2010, close to fifty nations attended a Nuclear Security Summit in Washington, D.C. The objectives of the summit were to arrive at a common understanding of the threat posed by nuclear terrorism and enhance international cooperation to prevent it, agree to effective measures to secure nuclear material, prevent nuclear smuggling and terrorism, and push for the development of nuclear detection and forensics. For details, see http://fpc.state.gov/c35775.htm.

23. Joint Declaration of Leaders, 2012 Nuclear Security Summit, reprinted in "World Leaders to Strengthen Nuclear Security: Statement Text," *Bloomberg News*, March 27, 2012, found at: http://www.businessweek.com/news/2012-03-27/ world-leaders-to-strengthen-nuclear-security-statement-text.

24. Institute for Foreign Policy Analysis, *A Comprehensive Approach to Combating Illicit Trafficking* (IFPA: 2010), http://www.ifpa.org/pdf/IFPA-GCSPTrafficking Report.pdf.

25. On October 29–30, 2006, under the auspices of the Proliferation Security Initiative, the exercise Leading Edge was conducted off the coast of Bahrain. The exercise was notable for being the first PSI exercise to include the participation of an Arab state and the first conducted in the Persian Gulf in geographic proximity to Iran. Bahrain acted as the host for the maneuvers and was a full participant while all the other GCC states except Saudi Arabia joined as observers. Leading Edge was also the first PSI exercise that South Korea observed. The exercise placed pressure on Iran during a crucial point of diplomacy seeking a new UN Security Council resolution to sanction Iran for refusing to heed earlier resolutions demanding a suspension of uranium-enrichment and plutonium-separation activity. Leading Edge was closely monitored by the Iranian navy. See Guy Dinmore, "WMD Intercept Exercise Set to Begin in the Gulf," *Financial Times*, October 30, 2006, www.ft.com/ intl/cms/s/0/8b0a05b8-678b-11db-8ea5-0000779e2340.html#axzz2Ayfqmwqy; and Hassan M. Fattah, "U.S-Led Exercise in Persian Gulf Sets Sights on Deadliest Weapons," *New York Times*, October 31, 2006, www.nytimes.com/2006/10/31/world/ middleeast/31gulf.html.

8. U.S. DETERRENCE PLANNING AND IRAN

1. According to *New York Times* correspondent, David E. Sanger in his book *Confront and Conceal: Obama's Secret Wars and Surprising Use of American Power* (New York: Crown, 2012), the United States and Israel collaborated on the development of Stuxnet. Sanger's book (chapter 8) contains an extensive discussion of the planning and deployment of Stuxnet.

2. Bernard Brodie, ed., *The Absolute Weapon: Atomic Power and World Order* (New York: Harcourt, Brace, 1946), 76.

INDEX